CONCENTRATE Q&A
CONTRACT LAW

CONCENTRATE
Q&A
CONTRACT LAW

James Devenney

Head of School and Professor of Transnational
Commercial Law, School of Law, University of Reading, UK
and
Visiting Full Professor, UCD Sutherland School of Law,
University College Dublin, Ireland

THIRD EDITION

OXFORD
UNIVERSITY PRESS

OXFORD
UNIVERSITY PRESS

Great Clarendon Street, Oxford, OX2 6DP,
United Kingdom

Oxford University Press is a department of the University of Oxford.
It furthers the University's objective of excellence in research, scholarship,
and education by publishing worldwide. Oxford is a registered trade mark of
Oxford University Press in the UK and in certain other countries

First edition 2016
Second edition 2019

Impression: 1

Public sector information reproduced under Open Government Licence v3.0
(http://www.nationalarchives.gov.uk/doc/open-government-licence/open-government-licence.htm)

Published in the United States of America by Oxford University Press
198 Madison Avenue, New York, NY 10016, United States of America

British Library Cataloguing in Publication Data
Data available

Library of Congress Control Number: 2022943094

ISBN 978–0–19–286562–5

Printed in the UK by
Bell & Bain Ltd., Glasgow

Contents

Guide to the book

Every book in the Concentrate Q&A series contains the following features:

ARE YOU READY?

Are you ready to face the exam? This box at the start of each chapter identifies the key topics and cases that you need to have learned, revised, and understood before tackling the questions in each chapter.

KEY DEBATES

Demonstrating your knowledge of the crucial debates is a sure-fire way to impress examiners. These at-a-glance boxes help remind you of the key debates relevant to each topic, which you should discuss in your answers to get the highest marks.

QUESTION

Each question represents a typical essay or problem question so that you know exactly what to expect in your exam.

CAUTION!

Don't fall into any traps! This feature points out common mistakes that students make, and which you need to avoid when answering each question.

DIAGRAM ANSWER PLANS

Not sure where to begin? Clear diagram answer plans at the start of each question help you see how to structure your answer at a glance, and take you through each point step-by-step.

A SUGGESTED ANSWER

What makes a great answer great? Our authors show you the thought process behind their own answers, and how you can do the same in your exam. Key sentences are highlighted, and advice is given on how to structure your answer well and develop your arguments.

LOOKING FOR EXTRA MARKS?

Don't settle for a good answer—make it great! This feature gives you extra points to include in the exam if you want to gain more marks and make your answer stand out.

TAKING THINGS FURTHER

Really push yourself and impress your examiner by going beyond what is expected. Focused further reading suggestions allow you to develop in-depth knowledge of the subject for when you are looking for the highest marks.

Additional online materials to aid your study and revision can be accessed at www.oup.com/lawrevision.

Table of cases

Table of primary legislation

Table of secondary legislation

Table of European legislation

EU Secondary Legislation

Directives

Exam Skills for Success in Contract Law

This book is designed to give students of the law of contract an insight, on the one hand, into how answers to essay and problem questions are to be written and, on the other, what examiners expect to see in well-crafted answers. It is presupposed that you, as the user of the book, will have a familiarity with the topic areas of the law of contract. The book can be used throughout your course of study, on a chapter-by-chapter basis, or at the end of your module to support your preparation for assessment. The book offers support in relation to assessment by coursework and examination but does not provide a comprehensive revision guide for the law of contract. The key to using this book is to understand that assessment is a process and once you understand the process it can be employed in relation to any subject area. So the answers given in each chapter demonstrate the process of answering problem and essay questions but do not seek to be exhaustive of all areas of the law of contract.

Answering Problem Questions

The primary expectation of the examiner in relation to an answer to a problem question is that you will demonstrate an ability to analyse and apply the law. In so doing your answer should be relevant, have a clear structure, demonstrate legal scholarship, and be understandable. A simple approach to analysis is to adopt the 'IRAC' approach. This is an acronym with four stages: Identification, Relevant law, Application, and Conclusion. First, *identify* the legal issue raised by the question. An initial inquiry will be what is the general area raised by the question. Often, although not always, questions will focus on one area of the syllabus, for example offer and acceptance or consideration. At the outset of your answer, identify the overall area. Then identify specific issues raised in the area; this might be, in an offer and acceptance question, finding an offer, finding an acceptance, etc. Secondly, state the *relevant law*. For example, in relation to offer you will need to define the term and then explain what the law requires for the existence of an offer. Statements of law are to be supported by reference to authority, for instance a case or statute as appropriate. Note that you will have choices to make, in that there are numerous cases on the meaning of offer, but you must choose the cases relevant to the question posed. Having stated the relevant law you must then seek to *apply* the law to the facts demonstrating that you are aware of any arguments for and against a particular interpretation. In doing this you are showing that you understand how the law may be used. Problem questions quite often introduce uncertainty in the factual scenario by omitting certain facts. Ensure that you address all the possibilities raised. Finally, reach a *conclusion* on the point identified. Note that your conclusion may not be definitive of an issue and may have to be couched in terms of the strength of opposing arguments or, if the facts of the problem are vague, what would be argued if particular facts exist. In other words, there may be no right answer but what is important is to employ a full and consistent argument or arguments given the facts that exist in the question.

What is essential to an understanding of IRAC is that it is to be used more than once in an answer. For every legal issue raised by a question IRAC is to be used. So if there are five issues raised by a question then IRAC may be used in relation to each of the five issues. This avoids having a block of law in an answer and then a short final paragraph seeking to apply the law. In this way the law and application are intertwined throughout your answer. See, for example, answer 1 in Chapter 2 'Offer and Acceptance'.

An examiner will also want to see that there is a logical organization of material in your answer. With problem questions, using the inherent structure of the law will help you order your thoughts. In relation to a question on offer and acceptance the logic of your answer must include the identification of an offer before you discuss the presence or otherwise of an acceptance. The chronology of offer and acceptance problems usually provides a structure for using the offer and acceptance analysis. The answers to the problem questions in this book will impose a legal order on the facts of a scenario and you will see that they follow the order that exists in the law. Understanding the structure of a legal area also has the spin-off that you have a ready-made plan for problem questions that you may encounter in an examination, where time is at a premium. So a little time spent reflecting on the structures of subject areas you will encounter in a contract module will be well rewarded.

Relevance is important in answering a question. Only deal with the legal issues raised by the facts of a question. Be careful to identify what the question expects you to discuss. Equally, only explain law which is relevant to the issue identified. Certainly, do not deal with issues if there is no problem on the facts, for example discussing the law relating to agreement when the question clearly states 'the parties agree . . .' If a question states that a document has been signed, raising an issue of incorporation of terms, explain and apply the rule relating to signature (***L'Estrange v F Graucob Ltd* [1934] 2 KB 394**) but do not explain and apply the other methods of incorporation; that is, notice and previous course of dealings.

When looking at the answers in this book, take note of how authority is used to support an explanation of a particular rule. While full citations are given in the answers, for example [1983] 2 AC 34, this would usually not be expected of you in an exam; the citations are only included here for ease of reference. Usually all that will be required is that you state the name of a case or a statute.

Answering Essay Questions

Much of the previous advice is also applicable to answering essay questions. However, the starting point with an essay question is to deconstruct the sentence or sentences. Part of the essay title will indicate the scope of the question—that is, the subject matter to be examined—the remaining words will refer to concepts or rules, for example, and then instruct you as to what to consider about this subject area. Always remember that mention of a concept or rule in an essay title is an invitation to give an explanation of the concept or rule. Once you have identified the areas, then the approach to adopt is 'PEA' that is, in relation to each issue raised by the essay, make a Point, then provide Evidence (in law essays this may consist of relevant law), and then undertake Analysis. This approach may be used several times in an answer as you address each point in turn.

Ensure that throughout your essay you keep linking the material you are discussing to the requirements of the question.

The use of IRAC and PEA gives you templates to follow in analysing a question but as your writing skills develop you may find the stages of each blending into one another. The important point is that by dealing with matters raised by IRAC and PEA you will be addressing the issues raised by the question.

General Guidance

In relation to questions broken into parts, a mark allocation may give some guidance on where to concentrate your efforts, for example if a marks split is part (a) 60% and part (b) 40%, it is clear that more time should be expended in relation to part (a). If no marks split is given, then it may be that each part is to be treated equally. It is advisable to look at past questions and, if in doubt, to consult your tutor for guidance.

Questions may focus on an area of contract law, for example offer and acceptance or remedies for breach of contract, and not mix areas, for instance offer and acceptance and consideration. However, questions may also link areas, such as terms and misrepresentation or breach and damages. **Chapter 14** includes some questions that do link areas together to illustrate how such questions may occur. Again, the advice is to look at how your module has been assessed in past papers and to consider how the subject is taught through the lectures and seminars.

Finally, a few words relating to assessment in general. First, you should listen carefully to your contract lecturer and seminar tutor as they will guide you as to their expectations in relation to written work. They may indicate a particular form or style that they want to see in assessments. Ensure you are aware and follow closely any specific instructions given both in teaching sessions and assessment notifications. Secondly, when referring to the decision of a court you are to use the word 'judgment', but when referring to, for example, an estimate or opinion employ the spelling 'judgement'. Thirdly, the answers in this book are suggested answers; there may be other ways to answer the questions posed, especially essay questions. The important point is that the answers indicate an approach and include the type of information that must be present in an answer. Fourthly, in problem questions avoid concluding with the obvious statement that the issue is one for a court to decide. This is undoubtedly true, but a client would expect to be given more guidance as to the relevant law, its application, and the likely success of an argument or arguments should a case be pursued before the courts.

2 Offer and Acceptance

ARE YOU READY?

In order to attempt the questions in this chapter you must have covered the following areas in your revision:

- The principles used to determine the existence of an agreement;
- The distinction between an offer and an invitation to treat (ITT);
- What constitutes acceptance;
- The problems arising from the 'battle of forms';
- Communication of acceptance;
- Methods of terminating an offer;
- The problems relating to unilateral contracts;
- What is meant by certainty of terms.

KEY DEBATES

Offer and acceptance is a fairly settled area of law, but a number of questions arise in relation to the application of the relevant principles.

Debate: communication of acceptance.

When does the postal acceptance rule apply, and does it apply to methods of communication other than letters of acceptance sent through the post?

Debate: unilateral contracts.

On what basis will the law prevent the revocation of an offer in respect of a unilateral contract once performance of the requested act has commenced but before the requested act is complete?

QUESTION 1

Andrea has decided to sell her caravan. She parks it outside her house with a notice on the front windscreen stating: 'For sale. Pristine example—one owner. £4,750 or near offer. Please call at number 34 or tel: 713850, only. First person to agree a price WILL get the caravan.'

On Monday at 9am, Bernice sees the caravan but, as she is late for the dentist, she telephones Andrea from work at 10am and makes an offer of £4,500 which Andrea says she would like to consider. Bernice says that she will assume Andrea has accepted unless she hears from her by 9pm that evening, a proposal to which Andrea agrees.

At 11am on Monday, Curtis calls at Andrea's house, but she is not at home. He leaves a note reading: 'Monday 11am. Please keep caravan for me—here is a cheque for £4,750, Curtis.'

At 2.15pm on Monday, David sees the notice and, within a few minutes, has posted a letter of acceptance and cheque for £4,750, using the post-box at the end of the street. Unfortunately, David misaddresses his letter, so it only arrives on Friday.

At 3pm on Monday, Andrea decides to accept Bernice's offer and posts a letter to Bernice's business address saying: 'I agree to sell on your terms. Because of the lower price can you pay in cash?'

At 9.30pm on Monday, Andrea reads Curtis's acceptance and immediately telephones Bernice's business address, leaving a message on the recorded answering service: 'Ignore the letter you will receive—deal off. Andrea.' Bernice is away on business and only listens to the tape on Wednesday evening.

Advise each party as to their legal position.

CAUTION!

- The topic of offer and acceptance at one level seems quite straightforward but the applicable law depends upon assessing the intention of the parties which is not so straightforward.

- Always establish that there is, at least, an argument for the existence of an offer *before* you consider any possible argument for the existence of an acceptance. In problem questions it is illogical to consider acceptance in the absence of an offer.

- With offer and acceptance questions a number of possible answers may arise, depending upon how the facts of the question are interpreted (for example, one party may have an *arguable* case that a particular statement is an offer, whereas the other party may have an *arguable* case that the same statement is actually an invitation to treat). It is advisable that a draft plan is used to identify the pathways for an answer and so that your answer can be structured in a logical way.

DIAGRAM ANSWER PLAN

Identify the issues
- Identify the legal issues—formation of contract.
- Offer or invitation to treat?
- Consequences if invitation to treat; consequences if offer.

Relevant law
- Outline the relevant law together with authority from case law.
- Offer or invitation to treat—*Carlill* and *Partridge* cases.
- Acceptance—unequivocal assent to terms of offer and communication of acceptance.

Apply the law
- Effect of advert being an invitation to treat—need for an offer and then acceptance for contract.
- Effect of advert being an offer—need for acceptance.

Conclude
- If ITT, has an offer subsequently been made and accepted—Bernice's offer may have been accepted.
- If Curtis can successfully argue that the original notice in the caravan was an offer and he had effectively communicated his acceptance, then he may have a contract.
- David's purported acceptance—is subject to the postal rule and does it follow the prescribed mode of communication?
- Bernice possibly has a contract formed Monday 9pm on the basis of Andrea's failure to contact Bernice before that time with a rejection of the offer.
- Overall conclusion.

SUGGESTED ANSWER

[1] Indicate in your opening sentence what is the overall subject area raised by the question.

[2] Here there is the identification of the first legal issue for consideration.

This question concerns formation of contract, particularly agreement. In order to determine the existence of an agreement it is usually necessary to find an offer and acceptance of that offer (*Gibson v Manchester City Council* **[1979] 1 WLR 294**).[1] The first issue is whether the wind-screen notice constitutes an offer or an invitation to treat (ITT),[2] for if it is an ITT Curtis's and David's offers are never accepted. Does the notice demonstrate a clear willingness to be bound without any need or desire for further negotiations? The notice states a definite price, the caravan is subject to an external inspection and there is a prescribed method of communication. Use of the word 'WILL get the caravan' arguably demonstrates clear intent and is similar to *Carlill v Carbolic Smoke Ball Co. Ltd* **[1893] 1 QB 256** where an offer was held to have been made. Moreover, the stipulated methods of communication allow Andrea to vet each acceptance personally and thereby avoid any confusion as to who is the 'first person'. The notice may be an offer.

Conversely, the price stated invites different bids ('or near offer'), it is unlikely that a buyer would come forward without an *internal* inspection of the caravan and test drive, and an advertisement is normally considered to be an invitation to treat. Following *Partridge v Crittenden* **[1968] 1 WLR 1204**, there is a presumption that where individuals attempt to conclude private contracts, they will prefer to make the final decision as to whom they will sell, particularly where there is a limit on available stock[3] (although Andrea's comment that only the 'first person gets the caravan' potentially eliminates this problem). Moreover, is a notice on a windscreen any different from a displayed price in a shop window (eg *Fisher v Bell* **[1961] 1 QB 394**)?

Consequently, as the contractual status of the notice is debatable, the following answer will assume that either proposition is valid.[4]

Assuming the Windscreen Notice is an ITT

Andrea v Bernice

If Bernice is making an offer to buy the caravan for £4,500, Andrea attempts to accept this offer by posting a letter asking that payment be made in cash. What is the effect of this letter? First, by introducing this new element of payment in cash, Andrea's response may be a counter-offer, rather than an acceptance.[5] If so, the counter-offer destroys Bernice's original offer (*Hyde v Wrench* **(1840) 3 Beav 334**) and Bernice would need to accept this counter-offer before any contract came into existence (of which there is no evidence). Moreover, Andrea's subsequently recorded telephone message would effectively revoke this counter-offer, at the very latest when Bernice listened to it on Wednesday morning. An alternative interpretation is that by asking whether payment could be made in cash, Andrea may simply be clarifying the position.

Assuming Andrea's acceptance to be unqualified, when is it effective? As the letter is posted, the postal rule may apply, whereby acceptance is effective on posting (*Adams v Lindsell* **(1818) 1 B & Ald 681**).[6] If so, case law would lean towards Andrea's subsequent retraction being ineffective (eg *Wenkheim v Arndt* **(1873) 1 JR 73 (NZ)**). However, one should question the reasonableness of using the postal rule in these circumstances. The notice on the caravan required would-be purchasers to visit Andrea's home or telephone her personally.

[3] An explanation of a key case is given here.

[4] A conclusion is reached. Note that due to the facts of the question being unlike any decided case, arguments may be raised, but no definitive conclusion reached. The answer then considers the consequence of each possible interpretation, ie is the notice an offer or is it an ITT?

[5] Identification of the next issue, ie what is acceptance.

[6] Note that when a rule is stated it is immediately followed by authority. Remember, the case name will often suffice so there is often no need to include the full reference.

An instantaneous communication is arguably contemplated by the parties. A court might declare the postal rule inapplicable, particularly as Bernice (the offeror) would not have expected a posted response. If so, the letter cannot be effective prior to its receipt, making the final result dependent upon whether the letter was delivered *before* or *after* Bernice listened to Andrea's recorded message on Wednesday.[7]

One final possibility must be considered, when Bernice offered to pay £4,500 she stated that unless Andrea responded by Monday 9pm she would assume that her offer had been accepted.[8] Imposing silence as a means of acceptance is not normally permissible (***Felthouse v Bindley*** **(1862) 11 CB NS 869**) and should therefore leave Andrea free to sell to anyone else. However, in ***Re Selectmove Ltd*** **[1995] 1 WLR 474**, the Court of Appeal recognized, *obiter*, that if an offeree *agrees* to silence being a means of acceptance, then failure to communicate with the offeror is equivalent to acceptance. As Bernice did not *receive* any further communication from Andrea before Monday 9pm, a court is entitled to conclude that Bernice had bought the caravan at that moment in time.

Andrea v Curtis

If the windscreen notice is only an ITT, Curtis will actually be making an offer to Andrea and, in the absence of acceptance, no contract can yet exist. Andrea's mental acceptance of Curtis's offer would be insufficient.

Andrea v David

David is in the same position as Curtis.

Assuming the Windscreen Notice is an Offer

Andrea v Bernice

Should the notice be an offer, Bernice's reply would probably constitute a counter-offer as she offered a lower price. Andrea's subsequent request for payment in cash would either be another counter-offer, in which case no contract would yet exist, or an acceptance of that counter-offer. If the latter, the final result would be determined by the following two points: (a) whether Andrea's acceptance was communicated to Bernice before Andrea's attempted retraction, or afterwards (see the previous section); and (b) whether Andrea's failure to communicate with Bernice before Monday 9pm resulted in a contract coming into existence anyway on grounds of acceptance by conduct (following ***Re Selectmove Ltd***).

Andrea v Curtis

Curtis has accepted Andrea's offer without qualification. When is his acceptance effective: when the note is left at Andrea's house (ie delivery) or when Andrea actually reads it (ie actual receipt)?

[7] You might also wish to consider whether Andrea's retraction is effectively communicated when it was recorded or only when Bernice heard it—see extended analysis of this point in **Question 2**.

[8] Another legal issue is identified. The remainder of the paragraph briefly explains the rules, applies the law to the facts of the question, and reaches a conclusion.

In support of the delivery theory it could be argued that Curtis complied with the terms of the notice, by leaving an acceptance at Andrea's house. There is nothing to suggest that Andrea's notice required face-to-face communication. If this argument is successful, then a contract is formed at 11.05am Monday, leaving other prospective purchasers with no redress as Andrea's offer will have impliedly lapsed in accordance with the notice on the caravan which specified 'first person'. It is unlikely that Curtis could rely upon any *obiter dictum* in **The Brimnes** [1975] **QB 929** to the effect that a letter that has been delivered will normally be deemed to have been opened within a reasonable time as this probably applies to communications with businesses rather than with private individuals (compare **Newcastle Upon Tyne NHS Foundation Trust v Sandi Haywood** [2017] **EWCA Civ 153**).

If this argument fails, Curtis's acceptance may only be effective when it has been communicated to Andrea—presumably when she read it on Monday at 9.30pm (see **Entores v Miles Far East Corp.** [1955] **2 QB 327**, a case which, although subjected to some criticism, in the context of instantaneous communications, by Lord Sumption JSC in **Brownlie v Four Seasons Holdings Inc** [2017] **UKSC 80** and Leggatt JSC (in his partial dissent) in **FS Cairo (Nile Plaza) LLC v Lady Brownlie** [2021] **UKSC 45**, probably still governs this situation). By this time Andrea has potentially formed a contract with Bernice (eg if the postal rule applies to Andrea's 'acceptance' sent at 3pm on Monday), or Andrea is deemed to have accepted Bernice's offer by not communicating with Bernice before Monday 9pm. If so, either Andrea's advertised offer will have impliedly lapsed or, if a court felt that the offer remained in force until it had been positively withdrawn, Andrea would be in breach of contract to Curtis by selling the caravan to Bernice.

Andrea v David

David will argue that his posted acceptance has created a contract with Andrea. Two questions arise: (a) does the postal rule apply to his letter of acceptance; and (b) by using a different means of communication than specified in the notice, was his acceptance valid?

[9] This paragraph makes plain the limits to the operation of the postal rule.

For the postal rule to apply, the acceptance must be properly addressed, the rule must not be excluded by the terms of the offer (eg **Holwell Securities Ltd v Hughes** [1974] **1 WLR 155**), and the post must be a reasonable means of communication.[9] In the present case David fails on all three counts. First, he has misaddressed his letter. Secondly, the terms of the offer stipulate a personal visit or a telephone call. Thirdly, as the situation presumably requires direct communication between the parties (in order to avoid unknown acceptances in the post creating unexpected liabilities), it would appear unreasonable for the postal rule to apply.

If the postal rule does not apply, perhaps David's letter is effective when it is delivered on Friday morning? The general rule is that the offeree must adhere to the prescribed mode, otherwise the acceptance is invalid; whereas if the offeror's intentions are at all ambiguous, the offeree may choose an equally expeditious means of communication (*Yates v Pulleyn* (1975) 119 Sol Jo 370). In the present case, Andrea has used the word 'only' in her offer, thereby arguably excluding use of the postal service, so David's acceptance is unlikely to be valid on receipt. Moreover, even if alternative forms of communication were not excluded by the terms of the offer, one would still expect an instantaneous means of communication to be used. As the post is not as fast as the telephone, nor as immediate as a personal visit, David's attempted acceptance appears invalid.

[10]Remember to include an overall conclusion to your answer.

In conclusion,[10] unless Curtis can successfully argue that the original notice in the caravan was an offer and that he had effectively communicated his acceptance by delivering it to Andrea's house, it seems that Bernice has the best chance of securing the caravan at a price of £4,500, with the contract probably being formed at 9pm on Monday on the basis of Andrea's failure to contact Bernice before that time with a rejection of the offer.

LOOKING FOR EXTRA MARKS?

- Use the IRAC method to ensure that you demonstrate the relevance of the law and how it applies to the facts.

- When a question begins with an advert, never assume it is definitely an offer or an invitation to treat. Explain why either is possible, explicitly stating your analysis.

- Make sure you send a clear signal to the examiner that you do not expect the answer to be clear-cut, with only one possible solution. For example, it is arguable that Curtis's acceptance is effective either when it physically arrives at Andrea's house or when she actually reads it.

QUESTION | **2**

Margaret, the sales director at TechMech, is approached by Philip, a local businessman, who outlines the size and nature of his business enterprise and asks Margaret to quote a price for the installation of TechMech's new accounts software system. Margaret, realizing that her monthly sales quota has not yet been reached, replies: 'I am sure that for a business of your size we can guarantee a price of £3,000, covering all installation costs and appropriate staff training. But please get back to me quickly; I cannot hold that price for more than a week.'

Later that day, Philip receives an advertisement by email from CostPlus Ltd which states: 'We can offer "state-of-the-art" accountancy software for small businesses at a price guaranteed not to exceed £2,500.' He immediately telephones CostPlus and places an order. However, after discussing the matter further with a CostPlus representative, it becomes apparent that the actual costs of installation would exceed £4,000. Philip thereupon withdraws his order.

The next day, Philip telephones TechMech. He leaves a message on the answering machine accepting the offer of £3,000 made by Margaret, at the same time asking whether the cost could also include on-site training for any new staff he takes on over the next six months.

Subsequently, Philip has second thoughts and telephones TechMech to cancel his order. The secretary, now on duty, points out that she has passed all the answering service tapes over to Margaret who would be listening to them shortly, but that she would make a note of his wishes.

Advise Philip whether he has concluded a contract with TechMech and/or CostPlus and, if so, on what terms?

! CAUTION!

- Do not make assumptions, for example there is an advert, therefore it must be an invitation to treat (it may be an offer!). Explain the law and explain how it might apply to the facts of the problem.

- The facts of offer and acceptance questions may lack clarity. This is deliberately so to allow room for discussion of alternatives.

- In complicated questions of this nature, an examiner will place a premium on answers that adopt a logical structure. Consider the possible use of subheadings as a means of avoiding unnecessary confusion. It is best to check with your module tutor that this an acceptable format to employ.

DIAGRAM ANSWER PLAN

Identify the issues	■ Offer and acceptance. ■ CostPlus Ltd advert—invitation to treat (ITT) or offer? ■ Margaret's quote—ITT or offer? ■ Philip's response to CostPlus and Margaret—offer, counter-offer, or acceptance?
Relevant law	■ Offer or ITT—look at language, terms of proposal, and inferences to be drawn from circumstances, eg *Partridge v Crittenden*. See also *Carlill, Fisher v Bell*, and *Grainger & Son v Gough*. ■ Counter-offer—*Hyde v Wrench* ■ Acceptance—communication of acceptance, as a general rule needs actual communication of acceptance: *Entores v Miles Far East Corp., Brinkibon*, and *The Brimnes*.
Apply the law	■ CostPlus Ltd advert—if offer, has Philip accepted; if ITT, does Philip make offer and CostPlus then accept? ■ Margaret's quote—if offer, did Philip accept or make a counter-offer? If Philip seeks to accept, did communication take place before the attempted withdrawal of acceptance? If ITT, did Philip make an offer which was accepted by Margaret?
Conclude	■ Unclear whether advert and quote are offers or ITTs—the consequences of both possibilities to be considered. ■ CostPlus Ltd advert—if ITT no contract; if offer Philip appears to accept so contract. ■ Margaret's quote—if ITT, Philip makes an offer, if accepted then a contract; if offer, does Philip reject the offer by making a counter-offer? If Philip's assent communicated to Margaret, then acceptance. But might Philip withdraw assent before Margaret receives communication and so no contract?

SUGGESTED ANSWER

In advising Philip it is necessary to discuss formation of contract, particularly an analysis of offer and acceptance. The question is whether Philip is contractually bound to purchase the relevant accounts software from either/both of the two firms, CostPlus Ltd or TechMech.

CostPlus Ltd Advertisement

Does the advertisement constitute an offer or an invitation to treat (ITT)? Whereas an ITT merely represents a preliminary stage in negotiations, an offer is a definite proposition by the offeror signifying a willingness to be bound by the terms stated as soon as it has been accepted by the offeree. The basic distinction between an offer and an ITT is that an ITT lacks the required objective intent and specific terms of an offer.[1] Traditionally, the courts have preferred to view an advertisement as an ITT for two reasons. First, the wording of advertisements is often too vague (compare *Grainger & Son v Gough* [1896] AC 325).[2] Here the advertisement states a maximum price that presumably means that a lower price might be negotiated; moreover, no precise details are included about the software specifications, nor its inherent limitations or performance targets relevant to its intended business use. Secondly, sound business sense may dictate that a business 'supplier/seller' would prefer to choose its customers so as to avoid being inundated with acceptances that could not be fulfilled from existing stock (see *Partridge v Crittenden* [1968] 1 WLR 1204). Moreover, there seems little difference between shops advertising goods in windows or on shelves, either of which are normally viewed as ITTs (see *Fisher v Bell* [1961] 1 QB 394) or advertising them via some other medium. This reasoning points to the advertisement being an ITT, reinforced by the subsequent conversation which demonstrates that CostPlus required further information before it could actually quote a definite price. Indeed, if the advert was an offer, what is the price at which Philip is accepting—£2,500, or less? The fact that no definite answer can be given again suggests that the advert lacked the certainty required of an offer.[3]

However, there are two points that might arguably alter the position here.[4] First, in *Partridge v Crittenden*, Parker LJ, in a strong *obiter dictum*, excluded manufacturers' catalogues from the presumption that an advert represented an ITT. Should this approach be extended to the supplier of specialist software who quotes a definite upper limit? Secondly, in *Carlill v Carbolic Smoke Ball Co. Ltd* [1893] 1 QB 256 an advert was held to be an offer because the clarity of its wording, linked with an intention to be bound as evidenced by the deposit of money with the bank, demonstrated the required degree of intent and specificity. Similarly, does CostPlus Ltd's advert incorporate a statement of clear intent or is it a mere advertising puff? One might emphasize, for example, that the words 'price guaranteed not to exceed £2,500' demonstrates a clear contractual intent and that any further discussions will result in a lower price being agreed.

In the end, the argument that an ITT was made initially is probably stronger, in which case no contract will result (at any price).[5] What is

---

[1] This paragraph is a good illustration of IRAC. In the opening sentences, there is identification of the legal issue, together with an explanation of the terminology.

[2] The use of IRAC continues with statements of relevant law and then immediate application to the facts.

[3] This is a running conclusion, ie the advert is unlikely to be an offer. This could be reinforced by using the facts of *Harvey v Facey* [1893] AC 552.

[4] The counter-arguments suggesting the existence of an offer are considered here. This shows an appreciation of the need to deal with counter-arguments.

[5] This paragraph concludes on the above arguments indicating the consequences of the advert being an ITT or an offer.

important here is that if the advertisement does constitute an offer, Philip has accepted its terms before CostPlus increased its quote (ie offer) to £4,000. Specifically, the normal rule is that an offer can be accepted, subject to the need for communication, at any time before notice of its withdrawal has reached the offeree (see *Byrne v Van Tienhoven* **(1880) 5 CPD 344**). Thus, if a contract was formed when Philip placed his order, any post-contractual attempt by CostPlus to increase the quote would represent a breach of contract.

Discussions with TechMech

Does Margaret's statement of price represent an offer or an ITT? Adopting the analysis in the previous section, the required degree of intent and clarity of language must be isolated. Margaret has used the words 'I am sure', arguably suggesting a clear intent to be bound. Compare this with *Gibson v Manchester City Council* **[1979] 1 All ER 972** where the defendants' statement that they 'may be prepared to sell' was viewed by the House of Lords as an ITT—especially when linked with the later statement in the letter inviting the tenant to 'make a formal application'. In our facts, a specific price has been given, with a definite time limit. It is therefore more likely that the price constitutes an offer.[6] One final point is that the offer can be withdrawn at any time before acceptance, unless Philip has provided consideration for the offer to be kept open (eg payment).

[6]Note that questions on offer and acceptance give rise to possible arguments on the facts of the question; if the communication from Margaret was definitely an ITT, the remainder of the question would have no purpose!

Unqualified Acceptance?

Has Philip unequivocally accepted the terms of TechMech's offer? At first glance, he appears to have added a new term; namely, that the cost includes the training of new staff recruited over the next six months. If this represents a counter-offer then the placing of his order cannot constitute an acceptance—TechMech can choose to accept or reject this counter-offer (see generally *Hyde v Wrench*).

Could Philip argue that he was simply requesting information in order to clarify the position; that is, is it clear that the quoted price applied only to the training of existing employees? This seems a weak argument as Philip's recorded message is not really phrased as a question of clarification, but rather as a request. However, he may use *Society of Lloyds v Twinn* **(2000)** *The Times*, **4 April** where the Court of Appeal recognized that there was no reason why an offeree should not unconditionally accept an offer while, at the same time, making a separate collateral offer to modify the contract. If the collateral offer was rejected, then the unconditional acceptance of the original offer still created a binding agreement. On the facts, Philip's acceptance seems unconditional with his plea for indulgence regarding the training of subsequently recruited staff representing a collateral offer that TechMech is free to accept or reject.

Communication of Acceptance

Philip attempts to accept by telephone. The general rule is that acceptance must be communicated to the offeror or their agent in order to be effective. In this case Philip's acceptance has been recorded on an answering machine: is it effective when recorded or when it has been listened to? In *Entores* the Court of Appeal suggested that, generally, if the offeror does not hear the acceptance, it is not effective.[7] On this basis no contract has yet come into existence. But there are arguable alternatives and, indeed, in *Brownlie v Four Seasons Holdings Inc* [2017] **UKSC 80** Lord Sumption JSC suggested that aspects of the *Entores* case may need to be reconsidered in the future.

First, it is possible that the answering machine is a mechanical agent (see *Thornton v Shoe Lane Parking Ltd* [1971] 2 QB 163). If so, a contract has been formed and Philip has no chance of withdrawing from it.

Secondly, in *The Brimnes* [1975] QB 929 where the plaintiffs exercised their right to withdraw from the contract, the question was whether the plaintiffs' telex of withdrawal was effective when it was received during designated office hours or when it was read the following morning. The Court of Appeal concluded that the telex was effective on receipt as the plaintiffs had been told that it was the defendants' ordinary practice to read such telexes immediately. Whether this reasoning can be applied to communications of acceptance is unclear.[8] If applicable the following arguments might be advanced: (a) if the answering service implied that recorded messages would be listened to before the end of normal business hours of that day, then acceptance would have been effectively communicated at some time during that day and a contract would come into existence, subject to the timing of Philip's attempted withdrawal; (b) if the answering service suggested that messages would be listened to on the following day, then it would seem (the facts are not entirely clear) that Philip's revocation would have already become effective; that is to say, no contract would come into existence (see *Mondial Shipping & Chartering BV v Astarte Shipping Ltd* [1995] CLC 1011).

In *Brinkibon Ltd v Stahag Stahl und Stahl* [1983] 2 AC 34 Lord Wilberforce said, *obiter*, the time at which a telexed acceptance was effectively communicated would depend on the intentions of the parties, sound business practice, and even a judgement as to where risks should lie.[9] Is the receipt of a telexed acceptance similar to the telephone recording of an order? If so, can one assume that the intention of the parties was that Philip's order would only be communicated when his recorded message was heard, thereby allowing him the freedom to withdraw the order until that time? Conversely, does the use of an answering machine imply that a busy company does not wish to miss any opportunity to receive an order and that tapes will be

[7] The answer here avoids a superficial consideration of communication of acceptance, ie communication is effective on receipt, by considering what in law is meant by receipt.

[8] As *The Brimnes* is a case on notice of withdrawal, it is possible to argue that the rule established should not extend to acceptance.

[9] In this paragraph, alternative arguments are raised, again showing the inherent flexibility in applying the normal rules of offer and acceptance.

listened to as quickly as possible, thereby suggesting that recording is tantamount to communication?

To conclude, if Philip's acceptance is effective only when his message has been listened to, then his revocation may be effective—an offeree can withdraw any acceptance provided the withdrawal is communicated prior to the acceptance. If his acceptance is effective when recorded, then a contract is immediately created, preventing him from attempting a revocation.

LOOKING FOR EXTRA MARKS?

■ Although a technical, schematic approach is demanded, there is considerable scope for better students to demonstrate their analytical abilities. For example, the average student will apply the general rule of communication of acceptance in *Entores v Miles Far East Corp.* **[1955] 2 QB 327** whereas the good student will explain the limitations possibly imposed upon this principle by the subsequent decisions in *The Brimnes* **[1975] QB 929** and *Brinkibon Ltd v Stahag Stahl und Stahl* **[1983] 2 AC 34**.

■ The ability to identify arguments and counter-arguments will reap rewards in terms of marks as this shows an appreciation of how to use the law effectively. Weighing up the strengths and weaknesses of opposing arguments is also an important part of this process.

QUESTION | 3

On Wednesday Oftmark Ltd offers to sell 100 tonnes of steel to Aftercool Ltd at £500 per tonne. The offer to Aftercool states: 'Please telephone or email an acceptance by noon today. Delivery will take place next Monday.'

Aftercool Ltd faxes an acceptance at 10am, the fax machine informing the clerical assistant that the message has been properly relayed to Oftmark. Unfortunately, the Oftmark fax machine has not been fitted with a new printing cartridge so the acceptance is not received. Moreover, as Aftercool Ltd believes that a firm contract exists, it enters into a binding contract with Torquecar Ltd to produce car body panels, using the anticipated delivery of steel on Monday.

Advise Aftercool Ltd whether there is a binding contract with Oftmark Ltd.

Would your advice differ in the following alternative circumstances?

a   **Aftercool emailed a withdrawal of its acceptance before noon, but the email was accidentally deleted by an Oftmark employee.**

b   **Aftercool telephoned an acceptance to Oftmark in the afternoon.**

c   **Instead of a telephoned acceptance Oftmark's offer had specified: 'Please notify us of your acceptance by first-class registered post sent before noon.' Aftercool sent a letter of acceptance before noon by unregistered post, which was never received by Oftmark Ltd.**

CAUTION!

- The question makes clear that there is an offer. In consequence, do not spend time explaining what is needed to establish an offer. The focus of the question is clearly upon problems relating to acceptance.
- The facts of problem questions are designed to raise a variety of legal issues. When reading a question, carefully note the issues raised by a particular fact or set of facts.

DIAGRAM ANSWER PLAN

Identify the issues	■ Identify the legal issues—outline the process of offer and acceptance. ■ Concentrate on acceptance.
Relevant law	■ Define and explain acceptance. ■ Prescribed mode of acceptance. What is the effect of Aftercool Ltd's employing a mode of acceptance different from that stipulated by Oftmark Ltd? ■ When does acceptance take place by fax? What flexibility does *Brinkibon* offer either party in these circumstances?
Apply the law	■ Communication of acceptance—application of *Entores* and *Brinkibon*. ■ (a) At what point was Aftercool's emailed rejection/withdrawal effective: when it was capable of being accessed or only when it was actually read? ■ (b) When did Oftmark's offer lapse, thereby negating any subsequent acceptance? ■ (c) Did Oftmark impliedly exclude the postal rule? What is the impact of a change to the prescribed mode of acceptance?
Conclude	■ If there is a valid mode of acceptance, arguably communication of acceptance when Oftmark should have received acceptance. ■ (a) Arguably the email rejection/withdrawal may be effective when it should have been read, subject to whether or not there had already been an effective acceptance. ■ (b) Offer made by Oftmark lapsed at 12 noon, 'acceptance' in the afternoon ineffective. ■ (c) If postal rule applies a contract is formed on posting, if the postal rule does not apply no acceptance and no contract. Even if the prescribed mode of acceptance rule is satisfied, there is no communication and no contract.

[1] The answer acknowledges the existence of an offer, as indicated in the question, but does not dwell on this.

[2] This sentence identifies the issue, ie what is the legal significance of an offer prescribing a mode of acceptance?

[3] The relevant rule of law is clearly stated and supported by authority.

[4] The possible application of the law to the facts is considered and a supportable conclusion drawn.

[5] This is the next legal issue.

It would appear that the requirements of an offer have been made out[1] in that there is sufficient certainty (price and quantity) and intention (business context). The question focuses on issues relating to acceptance of an offer. The significant feature here is that the offeror has clearly prescribed a mode of acceptance.[2] The general rule is that the offeree must adhere to the prescribed mode provided it is mandatory and if he/she does not, the acceptance is invalid (*Eliason v Henshaw* **(1819) 4 Wheat 225**).[3] However, if the prescribed mode of acceptance is not mandatory, it seems that the offeree may choose another equally expeditious means of communication (*Tinn v Hoffman & Co.* **(1873) 29 LT 271**). Into which category does this offer fall? On the one hand, the mode of acceptance is clearly specified but, on the other hand, use of the word 'please' suggests a degree of informality rather than a curt prescription. It is arguable that there is some room for manoeuvre here and, perhaps, the offeree is placed in a difficult position—does O want speed or a particular mode? If speed is of the essence, then A has clearly complied with O's wishes by an immediate near-instantaneous communication which should have the added benefit of a permanent record (ie the printed fax).[4] However, if the telephone or email mode is an absolute requirement, then Aftercool's acceptance is invalid.

Assuming A has employed a valid *mode* of acceptance, has a contract been formed? When does the acceptance take place?[5] The general rule is that acceptance is only effective once it has been 'communicated' to O (*Entores v Miles Far East Corp.*); normally this means receipt by O. In the instant case O does not receive any acceptance because of the malfunctioning fax machine. Does this mean that the acceptance is invalid?

Entores does not, however, provide an inflexible rule (and remember that in *Brownlie v Four Seasons Holdings Inc* **[2017] UKSC 80** Lord Sumption JSC suggested that aspects of the *Entores* case may need to be reconsidered in the future). The rule can be modified in various situations, for example if O is at fault with his defective communications equipment (turning off his 24-hour telex machine), then acceptance may be deemed to occur at the moment when it would have been received (see generally *Brinkibon v Stahag Stahl und Stahl* and *The Brimnes*). If this is the case then A may argue that, as O was at fault in failing to replace the printing cartridge on his fax machine, acceptance was deemed to be effective at 10am (subject to the following comments). As fault and business usage are the determining factors, a different answer might be forthcoming if A clearly recognized that the fax had not been properly transmitted.

There is a further line of argument based on estoppel. In *Entores*, Lord Denning considered the possibility of O's telex machine running out of ink and, therefore, being incapable of receiving A's acceptance. His Lordship suggested that if an offeree reasonably believed that the acceptance had been received, and the offeror was at fault, then the latter would be estopped from saying that the acceptance was not received. This estoppel might be more easily established on the present facts as Aftercool Ltd relied to its detriment upon the assumed communication by entering into a binding agreement with Torquecar Ltd (compare *Argy Trading Development Co. Ltd v Lapid Developments Ltd* **[1977] 1 WLR 444** where it was questioned whether a promissory estoppel could operate without a pre-existing contract).[6]

[6] This shows a wider appreciation of difficulties in using a concept.

Difference with (a)

The case law on the use of email communication in the context of offer and acceptance is still developing. To some extent one must seek to apply relevant principles from existing authority that might be appropriate to deal with the current situation. The basic principle stays the same: to be effective a revocation of an offer must be communicated prior to the time when any effective acceptance has occurred. In the context of faxes, we have seen that communication normally occurs on receipt (*Entores*) but that this rigid rule is subject to flexible interpretation (*Brinkibon*), taking account of the parties' intentions, sound business practice, and a judgement as to where risks should lie. In *Thomas v BPE Solicitors* **[2010] EWHC 306 (Ch)**, it was recognized, in a very strong *obiter* statement, that where email is an expected form of communication, an email sent during 'expected working hours' becomes effective very soon after transmission. Thus, Aftercool could argue that:[7] (i) sufficient communication of the withdrawal had taken place (relying on *Thomas v BPE Solicitors* **[2010] EWHC 306 (Ch)**); (ii) no estoppel could operate in Oftmark's favour as Aftercool's actions could not have induced any alteration of position; and (iii) neither party should be allowed to take advantage of their own fault in order to create or prevent the formation of a contract (see *The Brimnes*).

[7] Drawing on the previously stated law, a number of arguments are highlighted.

Difference with (b)

[8] Part (b) raises the issue of lapse of offer.

What is the effect of A telephoning an acceptance after the noon deadline?[8] An offer will lapse in accordance with its terms or, if this is unclear, a reasonable time after it has been made (see *Ramsgate Victoria Hotel Co. v Montefiore* (1866) **LR 1 Exch 109**). 'Reasonable' will depend on the circumstances, such as the implicit need for urgency displayed in *Quenerduaine v Cole* (1883) **32 WR 185** and the nature and perishability of the goods. On the present facts O has stipulated a reply before noon by telephone or email. It would seem, therefore, that the offer has impliedly lapsed by the time A attempted to accept the terms of the offer. (Note: the offeror would have expected to receive an acceptance before noon.) Another possible argument is that A, by not complying with the conditions of the offer, has made a counter-offer which was not accepted by O (*Wettern Electric Ltd v Welsh Development Agency* [1983] QB 796).

Difference with (c)

[9] This part raises two legal issues: operation of the postal rule; and the rule as to prescribed mode of communication. Note the use of IRAC.

Two issues arise to be discussed.[9] First, does the postal rule apply? The postal rule provides that acceptance is complete when a letter of acceptance is posted, *Adams v Lindsell* (1818) 1 B & Ald 681. The post is clearly contemplated as the expected medium for communicating acceptance. However, the postal rule can be excluded by express contrary intent, provided it is specified in the terms of the offer. For example, when completing a football pools coupon there is a clear statement that the coupon must be received by a certain time before any liability ensues. The present facts are similar to *Holwell Securities Ltd v Hughes* [1974] 1 WLR 155 where the offeree was requested to exercise his option by 'notice in writing'. These words were held to exclude the postal rule as the offeror was specifying the need to see the acceptance (ie have 'notice' of it) before any contract was formed. Equally, O appears to be imposing a similar condition. If so, no contract would come into existence as the postal acceptance never reached O.

The alternative argument is that the court in *Holwell* was applying the provisions of **s. 196 of the Law of Property Act 1925** in which, *inter alia*, the exercise of an option by post was deemed effective 'at the time at which the . . . letter would in the ordinary course be delivered'. Thus, *Holwell* is limited to contracts affecting interests in land. Moreover, whereas 'notice in writing' implies delivery, notification by post might suggest that the act of posting is sufficient; in particular, only O can 'notice' an acceptance, but only A can notify it. If this argument were accepted the postal rule would be applied; the acceptance would be effective on posting irrespective of its subsequent loss.

Secondly, by using unregistered post has Aftercool sent a valid acceptance? Previous comments have suggested that this will depend upon the contents of the offer. If registered post is a precondition for acceptance, no contract will exist, whereas if any equally expeditious means of communication is acceptable, a contract should be formed since registered and unregistered delivery have the same timescale for delivery, *Manchester Diocesan Council for Education v Commercial and General Investments Ltd* [1970] 1 WLR 241. Moreover, what is the purpose of stipulating registered post? It cannot help O as the acceptance is either delivered, in which case it is known, or not delivered, in which case it remains unknown. In *Yates Building Co. Ltd v RJ Pulleyn & Sons (York) Ltd* (1975) **119 Sol Jo 370**, the court concluded that the instruction to use registered post was intended to protect the offeree, so, if A took a risk by using unregistered post (thereby lacking proof of transmission if the letter was lost in transit), his acceptance would still remain valid on proof of delivery.

In conclusion, if the postal rule applied, then A's acceptance is effective on posting, provided there is sufficient evidence that the letter was actually posted. If the postal rule does not apply, no communication of acceptance has taken place so no contract can exist.

LOOKING FOR EXTRA MARKS?

- To provide a complete answer to this question, students must have a reasonable knowledge of the decisions in *Entores Ltd v Miles Far East Corp.* [1955] 2 QB 327, *The Brimnes* [1975] QB 929, and *Brinkibon v Stahag Stahl* [1983] 2 AC 34. In particular, the *obiter* comments made in the judgments will address the problem of Oftmark's fault in not maintaining the fax machine properly and the reliance of Aftercool Ltd in entering into a contract with Torquecar Ltd.

- This question requires an appreciation of the problems of adapting the rules of offer and acceptance to new developments in communications technology. Using existing authority, particularly an ability to use the various *obiter dicta*, will ensure top marks.

- A first-class answer might also include the following point: in **reg. 11(2) of the Electronic Commerce (EC Directive) Regulations 2002, SI No. 2013** (applicable to internet contracting rather than email exchanges), it is assumed that communications over the internet take place once the recipients 'are able to access them'. This might suggest a useful way of treating emails sent during or outside normal office hours—the former being effective almost immediately whereas the latter only becoming effective the following morning (as hinted at in *Thomas v BPE Solicitors*). On the other hand, what is meant by 'able to access'? Would this include remote access outside work hours?

QUESTION | **4**

Sweatshirt Ltd, which manages a chain of sports fitness centres, places the following advertisement on its website, dated 5 January:

Pay for one year's standard membership at a Sweatshirt Fitness Centre, and swim 400 consecutive lengths in one of our pools by 10 January, and you will be rewarded with a free one-year membership for your spouse. Happy Swimming and Good Luck!

Owing to bad publicity, resulting from some of its new members suffering heart attacks in its swimming pools, on the morning of 8 January Sweatshirt Ltd placed a prominent notice on its website withdrawing the promotional membership campaign contained on its website.

Discuss the legal position of the parties in the following separate situations:

a   Andrew paid for a year's membership at his local Sweatshirt Fitness Centre on 7 January. The following day he logged on to the Sweatshirt website and noticed the revocation. Nevertheless, he attempted to swim the 400 lengths that afternoon but found that he did not have the stamina to complete more than 25 lengths.

b   Bernice applied for a year's membership on the morning of 10 January. While arranging for payment of her membership fee she was informed of Sweatshirt Ltd's promotion. As Bernice was a long-distance swimmer, she immediately rushed into the changing rooms to prepare for the challenge. However, before entering the pool, she was told of Sweatshirt Ltd's revocation by the pool attendant.

CAUTION!

■ The nature of a unilateral contract and the associated difficulties should be explained in your answer.

■ Offers of a unilateral contract often require acceptance to be performed over a period of time, for example, *Carlill v Carbolic Smoke Ball Co Ltd*. This gives rise to the question of when does acceptance take place? An offeree may argue that commencement of the stipulated act is an acceptance, whereas the offeror's response will inevitably be that he/she bargained for nothing short of a completed performance.

■ A related difficulty is whether such an offer can be revoked legitimately once the offeree has commenced performance. An understanding of the competing interests and how the law seeks to protect them is necessary to successfully answer a question on unilateral contracts.

DIAGRAM ANSWER PLAN

Identify the issues	■ Identify the legal issues—outline the law relating to offer and acceptance. ■ What is a unilateral contract and when can an offer of such a contract be revoked?
Relevant law	■ Is Sweatshirt Ltd's advertisement an offer of a unilateral contract or an invitation to treat? Can you draw an analogy with *Carlill*? ■ If it is an offer, what act must be performed in order to accept it? ■ At what point is it too late for Sweatshirt to revoke its offer: once performance of the required act has commenced or after completion? See *Errington v Errington*. ■ What difficulties emerge when attempting to compensate the offeree for the offeror's revocation of his offer of a unilateral contract?
Apply the law	■ Advert appears to be an offer of a unilateral contract. ■ (a) Andrew—arguably Sweatshirt may not revoke offer: *Errington v Errington*, but note *Luxor v Cooper*. ■ (b) Bernice—acceptance in ignorance of offer not possible: *Williams v Carwardine*, but note *Gibbons v Proctor*. When is notification of a revocation by a third party effective? Does *Dickinson v Dodds* suggest that the third party must be reliable?
Conclude	■ Evaluate arguments on application of the law to the facts in relation to each party.

SUGGESTED ANSWER

This question focuses on the difficulties associated with the offer of a unilateral contract.

[1] This sentence identifies the first issue raised by the question.

The first issue to consider is whether the advertisement of Sweatshirt Ltd (S) was an offer or an invitation to treat (ITT).[1] An ITT is essentially an opening gambit in negotiations and is therefore incapable of acceptance, whereas an offer is an unequivocal proposition made with an intention to be legally bound.[2] The advertisement contains a definite proposal and, arguably, as it emanates from a business the court may be more inclined to construe it as an offer

[2] An explanation is given of the nature of an invitation to treat and an offer.

(see *Carlill v Carbolic Smoke Ball Co. Ltd* [1893] 1 QB 256). The language used by S in the advert is consistent with an intention to be bound by the specific proposal made. It would be difficult for S to argue that the advertisement's tone suggested a lack of relevant intent as it incorporates both an immediate benefit and detriment: earn free membership for a spouse in return for paying for your own membership and enduring the physical challenge of swimming 400 lengths.[3] Consequently, the advertisement appears to represent an offer of a unilateral contract which will be converted into a binding contract once an appropriate act of acceptance has occurred. Note that if the advertisement was held to be an ITT,[4] none of the parties would have any realistic prospect of claiming the reward as their swimming feats would simply be viewed, at most, as the making of an offer, with an unfettered discretion as to whether to allocate free membership to any of the parties' spouses.

[3] Note the immediate application of the law to the facts of the problem.

[4] An explanation is given of the consequences should the advert be viewed as an invitation to treat.

Andrew (A)

Assuming that the original advert was an offer, when does A's acceptance occur? The presumption in unilateral contracts is that only the completion of the stipulated act can amount to acceptance as, in the majority of cases, this is what the offeror bargained for. In our facts, Sweatshirt (S) does not therefore appear to be under any liability to A as he failed to complete the 400 lengths, nor was there any suggestion that S would compensate for any failed attempts. Support for this conclusion can be found in *Luxor (Eastbourne) Ltd v Cooper* [1941] AC 108 where the client (the offeror) agreed to pay the estate agent (the offeree) £10,000 if he could find a purchaser for two cinemas at a minimum price of £185,000.[5] The estate agent introduced a prospective purchaser who agreed, subject to contract, to pay that price. The client ignored this offer and, instead, sold the cinemas to a third party. The House of Lords held that any acceptance would necessarily entail a completed sale to the purchaser introduced by the estate agent and, accordingly, the client was free to revoke his offer at any time before that acceptance had been completed.

[5] Note that usually it is sufficient to state a rule and the authority for a rule, in this answer the facts of *Luxor v Cooper* are used to argue a particular point.

Moreover, the House refused to imply a term that the client would not revoke his offer in these circumstances as this was not necessary to give business efficacy to both parties' intentions. This appears to undermine any argument by A that S was prevented from withdrawing its offer (thus preventing A from completing, if there is time, by 10 January as originally stated).

However, A possesses a very strong counter-argument. In *Errington v Errington and Woods* [1952] 1 KB 290[6] a father promised his son and daughter-in-law that, if they paid the existing and future mortgage instalments on his house as they fell due, the house would belong to them. Various *obiter* statements in the Court of Appeal suggested that

[6] This is a key case in understanding the law concerning revocation of an offer of a unilateral contract once performance of an act has commenced.

the father's promise was irrevocable once the couple had 'entered on performance of the act' but that this limitation disappeared if they left it 'incomplete and unperformed'. Indeed, whereas in *Luxor* the extravagant commission (£10,000 on a sale price of £185,000) demonstrated the estate agent's acknowledgement of both the risk of not finding a purchaser and the client's right to revoke before completion, in *Errington* the couple would have never assumed an equivalent *business* risk while diligently paying off the instalments[7] (see also *Ward v Byham* [1956] 1 WLR 496 where a refusal to countenance any revocation by the father could be similarly justified). Moreover, the couple conferred a *tangible benefit* on the father with every payment made, thereby making any attempted revocation more inequitable as time progressed. Might it be argued that the payment of membership fees provides an equally important benefit to S?

In conclusion,[8] the court will need to balance three competing interests in reaching a satisfactory conclusion: *reliance* of the offeree (payment of fees in order to secure the advertised benefit), *benefit* conferred on the offeror (receipt of fees), and the inherent *risk* being accepted by the offeree (who may be unable to complete the stipulated challenge). The current weight of authority (eg *Daulia Ltd v Four Millbank Nominees Ltd* [1978] 1 Ch 231) is that once the offeree has 'embarked upon a course of performance' that is intended to lead to completion of the required act, the offeror will be prevented from revoking the offer (see also *United Dominions Trust (Commercial) Ltd v Eagle Aircraft Services Ltd* [1968] 1 All ER 104). On the facts, it must surely be the case that A did embark upon the required course of performance once he had signed a contract to pay membership fees for one year. Consequently, the subsequent revocation will not have an immediate effect as A will have until the end of 10 January to improve his swimming performance and comply fully with the terms of the offer!

Bernice (B)

B's position is different from that of A. In S's favour is the uncertainty of whether B entered a contract of membership before being told of S's advertisement.[9] The general rule is that one cannot accept an offer without knowledge of it (eg *Williams v Carwardine* (1833) 5 C & P 566). On our facts, B was informed of the promotion 'while arranging for payment of her membership fee'. If knowledge of the promotion was acquired *after* the offer and acceptance had taken place, S would rely upon *Williams* to argue that B had no right to claim free membership for her spouse, even if she had actually completed the required number of lengths. B's only defence would be to cite *Gibbons v Proctor* (1891) 64 LT 594 which suggests that, where an offer of

[7] This section demonstrates an appreciation of the interrelationship of the cases of *Luxor v Cooper* and *Errington v Errington*.

[8] The conclusion states the interests that have to be considered in determining whether an offer of a unilateral contract may be withdrawn and potential consequences.

[9] This is the next legal issue that needs to be considered, ie is it possible to accept in ignorance of an offer?

reward is advertised, a person can claim the reward provided he/she was informed of this offer *before completion* of the required act. As B was notified of the reward *before* embarking upon her marathon swim, she may yet succeed on this point. At present the law is very unclear on these matters (especially as *Gibbons* has been doubted) so a definitive answer is not possible.[10]

If the decision in *Gibbons* prevails, and B is entitled to accept S's offer, she will presumably adopt the same argument as Andrew with regard to the timing of S's revocation; namely, that she had already embarked upon performance before being notified of any attempted revocation. However, B can strengthen this argument by pointing to the manner in which S's revocation was communicated to her. It was held in *Shuey v US*, **92 US 73 (1875)** (a US decision and therefore of only persuasive authority) that an offer of reward was revocable by giving the revocation 'the same notoriety' as that given to the offer, even if the offeree A had no actual knowledge of it. This is justifiable where the offeror does not know the potential offerees (in *Shuey* the offer was made to the public) but S will have a record of all of its new members (names, addresses, and telephone numbers presumably). Indeed, B was actually present in the fitness centre when signing up for membership. In such circumstances the court may decide that S should have communicated directly, and individually, with all of its new members, including B. If B failed on this point her case would be weakened, since it was recognized in *Dickinson v Dodds* **(1876) 2 Ch D 463** that a reasonable third party may communicate the offeror's revocation even though not authorized by the offeror to perform this task. One must assume that knowledge of revocation acquired from a paid employee of S would be covered by the same principle.

Finally, there is the problem of the measure of damages. If B is entitled to accept S's offer, and S's revocation is ruled ineffective, how should B be compensated now that she has been discouraged from swimming the required lengths within the stipulated time? The contract for the free one-year membership does not exist until B has completed all of the stipulated acts, so S cannot be in breach of that contract. In the light of B's manifest ability to comply with the swimming challenge, the court may consider S to be in breach of a *collateral* contract not to revoke. Alternatively, perhaps a compromise can be reached which allows S to revoke its offer subject to an obligation to reimburse B to the extent of her justifiable reliance on the offer. While not a perfect solution, in that it leaves open the question of how reliance is to be quantified, it would enable a court to *apportion* loss rather than take the all-or-nothing approach evidenced in *Errington* and *Luxor,* respectively (see also certain *obiter* comments regarding a *quantum meruit* raised in *Morrison SS Co. v Crown* **(1924) 20 Ll LR 283**).

[10] This sentence sums up the legal position noting that the authorities appear inconsistent. Commentary on authority is a good way to get extra marks.

LOOKING FOR EXTRA MARKS?

- Questions concerning unilateral contracts require an appreciation of what constitutes acceptance and when revocation of an offer may take place. The general rule is that revocation of an offer is permissible at any time prior to its acceptance (completion of the stipulated act), but strict adherence to this rule might appear inequitable in unilateral contracts once the offeree has begun to perform the stipulated act (and potentially incurred expenditure on the faith of the offer remaining open). Should the offeree be afforded some measure of protection against a premature revocation?

- If the relevant cases are unclear or the rules in cases need to be reconciled or you are relying on an *obiter dictum* rather than a *ratio decidendi*, it is important to make a comment. This shows an appreciation of the rules of judicial precedent in presenting an argument.

Q   QUESTION | 5

It is a basic axiom of the Law of England and Wales that, although the courts cannot make a contract for the parties, they will strive to uphold a bargain wherever possible.

Discuss in relation to the principles of certainty of terms.

CAUTION!

- When answering an essay question, avoid writing all you know about the topic in an indiscriminate fashion. Tailor your knowledge to the specific question being posed. To this end it is important to take the essay title apart and identify its constituent elements.

- With essay questions, careful attention must be paid to planning your answer. Unlike problem questions, which will usually have an inherent structure, answers to essay questions may be organized in a variety of ways.

DIAGRAM ANSWER PLAN

General policy of upholding agreements.

▼

Explore circumstances in which courts are prepared to clarify vagueness.

▼

Courts' approach to agreements providing machinery for future clarification of terms.

▼

> Vagueness the courts will not clarify.

▼

> Striking an appropriate balance.

▼

> Conclusion.

 SUGGESTED ANSWER

[1]This paragraph outlines the issue of certainty of terms and the effect of a lack of certainty.

In general terms, it is the parties who make the contract and fix its boundaries, while the courts enforce the bargain thus created. It follows that if the agreement is too uncertain or imprecise the courts will be unable to enforce it.[1] For example, in *Scammell (G) and Nephew Ltd v Ouston* **[1941] AC 251** there was an agreement to acquire goods 'on hire-purchase terms' but the House of Lords held that this could not be a binding contract as it was 'so vaguely expressed that it cannot, standing by itself, be given a definite meaning' (as there are many different types of hire-purchase terms!).

[2]The main point of the essay is outlined here.

Nevertheless, the courts have traditionally sought to uphold bargains where possible and, as Lord Wright emphasized in *Hillas & Co. Ltd v Arcos Ltd* **(1932) 147 LT 503**, have not been 'too astute or subtle in finding defects', even where the commercial agreement has been crudely drafted by businessmen.[2] In *Hillas*, the plaintiffs agreed to buy from the defendants a quantity of Russian softwood timber of a particular quality, the agreement containing an option for the plaintiffs to buy more timber at a later date but with no particulars of size or quality. When the plaintiffs sought to exercise the option, the defendants argued that the clause was vague and indeterminate. The House of Lords held that, having regard to previous dealings, there was sufficient intention to be bound and the agreement could be rendered certain by referring to the parties' previous dealings and the normal practice in the timber trade. *Hillas* was considered in *Baird Textile Holdings Limited v Marks & Spencer Plc* **[2001] EWCA Civ 274** where the Court of Appeal, focusing on Lord Thankerton's speech in *Hillas*, made a distinction 'between cases where the contract provides for an objective standard which the court applies by ascertaining what is reasonable and those where, there being no such standard, the test of reasonableness is [illegitimately] being used to make an agreement for the parties which they have not made for themselves'.

[3] The point concerning defects in an agreement is explained with reference to cases by way of example.

Hillas is illustrative of the courts' willingness to sometimes imply terms that make commercial sense of the agreement, but an alternative method of resolving uncertainty is to delete a meaningless, subsidiary provision, leaving the remainder of the contract complete and enforceable.[3] In *Nicolene Ltd v Simmonds* **[1953] 1 QB 543,**[4] the words 'we are in agreement that the usual conditions of acceptance apply' were held to be meaningless. As Denning LJ commented, if the opposite conclusion had been reached in *Nicolene,* defaulters would be 'scanning their contracts to find some meaningless clause on which to ride free'. However, the *Nicolene* principle cannot function if the meaningless clause is intended to govern an undertaking *central* to the agreement, for such uncertainty would potentially vitiate the whole agreement.

[4] The discussion of this case follows the PEA formula.

[5] A new point is raised by this paragraph and then explained and analysed.

The courts also look favourably on agreements which, although leaving some issue to be resolved in the future, provide the machinery or criteria for its resolution.[5] Thus, an agreement will normally be upheld if it provides for the resolution of outstanding issues by arbitration (*Brown v Gould* **[1972] Ch 53**). This approach was extended in *Sudbrook Trading Estate Ltd v Eggleton* **[1983] 1 AC 444** where a lease gave the tenant an option to purchase the premises 'at such price as may be agreed upon by two valuers' who were to be appointed by each party. The landlord refused to appoint a valuer, but the House of Lords held that the option did not fail for uncertainty. *The substance of the undertaking was an agreement to sell at a reasonable price*, to be determined by valuers, and the extra stipulation that each party should nominate a valuer was 'subsidiary and inessential'. But while a court may choose to follow this analysis and substitute its own procedures for resolving uncertainty where the original machinery breaks down, the Court of Appeal decisions in *Gillatt v Sky Television Ltd* **[2000] 2 BCLC 103** and *Infiniteland Ltd v Artisan Contracting Ltd* **[2005] EWCA Civ 758, [2005] All ER (D) 236** suggest that such discretion is severely circumscribed as it is not always easy to separate the *process* by which an agreed price is to be reached (eg *Sudbrook*), from the essential *criteria* for determining that price (which a court will not substitute in accordance with *May and Butcher v R* **[1934] 2 KB 17**).

[6] These words raise the difficult issue of agreements to agree and are then followed by an explanation of case law relevant to the issue.

On the other hand, the courts have not always been deterred from clarifying uncertainty where the vagueness in question relates to a fundamental obligation which the parties have deliberately left open-ended.[6] This may occur, for example, where both parties are reluctant to finalize every aspect of a long-term agreement, preferring to leave some flexibility around questions, such as the price (which may, of course, be affected by changing market conditions) and the manner of payment. In such cases, the parties may agree to agree the outstanding aspects of the agreement at a later stage. In *May and Butcher v R*, an agreement for the sale of tentage provided that the price should be agreed 'from time to time'. The House of Lords held that the agreement was incomplete as it was an agreement to agree in the future. If the agreement had been silent on these issues, the House said s. 8(2) of the Sale of Goods Act 1893 (**now** 1979*)* might have led to a reasonable price being payable, but the parties had shown that this was not their intention by providing for a further agreement. However, *May and Butcher* has been distinguished and, although it is difficult to generalize in this area, it seems that if the courts identify substantial agreement between the parties some points may be left for future resolution without vitiating the agreement. For example, in *Foley v Classique Coaches Ltd* [1934] 2 KB 1, the plaintiff owned a petrol station and adjoining land which he agreed to sell to the defendants on condition that they should agree to buy all the petrol for their coach business from him. The agreement regarding the petrol was executed and provided that it was to be supplied 'at a price to be agreed by the parties in writing and from time to time'. The land was conveyed and the petrol agreement was acted on for three years but the defendants then argued that it was incomplete in relation to the price of the petrol. The Court of Appeal held that the agreement was enforceable and that, consequently, the defendants must pay a reasonable price for the petrol. The most influential factors in the decision appeared to be that the contract had been acted upon for several years[7] and that the petrol agreement formed part of a linked bargain with the sale of the land, the defendants paying a price for the land which no doubt reflected the fact that they would buy their petrol from the plaintiffs. However, performance may not be sufficient to save an agreement where the evidence shows that the parties have failed to reach any agreement on particular essential terms, for example *British Steel Corp. v Cleveland Bridge and Engineering Co. Ltd* [1984] 1 All ER 504.

[7] An important factor is that of performance of the agreement, but performance within itself may not be enough to render an agreement enforceable.

Case law has also cast doubt upon the notion that the courts will strive to uphold the parties' bargain where possible.[8] In *Walford v Miles* [1992] 2 AC 128 parties were negotiating over the sale of the defendant's business. An agreement was reached by which the plaintiff would provide the defendant with a letter of comfort from their bankers confirming that a loan would be granted to the plaintiff and, in return, the defendant agreed to terminate any negotiations with third parties and not to consider any alternative offers.

[8] The answer then explores the limits on the enforceability of agreements. The key case of *Walford v Miles* is explored in some detail.

The comfort letter was provided but the defendant withdrew from the negotiations and sold the business to a third party. The House of Lords held that the plaintiff's action must fail. The House of Lords said it was possible to have an enforceable lock-out contract (ie an agreement *not* to negotiate with third parties) provided the duration of the 'lock-out' was specified expressly (which was not the case here). Moreover, the House of Lords held that the parties could not be 'locked in' (as the plaintiff had also argued) to negotiate *positively* as this would amount to an uncertain and unenforceable contract to negotiate.

[9] The implications of *Walford v Miles* are addressed in this paragraph and the primacy of the intention of the parties considered.

Walford arguably illustrates the laissez-faire principles of self-reliance and judicial non-interventionism.[9] It is suggested that such decisions ignore English law's basic tenet that agreements should be validated wherever possible and, in so doing, potentially encourage bad faith in commercial transactions. Consequently, the Court of Appeal decision in *Petromec Inc. v Petroleo Brasiliero SA Petrobas (No. 3)* [2005] EWCA Civ 891 is to be welcomed. The facts involved a provision within an *existing* contract that required the parties to negotiate in *good faith* the costs of upgrading that contract (the possibility of upgrading was permitted and acknowledged within the contract). This provision was held to be enforceable. Longmore LJ was not put off by the difficulty of determining the result of 'good faith' negotiations (ie in calculating the costs of upgrading) as this would be a relatively easy task. Moreover, while withdrawing from negotiations in 'bad faith' (ie a potential breach of contract) would be difficult to ascertain, to ignore that possibility would unfairly undermine the expressed and reasonable intentions of the parties. However, it is not necessarily the case that an agreement to agree contained in an existing agreement will be enforceable (see *Morris v Swanton* [2018] EWCA Civ 2763).

[10] A conclusion is reached; seeking to link the discussion in the body of the answer to the requirements of the question.

In conclusion,[10] basic principles in the case law support the position taken by the question. The courts have sought to uphold 'uncertain' bargains through reference to the previous dealings of the parties, by disregarding meaningless clauses and, sometimes, even by substituting its own machinery to resolve uncertainty. Moreover, the courts have been reluctant to not enforce an agreement where there has been part performance of that agreement. However, there are limits and the courts have often been unwilling to enforce agreements where further negotiation or agreement is required. Nevertheless, the case law developments question whether such a position is absolute. So, while the traditional notion that courts seek to uphold rather than destroy contracts has, to some extent, come under attack in recent times, the sentiments expressed in the original question still retain validity in the law today.

LOOKING FOR EXTRA MARKS?

■ This question calls for an understanding of certainty of terms. Students must be able to make an accurate analysis of the lengths to which the courts will go in enforcing contracts. The decisions tend to make technical distinctions, but students should be aware of the important substantive issues raised in *Walford v Miles* **[1992] 2 AC 128**.

■ The tension in the law between the courts refusing to write contracts for parties but also not wanting to be perceived as the destroyer of bargains should inform your answer. The limits that the courts will go to in order to uphold a bargain should be clearly drawn and any underlying principles revealed.

 TAKING THINGS FURTHER

■ Brown, I. and Chandler, A., 'Intent and Contract Formation' [1991] Conv 149.

*Explains the decision and implications of Blackpool and Fylde Aero Club Ltd v Blackpool Borough Council **[1990] 1 WLR 1195**.*

■ Hill, S., 'Flogging a Dead Horse—The Postal Acceptance Rule and Email' (2001) 17(2) JCL 151.

Considers whether the postal rule of acceptance extends to communication of acceptance by email.

■ Macdonald, E., 'Dispatching the Dispatch Rule? The Postal Rule, E-Mail, Revocation and Implied Terms' (2013) 19(2) Web JCLI; http://webjcli.org/article/view/239.

Considers the basis of the postal rule and its merits in the light of modern forms of communication; especially email.

Consideration and Intention to Create Legal Relations

3

In order to attempt the questions in this chapter you must have covered the following areas in your revision:

- Understanding the nature and development of the doctrine of consideration;
- The types of consideration: executory and executed;
- The rule that consideration must move from the promisee;
- The rules on past consideration;
- The rule that consideration must be sufficient but need not be adequate;
- Understanding of the actions or promises which the courts do not recognize as valuable consideration;
- The principle and operation of promissory estoppel;
- Awareness that as well as the other elements necessary for the formation of a contract, there must be an intention to create legal relations.

KEY DEBATES

Debate: should both consideration and an intention to create legal relations be necessary for an agreement to be enforceable under the Law of England and Wales?

Debate: should it be necessary to establish consideration to modify contracts?

Should parties be free to modify a contract in situations where it is, in effect, advantageous to both parties even where this leads to 'invented consideration' (as was arguably the case in *Williams v Roffey Bros & Nicholls (Contractors) Ltd* [1991] 1 QB 1)?

ⓘ

Debate: the scope and effect of promissory estoppel under English law.

Should the Law of England and Wales adopt a different theoretical approach such as that taken in *Walton Stores (Interstate) Ltd v Maher* **(1988) 164 CLR 387** (Australia)?

QUESTION | 1

Gaia is a successful technology consultant who is about to launch a new business, RoboWiz, that specializes in the sale and supply of 'intelligent industrial robots' to the manufacturing sector. She hires a stand at the prestigious World Industrial Technology Exhibition (WITE) in London, to demonstrate the range and capabilities of the robots.

Exprop contracts with Gaia to erect the exhibition stand for £10,000. Gaia also persuades *Tech Weekly*, a new London-based publication that is seeking to raise its profile among the business community, to advertise the presence of RoboWiz's exhibition stand at the WITE for free.

Gaia is determined that her WITE exhibition stand projects the right image so she subsequently promises to pay Exprop an extra £2,000 to make sure 'it has a wow factor'. She also promises to pay £1,000 to Securefest, a company employed by WITE to provide security for the exhibition, if its employees can keep a 'watch' on her stand.

The RoboWiz stand is a great success but Gaia refuses to pay Exprop the extra £2,000 and also refuses to pay Securefest its £1,000. *Tech Weekly* is being pursued by some creditors so Gaia promises to pay it £3,000 for the advertising of her exhibition stand. However, she later withdraws her promise to *Tech Weekly* after looking at the state of her private finances, despite *Tech Weekly* having already incurred additional costs in anticipation of receiving that money.

Discuss the legal position of all the parties involved.

CAUTION!

- Do not write everything you know about consideration: be selective to keep your answer relevant to the question.
- Address all of the areas raised by the question.
- Using the IRAC method should ensure that you demonstrate the relevance of the law and how it applies to the facts.
- Make sure that you advise all of the parties.

DIAGRAM ANSWER PLAN

Identify the issues	■ Identify the legal issues—the question relates to the rules of consideration, particularly where parties change existing contractual arrangements once performance has begun. ■ Need to address several potential claims.
Relevant law	■ Outline the relevant law: the rules of consideration. ■ In relation to each party, you need to assess what, if any, consideration was received.
Apply the law	■ G v E—did E exceed its duty to G? If not, did E provide G with a practical benefit? ■ Did S exceed its duty to G? If not, can S take advantage of the third-party exception? ■ Did *Tech Weekly* (TW) provide any consideration to G? Was TW's consideration past?
Conclude	■ Available remedies? ■ Conclusion.

SUGGESTED ANSWER

¹Answers to problem questions do not need the same type of formal introduction as essay answers. In the IRAC structure, an opening paragraph should analyse the facts to identify the legal issues raised, outlining the questions the answer will address.

²In problem questions with a number of parties and a complex factual scenario, using subheadings can help to separate out the various relationships. Apply the IRAC structure for each.

³The question does not raise any specific issues regarding the intention of the parties to create legal relations, but making this statement and perhaps referring to an appropriate legal authority could bring extra marks.

This question concerns sufficiency of consideration, past consideration, third party consideration, and promissory estoppel.[1]

Gaia (G) v Exprop (E)

G and E[2] clearly initially entered into an enforceable contract: intention to create legal relations will be presumed where two businesses have reached an agreement[3], while G's promise to pay E £10,000, in return for the erection of the stand, clearly constitutes consideration on both sides. Can E claim the additional £2,000? This will depend on whether or not E has provided separate consideration for this additional promise.

[4] Identify and explain the law relevant to the issues. When deciding whether a contract modification is enforceable, treat 'exceeding one's duty' (*Hartley v Ponsonby*) separately from 'acquiring a practical benefit' (*Williams v Roffey*).

Courts do not normally inquire into the **adequacy** of the consideration[4] provided by either party as long as there is clear evidence that both have contributed *something of value in the eyes of the law* to their bargain (the *sufficiency* of consideration rule). However, where A performs an existing contractual duty to B it is normally assumed this does not represent sufficient consideration for any additional payment from B, particularly as A has not suffered any further legal detriment in doing so. For example, in **Stilk v Myrick (1809) 2 Camp 317**, some crew members deserted during a voyage so the captain promised to share their wages among the remaining crew if they stayed on board until the final destination. It was held that the sailors had not provided additional consideration as they were merely performing their existing contractual duty.[5]

[5] Explaining a key case here.

However, if the promisee *exceeds* their contractual duty (or promises to do so) a court will treat this as sufficient consideration for an additional payment. In **Hartley v Ponsonby (1857) 7 E & B 872** the scale of desertion by the crew was so great that it became dangerous to continue the voyage. This freed the sailors from their existing contractual commitments and enabled them to negotiate a new contract with increased remuneration. On the facts of this question it is unclear whether E has exceeded its existing contractual duty[6]. Arguably E is simply performing an existing contractual duty in erecting the exhibition stand, but if it agrees to incur extra costs beyond those set out in the contract and/or it agrees to exceed the level of performance stipulated (in order to give the stand a 'wow factor'), E could claim the additional £2,000.

[6] Apply the law. The facts of questions may lack clarity: this is to encourage you to discuss alternatives.

Assuming E fails on that point, what other options might it pursue? More recent case law has suggested[7] that if G (the promisor) has obtained a factual benefit, enforcement of the additional promise is possible as acknowledging commercial reality and the underlying intentions of the parties. For example, in **Williams v Roffey Bros & Nicholls (Contractors) Ltd [1991] 1 QB 1**,[8] the defendant building contractors were refurbishing a block of flats. The carpentry work was subcontracted to the plaintiff who subsequently encountered financial difficulties and was unable to complete the work. The defendants offered the plaintiff an additional £10,000 to complete the (contracted) work on time, thereby potentially avoiding payment to a third party of any liquidated damages for late completion of the overall contract or the need to hire alternative carpenters. As there was no evidence of economic duress, the Court of Appeal concluded that the defendants had obtained a practical benefit from the arrangement, making payment of the additional £10,000 enforceable. In G's case, there seem to be three possible conclusions.[9] First, if E agreed to exceed the original contract specification, E will have provided consideration in the traditional sense (a *legal* benefit). Accordingly, E could rely on **Hartley v Ponsonby** to claim the extra money. Secondly, if E did not agree to exceed the original contract specification, E might argue, applying **Roffey**, that G has nevertheless secured a *practical* benefit from

[7] A key point in this area of law.

[8] Explain this key case.

[9] Having applied the law, here conclude and advise. Where the facts are not clear, identifying alternative outcomes can bring additional marks.

taking possession of an exhibition stand that matches her enhanced expectations. If so, G's promise to pay the additional £2,000 may be enforceable. Thirdly, if the exhibition stand conforms to the original contract and G secures no other practical benefit E will be unable to claim the extra money. The final decision will depend on the court's interpretation of the actual wording used in the contract to describe the exact features of the desired exhibition stand.

Gaia (G) v Securefest (S)

When G promises to pay S £1,000 for keeping an eye on her stand she is, effectively, paying S to perform an existing contractual duty that it owes to WITE (a third party). Performance of an existing duty owed to a third party is a good consideration: the question is whether S provided sufficient consideration to support this separate contract.[10] Assuming the court decides that the 'agreement' between G and S was sufficiently clear and intended to be legally binding, it would likely follow the decisions in *New Zealand Shipping Co. Ltd v AM Satterthwaite & Co. Ltd (The Eurymedon)* **[1975] AC 154** and *Pao On v Lau Yiu Long* **[1980] AC 614** and find the presence of consideration: S has suffered a detriment by making itself potentially liable to two different parties if it fails to perform its security duties and G has secured a benefit by being able to sue S directly.[11] On this reasoning G must pay S the £1,000.[12]

> [10] Identify the legal issues raised.

> [11] Apply the law to this aspect of the problem.

> [12] Advise G.

Gaia (G) v *Tech Weekly* (TW)

Have the parties entered into an enforceable contract?[13] G promised to pay TW *after* it had advertised her exhibition stand. The doctrine of consideration demands a contemporaneous exchange of consideration by the parties; where one party performs an act constituting consideration *before* any promise to pay for it has been given, the consideration is said to be 'past' and unenforceable (see *Roscorla v Thomas* **(1842) 3 QB 234**—a promise that a horse was 'sound' *after* it had been sold was treated as past consideration). G's promise may therefore be unenforceable. However, there is an exception to this rule,[14] where: first, the promisor must have asked the promisee to perform the act; secondly, it must reasonably be assumed that the promisee would be remunerated; finally, the payment must have been legally enforceable had it been promised in advance. If these three conditions are met, the subsequent promise becomes enforceable (see *Lampleigh v Braithwaite* **(1615) Hob 105**; *Re Casey's Patents* **[1892] 1 Ch 104**; *Pao On*). Unfortunately, on this basis TW is unlikely to succeed[15] as it agreed to act without payment, thereby undermining any argument that it expected to be remunerated. Arguably, therefore, no enforceable contract would exist. TW would not then fall within the exception to the rule on past consideration, making G's promise unenforceable.[16]

> [13] Identify the legal issues raised.

> [14] Explain the relevant law.

> [15] Apply the law.

> [16] Having applied the law, conclude and advise on this aspect of the problem.

However, when courts consider sufficiency of consideration by both parties they tend to adopt a reasonably flexible approach. Consider *De La Bere v Pearson* **[1908] 1 KB 280** where the defendant owners of a newspaper invited readers to submit letters requiring the advice of a financial expert. The plaintiff sent in a question that was printed, received some advice, acted upon said advice, and lost money as a consequence. The court found that there was sufficient consideration to support a contract. The plaintiff had allowed his letter to be published, thereby receiving the benefit of some advice. The defendant had benefited from being able to print readers' letters, which might have improved the circulation of its newspaper. Applying this reasoning to our facts suggests a similar outcome. G received consideration via the free publicity of her exhibition stand while TW potentially raised its profile among potential advertisers and thereby gained an important commercial advantage. If a contract did exist, G's subsequent promise of payment is clearly attempting to modify her *existing contract* with TW but what consideration does TW, at that stage, give in return?

LOOKING FOR EXTRA MARKS?

■ A good answer may briefly discuss whether Gaia's request for 'a wow factor' was too vague to be legally enforceable.

■ Extra marks are possible for noting a public policy dimension to *Stilk*: it discouraged sailors from threatening mutiny to increase their wages (see the Espinasse report of *Stilk* (1809) 6 Esp 129).

■ Critiquing the decision in *Williams v Roffey Bros & Nicholls (Contractors) Ltd* and its treatment in subsequent cases might gain additional marks, but try to avoid 'essay-style' discussion in answers to problem questions.

■ Identifying alternative outcomes can bring additional marks. TW may argue that G is estopped from withdrawing her promise of payment but remember that promissory estoppel is not a principal cause of action but is primarily a 'defence'.

QUESTION 2

Cheatham & Steele wish to expand the productivity and efficiency of their manufacturing processes. They borrow £100,000 from Grabbit & Runne, merchant bankers. The agreed period of the loan is five years: £20,000 to be repaid each year together with interest at 40 per cent on the capital outstanding.

After repayment of £20,000 with interest, Cheatham & Steele suffer a lengthy industrial dispute which makes it impossible for them to pay the next £20,000 due. There is a possibility that the company may become insolvent. Cheatham & Steele draw the attention of Grabbit & Runne to this and the consequential risk to their unsecured loan. With this in mind, Grabbit & Runne agree to the postponement for a year of payment of the £20,000 due and the waiver of all interest payable.

However, four months later Grabbit & Runne also experience severe financial problems and request Cheatham & Steele to pay the outstanding instalment and interest owing without further delay. Cheatham & Steele refuse to do this and suggest that only £10,000 of the loan could be paid but that this would cause them severe hardship in the circumstances.

Advise Grabbit & Runne.

CAUTION!

- The facts of problem questions are often designed to raise a variety of legal issues. Read the question carefully and note all the issues raised. Use the IRAC method to make sure your answer has a clear structure and deals with all of the issues.

- Many students find estoppel perplexing. Read the leading decisions and, in particular, the judgments of Lord Denning for their clear explanations.

- Merely setting out the requirements of estoppel with little or no application to the problem will lead to a poor mark.

DIAGRAM ANSWER PLAN

Identify the issues	▪ Identify the legal issues—the interaction of the rules on part-payment of a debt and promissory estoppel.
Relevant law	▪ Outline the relevant law on part-payment of a debt (see *Foakes v Beer* and *Rock Advertising Ltd v MWB Business Exchange Centres Ltd* [2018] UKSC 24). ▪ Outline the requirements for promissory estoppel.
Apply the law	▪ If no exceptions to the rule on part-payment of a debt apply, consider promissory estoppel. ▪ Does GR's promise support the existence of a promissory estoppel? ▪ If an estoppel exists, is the effect suspensory or extinctive?
Conclude	▪ Available remedies? ▪ Conclusion.

SUGGESTED ANSWER

[1] This paragraph is a good illustration of IRAC. Opening sentences clearly identify the legal issue(s), then identify and explain the relevant law.

This problem concerns the doctrines of consideration and promissory estoppel.[1] The question here is whether Grabbit & Runne (G&R) can request Cheatham & Steele (C&S) to pay the outstanding loan instalment and interest owing without further delay. Under the original contract between C&S and G&R it is clear that G&R is entitled to the outstanding loan instalment and interest without further delay. However, there has been an attempted variation of that contract. Is the variation enforceable (with the result that G&R would not be entitled to *immediately* claim the outstanding loan instalment and G&R may not be able to claim the relevant amount of interest at all)? Presumably, as the parties are acting in a commercial capacity, there is an intention to create legal relations. However, did C&S provide consideration to G&R for the postponement of the loan instalment? Did C&S provide something different or extra (a *legal* benefit) in return for the variation promise? It would seem that G&R have not received a legal benefit as they have a pre-existing contractual right to full and prompt payment in any event. The long-established rule for payment of debts is that a creditor is, generally, not bound by a promise to accept a partial payment in full settlement and may claim the remainder from his/her debtor (see *Pinnel's Case* **(1602) 5 Co Rep 117a**; *Foakes v Beer* **(1884) 9 App Cas 605**). Has this rule been softened by *Williams v Roffey Bros & Nicholls (Contractors) Ltd* **[1991] 1 QB 1**? In other words, would it be sufficient for C&S to demonstrate that G&R obtained a *factual* benefit (perhaps on the basis that if C&S were to become insolvent, G&R would be unlikely to recover most/all of the loan)? Following the Court of Appeal decision in *Re Selectmove* **[1995] 1 WLR 474** it was generally understood that *Williams v Roffey Bros & Nicholls (Contractors) Ltd* **[1991] 1 QB 1** did not apply to promises to accept *less* (as opposed to promises to pay *more*). However, the decision of the Court of Appeal in *Rock Advertising Ltd v MWB Business Exchange Centres Ltd* **[2016] EWCA Civ 553** has challenged that understanding (the case involved a promise to reduce the fee for a licence of some business premises). In *Rock Advertising Ltd* the Court of Appeal were of the opinion that part-payment was not per se sufficient consideration. Nevertheless, the Court of Appeal were of the opinion that *Williams v Roffey Bros & Nicholls (Contractors) Ltd* **[1991] 1 QB 1** could apply to promises to accept less *if* the promisor received *some factual benefit beyond part-payment*. On the facts of *Rock Advertising Ltd* such a factual benefit was found in the promisor not having to find another occupier for the premises. The case was appealed to the Supreme Court (**[2018] UKSC 24**) but the Supreme Court declined to discuss the relationship between *Williams v Roffey Bros & Nicholls (Contractors) Ltd* **[1991] 1 QB 1** and *Foakes v Beer* **(1884) 9 App Cas 605** (the 'tension' between these lines of authority continues to cause difficulty for trial judges: see *Simantob v Shavleyan (t/a Yacob's Gallery)* [2018] EWHC 2005 (QB) (appealed [2019] EWCA Civ 1105)).

[2]Using IRAC, apply the part-payment rule to the facts.

Arguably the variation promise is not supported by consideration (*legal* or *factual*),[2] which, prima facie, would mean that G&R is not bound by their promise to accept partial payment from C&S (ie postponing the loan instalment). However, the possibly harsh effect of the rule in *Pinnel's Case* is mitigated by a possible means of bypassing the part-payment rule: the doctrine of promissory estoppel.

[3]In setting out the conditions for a promissory estoppel, identify and explain the law relevant to the issues.

The basic notion of estoppel is that A makes certain representations or promises to B upon which B relies or acts in some way.[3] If A wishes to change his/her mind, to go back on his/her representation or promise, he/she *may* be prevented or estopped from doing so. In *Central London Property Trust Ltd v High Trees House Ltd* **[1947] KB 130**,[4] Denning J famously applied the notion of promissory estoppel to the law of contract by drawing on the equitable principles in *Hughes v Metropolitan Ry* **(1877) 2 App Cas 439**. In *High Trees*, the plaintiffs leased a block of flats to the defendants in 1937 at a ground rent of £2,500 *per annum* but in 1940 agreed to reduce this rent by half because few of the flats were let in the wartime conditions. At the start of 1945 most of the flats were let again but the defendants were still paying the reduced rent. The plaintiffs then demanded the full rent, testing their claim by suing for the last two quarters of 1945. It was held that the claim should succeed as the agreement of 1940 was only intended as a temporary arrangement for wartime conditions and it had ceased to operate early in 1945. Denning J also said that, although the defendants had provided no consideration for the plaintiffs' promise to reduce the rent, the plaintiffs could not have recovered the full rent for the period covered by the 1940 agreement. The plaintiffs would be estopped from denying the force of the 1940 agreement where the promise was 'intended to be binding, intended to be acted on, and in fact acted on' (per Denning J).

[4]Explain this key case.

[5]Apply the law to the facts of the problem.

If this principle were to be applied here,[5] it may mean G&R would be estopped from going back on their promise to postpone for a year payment of the £20,000 due and the waiver of all relevant interest payable. The requirements for promissory estoppel are: the parties must have a legal relationship which gives rise to rights and duties between them: here C&S and G&R do have a contractual relationship. There must be a promise or representation that the promisor will not insist on his/her strict legal rights; this promise must be clear and unequivocal but it can be implied or made by conduct (eg *Hughes v Metropolitan Ry*) and need not be express: here this requirement is satisfied in an unambiguous, express promise. In *Combe v Combe* **[1951] 2 KB 215** it was established that promissory estoppel may be used 'as a shield but not a sword' (per Birkett LJ): here C&S are defending themselves against possible action by G&R. Finally, the promisee must have relied or acted upon the representation in some way and it must be inequitable for the promisor to revoke his/her promise. Here we can see that C&S relied on G&R's promise because they postponed paying the loan instalment.

Regarding reliance and equity, it seems that the promisee does not have to have acted to his/her detriment (compare *Rock Advertising Ltd v MWB Business Exchange Centres Ltd* **[2016] EWCA Civ 553** where Kitchin LJ felt that the key issue was whether or not it was inequitable for the promisor to go back on the promise). Indeed, Lord Denning consistently argued (see *WJ Alan & Co. Ltd v El Nasr Export & Import Co.* **[1972] 2 QB 189**; *Brikom Investments Ltd v Carr* **[1979] QB 467**) that repudiation of the promise was, in itself, inequitable. In *The Post Chaser* **[1981] 2 Lloyd's Rep 695**, Robert Goff J emphasized that a promisor will not be allowed to enforce his/her original contractual rights 'where it would be inequitable having regard to the dealings which have thus taken place between the parties', and that even if a promisee *benefited* from the promise it might still be inequitable to revoke. Here, C&S clearly benefit immediately from the postponed payment but suffer hardship when it is revoked, arguably suggesting that such revocation might be inequitable. Conversely,[6] in *Rock Advertising Ltd* Kitchin LJ stated:

> I do not for my part think that it can be said, consistently with the authorities, including … *Foakes v Beer* and … *Selectmove*, that in every case where a creditor agrees to accept payment of a debt by instalments, and the debtor acts upon that agreement by paying one of the instalments, and the creditor accepts that instalment, then it will necessarily be inequitable for the creditor later to go back upon the agreement and insist on payment of the balance.

Moreover G&R might point to their own dire financial position as a valid reason to retract the promise, leaving the court to balance G&R's alleged ability to withdraw against C&S's plea of estoppel.

In concluding, it is worth noting that the need to act equitably applies to the promisee as well as the promisor. Should the promisee extract the promise by duress it will not be inequitable for the promisor to resile. The promisee's conduct must be blameless for equitable protection: 'he who comes to equity must come with clean hands'. In *D & C Builders Ltd v Rees* **[1966] 2 QB 617**, the plaintiffs agreed to accept £300 from the defendant in settlement of £482, principally because of their desperate financial position; there was evidence that

[6] An examiner would expect an answer to deal with both argument and counter-argument.

the defendant knew of this and took advantage of it in getting the plaintiffs' promise to accept the lesser sum. Therefore, it was not inequitable for the plaintiffs to withdraw the promise. On the facts here, there is no clear evidence of duress. Although C&S 'draw the attention of G&R' to their financial position and the possible risk to G&R's loan, this is unlikely to be viewed unfavourably by the court assuming they were telling the truth.

[7] Identify and explain the law.

The final question raised by the problem is the effect of the *High Trees* doctrine on the obligations owed by the parties:[7] is the effect of the estoppel suspensory or extinctive? It is usually said that promissory estoppel suspends rights rather than extinguishing them. The promisor may revive his/her normal rights provided that he gives the promisee reasonable notice of his/her intention to do so (eg *Tool Metal Manufacturing Co. Ltd v Tungsten Electric Co. Ltd* **[1955] 1 WLR 761**). G&R may therefore be able—provided C&S was given reasonable notice—to request C&S to pay the outstanding instalment without further delay (although the law is unclear on what period of notice should be given before returning to the original contract).

[8] In applying the law, it is important to address any areas of uncertainty. This is an opportunity to address the authorities and discuss possible alternative outcomes.

However, the law in this area is unclear.[8] The suspensory nature of the doctrine can be seen in the *High Trees* case but estoppel may extinguish rights if it is impossible for the promisee to return to the previous position and perform the original obligation (eg *Birmingham & District Land Co. v L & NW Ry* **(1888) 40 Ch D 268**). There is authority that the doctrine may be extinctive, even though such performance is not impossible, if it would be inequitable to revoke the promise. In *Collier v P and MJ Wright (Holdings) Ltd* **[2007]**

[9] Note that *Collier v P and MJ Wright (Holdings) Ltd* [2007] EWCA Civ 1329, [2008] 1 WLR 643 was merely a preliminary (interlocutory) decision and such a decision is often regarded as a relatively weak authority. On the other hand, the Court of Appeal in *Rock Advertising Ltd* appeared to approve it.

EWCA Civ 1329, [2008] 1 WLR 643,[9] the majority of the Court of Appeal was controversially prepared to argue that a promise to accept part-payment of a debt in full satisfaction of the whole debt created a *permanent* estoppel, as reviving the remainder of the debt would invariably have been inequitable for the promisee in the circumstances. Nevertheless, if the court decides that an estoppel is only suspensory it is unclear how this might affect continuing obligations such as paying off a debt in instalments. If there is an agreed reduction in the debt and a postponement, on expiry of the notice can the promisor claim the full amount for the future only or is he/she entitled to future payments and the balance of those which fell due during the period of postponement? Much depends on the intentions of the parties. Here there seems to be an agreed postponement of time with an intended revival of full rights on its expiry, but arguably the right to interest on one year's payment might be extinguished.

[10] Conclude and advise.

In conclusion, the court must balance the deferment of payment sought by C&S against G&R's insistence on an immediate reinstatement of existing contractual rights.[10] This balance can normally be achieved by requiring the promisor to give reasonable notice before his/her rights can revive, thereby reconciling the rule in *Foakes v Beer* with the doctrine of estoppel in that the creditor's rights are not extinguished but merely suspended. However, the preliminary decision in *Collier* suggests that certain judges may to go further by, in effect, using promissory estoppel as another 'common law' exception to *Foakes*.[11]

[11] A first-class answer may speculate in this way, but always remember to keep it relevant to the facts of the question.

LOOKING FOR EXTRA MARKS?

- Difficulties in applying estoppel offer scope for better students to demonstrate their analytical abilities. To answer a question on this topic well you must understand the balance of interests between B's reliance on A's promise and whether it is inequitable for A to revoke his/her promise.

- Remember that promissory estoppel is a possible exception to the part-payment rule, so explain the main rules first.

- Extra marks may be available for noting that the rule on partial payment has been criticized for not reflecting commercial reality (see *Couldery v Bartrum* (1881) 19 Ch D 394), and there are several exceptions to it. In *Rock Advertising Ltd v MWB Business Exchange Centres Ltd* [2018] UKSC 24 at [18] Lord Sumption JSC stated that *Foakes v Beer* (1884) 9 App Cas 605 is 'probably ripe for re-examination. But if it is to be overruled or its effect substantially modified, it should be before an enlarged panel of the court and in a case where the decision would be more than obiter dictum'.

QUESTION | 3

Consideration is often a mere fiction devised to make a promise enforceable and, as such, serves little purpose. It would be advantageous to abolish consideration and leave the more satisfactory requirement of intention to create legal relations as the test of an agreement's enforceability.

Discuss.

CAUTION!

- Questions like this require you to think about the view expressed and discuss it. You must not merely reiterate all you know about consideration.

- Examiners like answers which show that you can think about, criticize, and reach sensible conclusions on the issues raised by the specific question.

- To ensure a clear structure for essays, use the PEA (point, evidence, and analysis) method to make sure you have dealt with all aspects of the question.

DIAGRAM ANSWER PLAN

Introduction.

▼

Point: what rules could a legal system adopt as tests for the enforceability of agreements and what rules does the Law of England and Wales in fact adopt as tests for the enforceability of agreements?

▼

Evidence: what is meant by the doctrine of consideration? What is the test of enforceability?

▼

Evidence: outline any problematic aspects of the doctrine of consideration and any rules arguably requiring amendment.

▼

Analysis: examine viability of intention to create legal relations as sole test for enforceability of agreement.

▼

Analysis: consider whether the common law is beginning to place greater emphasis on intent in contract formation.

▼

Conclusion.

 SUGGESTED ANSWER

[1] Try to keep introductions to essays quite short and relevant to the question.

The question suggests that consideration is a 'fiction' and an undesirable test of the enforceability of an agreement, and proposes intention to create legal relations as a preferable test of enforceability.[1] Consideration and intention to create legal relations both relate to the nature and substance of an agreement, which might suggest that they could perform a similar function. In fact, there are a number of tests which could be used to determine the enforceability of an agreement within a particular legal system.[2]

[2] Here is the first point. Following the answer plan, address what rules a legal system could adopt as tests for the enforceability of agreements. Support the answer with evidence.

First, in order to be enforceable, all contracts *might* require a degree of form such as writing or a deed. This would arguably provide a degree of certainty, deter fraud, and embody, almost as a necessity, that the parties intend legal relations; however, it would be virtually impossible to insist upon writing for *all* contracts today. Writing is demanded in certain exceptional cases; for example, contracts for the sale of land must be in writing, and strict formalities are sometimes necessary where one party may abuse the other's inexperience and lack of bargaining power (eg consumer credit agreements). At the other extreme, it is theoretically possible to make *all* agreements enforceable but this notion is equally impractical. Other options might look to the seriousness of intent alone or evidence of reliance on the promise, or a combination of both. In principle, many European countries view all lawful and serious agreements as contracts. On the other hand, English law uses consideration as a key test for a contract's enforcement and, in so doing, is said to look for a bargain or exchange between the parties. However, English law also demands intention to create legal relations as a separate requirement for a contract's enforcement (see ***Balfour v Balfour* [1919] 2 KB 571**). Consequently, the role played by consideration must be ascertained and it should be asked whether intention might perform it better.

A dominant theory of consideration is one of an exchange of values, or bargain, between the parties: A must show that he or she has bought B's promise.[3] However, the overall influence of the idea of freedom of contract means that, although some consideration is necessary, it need not be adequate. Bargains can be unequal, yet enforceable, as in ***Thomas v Thomas* (1842) 2 QB 851**, for example.[4] Under ***Chappell & Co. Ltd v Nestlé Co. Ltd* [1960] AC 87**, a contracting party may generally ask for whatever consideration he/she desires, even if it is valueless.[5] To this extent, perhaps, consideration could be viewed as a 'fiction'.[6] The doctrine of consideration evidently does not ensure fairness of bargains; rather, the doctrine of consideration distinguishes bargains from gratuitous promises by requiring a token exchange. Professor Atiyah argued ('Consideration: A Restatement' in *Essays on Contract* (1986)) that consideration was originally the *reason* for the enforcement of a promise.[7] It is a small step to see the token element in bargains as merely evidence that both parties take the agreement seriously; that is, as evidence of intention to create legal relations. One advantage in the token approach is that it provides a touchstone for intention. Consideration could therefore be seen as simply one test of enforceability which serves the same function as intent. However, to address whether consideration performs that function as efficiently as if intent were the sole test for enforceability, we must look at the established problems with the doctrine.[8]

In relation to adequacy of consideration, it is arguable that in supporting the notion of unequal consideration the law may wrongly invest an act of duress with the legitimacy of a so-called 'bargain'. Adequacy of consideration assumes there is valid consideration where A sells his/her Rolls-Royce to B for a nominal amount, but is it not more likely that some duress or blackmail might have prompted such an arrangement? In sufficiency of consideration, the cases which

[3] Here is another point. Explain what is meant by the doctrine of consideration in the law of England and Wales and the test of enforceability under the doctrine.

[4] The PEA structure can also work within paragraphs, aiding the clarity of the discussion. So, for example, here is the point.

[5] The point is supported by evidence from case law authority.

[6] Next, provide the analysis. Remember to keep demonstrating the relevance of the answer to the question.

[7] The quality of an answer can be improved by including a reference to academic views.

[8] Point: address any problems in the principles of consideration and discuss whether any rules should be amended.

establish that performance of an existing contractual duty are insufficient consideration (eg *Stilk v Myrick* **(1809) 2 Camp 317;** *Hartley v Ponsonby* **(1857) 7 E & B 872**) are really concerned with protecting the creditor from the economic duress of his/her debtor (as, at one time, the Law of England and Wales did not recognize a defence of economic duress). The rule was carried to a logical conclusion in *Foakes v Beer* **(1884) 9 App Cas 605**, a case which is traditionally regarded as authority for the proposition that part-payment of a debt cannot amount to consideration which would discharge the debtor from the remainder of the debt, thereby leaving the creditor free to claim the amount owing. Consideration achieves a purpose but at what cost? At its worst, the requirement of consideration prevents us from transparently distinguishing a 'desirable' agreement, which ought to be enforced, from an 'undesirable' agreement. Although, it seems, there has been some softening of the position following *Rock Advertising Ltd v MWB Business Exchange Centres Ltd* **[2016] EWCA Civ 553**, the starting point is that a part-payment of a debt is not, *per* se, sufficient consideration for the discharge of the remainder of the debt, even where the agreement was a freely negotiated and sensible business arrangement. It seems unduly restrictive that the discharge of a debt by payment of a lesser amount cannot be accommodated within the existing law on consideration. Certainly, the decision in *Re Selectmove Ltd* **[1995] 1 WLR 474** strongly suggests that the decision in *Foakes v Beer* should be reconsidered by the Supreme Court or addressed by legislation; and it is, perhaps, unfortunate that the Supreme Court in *Rock Advertising Ltd v MWB Business Exchange Centres Ltd* **[2018] UKSC 24** declined to explore this issue (this has left the law in an unsatisfactory state and difficult to apply: see *Simantob v Shavleyan (t/a Yacob's Gallery)* **[2018] EWHC 2005 (QB) (appealed [2019] EWCA Civ 1105)**).

The foregoing might be evidence that it could be advantageous to abolish consideration, but what could replace it?

If intention to create legal relations became the sole test, it would avoid some of the difficulties caused by the rigidity of the doctrine of consideration. For example, the courts could examine and enforce 'legitimate' bargains and invalidate 'illegitimate' bargains as having been exacted through improper threats or pressure. The evolution of a doctrine of economic duress, and an awareness that duress must be distinguished from commercial hard bargaining, has arguably removed one of the main justifications for retaining the rules of consideration.

A concern that gifts would become enforceable as promises if intention became the sole test of a contract's enforceability seems unrealistic. Intent would simply become the test for the enforceability of agreements; the parties would still not intend that most social and domestic gifts became binding contracts. However, the courts would have the ability to examine factors other than consideration in deciding whether promises should be enforceable. Much would depend on the nature of the promise and the promisee's response to it: for example, the presence of writing or other formalities might be significant, as would the promisee's direct reliance on the promise.

Similarly, the criticism that the courts would have to devise rules of intention to address new problems is unfounded: intention is an existing and established requirement for the formation of a contract. Why should intention not become the dominant requirement, retaining the essence of consideration but subservient to intent? The courts would not have to 'begin again' but would be required merely to adjust the concept of a bargain within the rules of intention. If the parties genuinely intended a token bargain it would not cease to be enforceable, but a freely negotiated part-payment of a debt, for example, would become enforceable provided there was intention evident in the mutual benefits received. This would appear to be a more modern approach.

The decision in *Williams v Roffey Bros & Nicholls (Contractors) Ltd* **[1991] 1 QB 1** may point the way ahead.[9] The defendants were building contractors with a contract to refurbish a block of flats; the carpentry was subcontracted to the plaintiffs who were in financial difficulties and falling behind with the work. Delays might have resulted in the defendants paying liquidated damages to a third party under the refurbishment contract, so they offered the plaintiffs extra money to complete the work on time. When the defendants refused to pay the extra sum, the Court of Appeal held that the plaintiffs should succeed, emphasizing that, although the plaintiffs were only performing their existing contractual duty, the defendants obtained a *factual*, real benefit and there was no duress tainting the bargain. *Stilk v Myrick* was subjugated to the rules of intent. The court enforced the freely negotiated variation, while the essence of consideration was preserved by focusing on the benefit received. Significantly, the court could almost certainly have found consideration in the revised methods of payment introduced by the parties (eg a restructuring of the payments' schedule): the decision might then have accorded more with established doctrine; however, the Court of Appeal deliberately chose a more radical route. *Roffey* has the potential to revolutionize the rules of consideration or, alternatively, remain limited to variations of existing contracts where a realistic benefit is obtained. Although the court in *Re Selectmove Ltd* was constrained by the House of Lords' decision in *Foakes v Beer*, Peter Gibson LJ saw 'the force of the argument' in extending *Roffey* to part-payment of debts; and in *Rock Advertising Ltd v MWB Business Exchange Centres Ltd* **[2016] EWCA Civ 553** the Court of Appeal limited the scope of

[9] The argument put forward here is quite sophisticated and likely to attract extra marks. Note that the overall argument remains coherent even without this paragraph.

Re Selectmove Ltd. Some critics have already argued that it is unde-sirable to substitute the vagaries of intent and duress for the certainty of consideration. This approach might wish to see the opposite conclu-sion reached on the facts of *Roffey* but it is arguably artificial and out-moded to justify such an outcome in the context of the modern law.

Why might there be apprehension in regarding intent as the sole test of contractual enforceability when, for example, criminal law is heavily reliant on the concept? The contract law doctrine of promis-sory estoppel functions well with the notions of intent, reliance, and inequity. It is therefore strongly arguable that intent should become the dominant principle in the formation of contract,[10] with the es-sence of consideration retained within a revised conception of a freely negotiated bargain.

[10] Conclusion relates to the specific question, demonstrating how your answer meets its requirements.

LOOKING FOR EXTRA MARKS?

- The essay concerns consideration and intention to create legal relations, so address both areas. You could also discuss the problem of past consideration and its exceptions, for additional marks.

- Recognize the importance of a clear conclusion which closely relates to the question set.

- Remember: regardless of your overall conclusion, you gain high marks for the quality of your argument, your evidence, and your analysis of the issues raised by the question.

QUESTION | 4

Build-High has a contract to build a new housing estate for Fields Trust. Each of the houses on the estate will have a conservatory and the erecting of these has been subcontracted to Clearview. Work begins but within two months Clearview is unable to pay the wages of its employees owing to a cash flow problem. The employees refuse to continue working until this problem has been resolved. Build-High, who have been informed of this strike, are already concerned about the pro-gress of Clearview in erecting the conservatories, especially as the Fields Trust recently disclosed that long delays might result in the loss of prospective buyers for the newly built houses. Build-High enter into a new agreement to pay Clearview an additional £10,000, thereby avoiding the inconvenience of finding an alternative builder to finish the conservatories. Clearview pays its employees all outstanding wages, and the employees return to work and complete two more conservatories. At this point Build-High refuse to pay the extra £10,000 as the Fields Trust has gone into liquidation.

Clearview's financial problems have been exacerbated by their dealings with another house builder, Lakeland. Clearview had been subcontracted by Lakeland to build conservatories for a number of recently completed houses, at a total price of £100,000. Lakeland now admits that it is encountering difficulties in selling these houses and therefore proposes to reduce their sale prices. However, this requires its subcontractors to agree to a reduction in their own previously agreed levels of remuneration. A number of the subcontractors, including Clearview, agree to reduce their outstanding claims by 20 per cent, thereby enabling Lakeland to reduce the sale price of its houses, a number of which are thereupon sold.

Discuss.

CAUTION!

- This problem question covers two of the more difficult aspects of consideration: performance of an existing contractual duty and the relationship with promissory estoppel.

- The question refers to two separate contractual arrangements, Clearview/Build-High and Clearview/Lakeland; you might find it sensible to deal separately with each contractual relationship. Make appropriate cross-references to avoid unnecessary repetition in your answer.

- A clear structure is important where there are a number of contractual relationships; following the IRAC method can help you demonstrate the relevance of the law and how it applies to the facts.

DIAGRAM ANSWER PLAN

Identify the issues	■ Identify the legal issues—performance of existing contractual duty; part-payment of a debt; and promissory estoppel. ■ Two separate contractual arrangements to be addressed: C and B; C and L.
Relevant law	■ Outline the relevant law on performance of existing contractual duty (including *Williams v Roffey Bros & Nicholls (Contractors) Ltd*). ■ Outline the relevant law on payment of a debt (including *Foakes v Beer*). ■ Outline the relevant law on promissory estoppel (including *Central London Property Trust Ltd v High Trees House Ltd*).
Apply the law	■ Analyse extra payment of £10,000 to C by B. ■ Can C claim full payment of the debt owed by L?
Conclude	■ Possible outcomes summarized. ■ Conclusion.

This question concerns the doctrines of consideration and promissory estoppel. Each contractual relationship will be addressed separately.

Clearview (C) v Build-High (B)

[1]Following the IRAC model, the first paragraph should analyse the facts of the question to identify the legal issues raised. Is the extra payment of £10,000 to C intended to ensure the continued performance of existing contractual duties, or is C being expected to exceed these duties?

The main problem for Clearview is that it does not appear to have done anything extra in return for the payment of £10,000 promised by Build-High.[1] *Stilk v Myrick* **(1809) 2 Camp 317** traditionally suggested that performance of a contractual duty must be exceeded to establish sufficient consideration for any additional payment (eg *Hartley v Ponsonby* **(1857) 7 E & B 872**). Here, it appears C did not agree to perform its contractual duties differently, or complete them earlier, or even use a different standard of materials; if C simply continued to perform its normal contractual duties, then prima facie C could not claim the additional £10,000.

[2]Next question: has B gained some practical benefit from paying C the extra money in order to secure continuing performance of its contractual duties? Apply the decision in *Roffey* to the facts of this problem.

However, C has a second argument based on *Williams v Roffey Bros & Nicholls (Contractors) Ltd* **[1991] 1 QB 1**, which refined and limited the *Stilk v Myrick* principle.[2] If C can show that B received a 'practical' benefit' (or obviated a recognizable disbenefit) from C's continuing to perform its existing contractual duty, then any promise of additional payment by B may become enforceable. In *Roffey* it was held that the main contractor (operating similarly to B) received certain practical benefits by promising to pay the plaintiffs an additional £10,000 in order to secure their continued performance of the contract: they avoided the inconvenience of finding other carpenters to complete the work (and the possibility of being charged more), circumvented the possible enforcement by their employers of a liquidated damages clause for late completion, and agreed a different method for paying the plaintiffs. Here the second point may be relevant[3]—there appears to be no liquidated damages clause enforceable against B for late completion although damages for breach of contract may be obtainable.

[3]The existence of a set completion date would strengthen C's argument as timely performance by C would avoid any claim by Fields Trust against B for late completion.

[4]The question may not give all the facts necessary to reach a firm conclusion; speculate up to a point, but not too far from the question facts.

Whether the avoidance of inconvenience is a sufficient 'practical benefit' for the decision in *Roffey* to be invoked is not clear for several reasons.[4] First, it is unclear whether the court in *Roffey* would have accepted that *each* of the benefits received by the main contractor was sufficient in its own right to demonstrate sufficient consideration. Secondly, it is unclear whether/when B could be sued by Fields Trust for late completion (avoidance of the penalty clause in *Roffey* was probably the most influential factor). Thirdly, C may have subjected B to some form of economic duress, which would undermine reliance upon *Roffey* and its requirement of a practical benefit (although this seems unlikely particularly if, as in in *Roffey*, it was B who offered the additional payment, rather than responding to any demand from C).

A further point is whether the parties formally rescinded their original agreement and replaced it with a new contract in which C would be paid more. In *Compagnie Noga D'Importation et D'Exportation SA v Abacha (No. 2)* [2003] EWCA Civ 1100, [2003] 2 All ER (Comm) 915, the Court of Appeal held that in such circumstances it is not the old agreement which compels the performance of any revised obligations but the new agreement. Consequently, *Stilk v Myrick* will not apply if (a) the old agreement was rescinded and (b) either the rescission/new agreement was underpinned by consideration. Here, point (b) applies as both parties had further duties to perform under the original agreement (B to complete the conservatories and C to pay for them)—the mutual surrender by B and C of their rights to enforce performance of each other's executory promises will amount to consideration for the new agreement.

[5] Can C use the principles of promissory estoppel to compel payment of the additional £10,000?

Finally, if C fails on all of these points, the only remaining argument is that B is estopped from revoking its promise to pay an additional £10,000.[5] Following the decision in *Central London Property Trust Ltd v High Trees House Ltd* [1947] KB 130, C must establish that it relied upon the payment to continue working, that it had not acted inequitably in obtaining B's promise (eg that the reason for stopping work on the conservatories was not misrepresented), that B's promise to pay was clear and intended to be binding, and that it was now too late to revoke the promise as some of the conservatories had been completed. However, although these conditions are met, the courts have stressed that promissory estoppel cannot create new rights (see *Combe v Combe* [1951] 2 KB 215); rather, it is a defensive measure to prevent inequitable conduct by the promisor (a 'shield, not a sword'). Therefore, C cannot rely upon promissory estoppel to claim the £10,000 as this would amount to *enforcing* the additional payment by B.

Clearview (C) v Lakeland (L)

[6] Does C have a right to claim full payment of the debt with L?

Lakeland's difficulty[6] is that the part-payment rule established in *Pinnel's Case* (1602) 5 Co Rep 117a and confirmed by the House of Lords in *Foakes v Beer* (1884) 9 App Cas 605 limits the ability to extinguish existing debts unless full payment has been made. In *Foakes*, the creditor mistakenly thought that the debtor had repaid the whole of an outstanding debt in full. In fact, as it was a judgment debt, the debt had attracted additional interest which had not yet been repaid. The House of Lords ruled that a creditor is not bound by either a promise to accept a smaller sum or its actual payment by the debtor. Such a promise amounts to nothing more than a promise to accept performance of *part* of an existing duty owed to the creditor, the debtor consequently providing no consideration. The position is then similar to *Stilk v Myrick* except that in part-payment of debts the debtor seeks to discharge an existing obligation rather than securing extra payment for its performance. Therefore, C should have a strong argument for entitlement to the full contract price (ie a sum equivalent to the amount by which the debt had been reduced). However, there are a number of exceptions to the part-payment rule; a possible exception that might apply here is that of a 'composition agreement by creditors'.[7] If all the creditors of L have agreed with each other, and with L, to reduce their debt claims against L, they may be bound by any ensuing debt-reduction arrangement (see *Good v Cheesman* **(1831) 2 B & Ad 328**). However, it is possible that L approached only some of its creditors (on an individual basis), rather than all of the creditors agreeing with each other to the debt reduction.

If C is not bound by any 'composition agreement', L's next argument would be that C derived a *practical* benefit from the agreed part-payment:[8] surely if L sells more of its properties C will have a greater chance of recovering the majority of its outstanding debt rather than none at all? However, the Court of Appeal decision in *Re Selectmove* seemed to suggest that the decision in *Roffey* cannot be used to undermine the part-payment of debt principle accepted by the House of Lords in *Foakes v Beer*. If so, L's argument on this principle would be unlikely to succeed.[9] However, the decision of the Court of Appeal in *Rock Advertising Ltd v MWB Business Exchange Centres Ltd* **[2016] EWCA Civ 553** has challenged that understanding of *Re Selectmove* (*Rock Advertising Ltd* involved a promise to reduce the fee for a licence of some business premises). In *Rock Advertising Ltd* the Court of Appeal were of the opinion that part-payment was not per se sufficient consideration. Nevertheless, the Court of Appeal were of the opinion that *Williams v Roffey Bros & Nicholls (Contractors) Ltd* **[1991] 1 QB 1** could apply to promises to accept less *if* the promisor received *some factual benefit beyond part-payment*. On the facts of *Rock Advertising Ltd* such a factual benefit was found in the promisor not having to find another occupier for the premises. The case was appealed to the Supreme Court (**[2018] UKSC 24**) but the Supreme Court declined to discuss the relationship between *Williams v Roffey Bros & Nicholls (Contractors) Ltd* **[1991] 1 QB 1** and *Foakes v Beer* **(1884) 9 App Cas 605**. On the current facts, it might be questioned whether C receives a benefit beyond part-payment.

L's final argument must be that C is estopped from recovering the full debt.[10] Using the *High Trees* principle, L can show that C made a clear promise which was intended to modify an existing contract, that L relied upon C's promise to accept less (ie L reduced the sale prices of its properties) and that there is no evidence of inequitable dealing

[7] What is the effect of other contractors also agreeing to accept a lower sum in full satisfaction of their own debts? Such a point may attract additional marks.

[8] No need to reiterate the facts of *Roffey* here.

[9] A conclusion such as this provides clear advice as required by the question.

[10] Addressing possible alternative arguments demonstrates understanding of the range of possible outcomes arising from the issues.

by L. This last point might be problematic if L unfairly pressurized its various subcontractors into subsidizing the proposed price reduction (see *South Caribbean Trading Ltd v Trafigura Beheer BV* [2004] **EWHC 2676 (Comm), [2005] 1 Lloyd's Rep 128**). Nevertheless, if an estoppel is established, the court must decide whether its effect is permanent or of only limited duration. The normal principle is that estoppel is suspensory rather than extinctive, and that once the promisor (C) has given reasonable notice the original contract will once again be enforceable (eg *Tool Metal Manufacturing Co. Ltd v Tungsten Electric Co. Ltd* [1955] 1 WLR 761). The only exceptions are where the promisee (L) would find it impossible to resume its original position (eg *Birmingham & District Land Co. v L & NW Ry* (1888) 40 Ch D 268) or it would be inequitable to insist upon such resumption in the circumstances (eg *Nippon Yusen Kaisha v Pacifica Navegacion SA (The Ion)* [1980] 2 Lloyd's Rep 245), in which case the promisor's original rights will be permanently extinguished. Here, L has already sold some properties at a discounted price and it therefore seems too late for C to withdraw its promise to accept part-payment from L. C's only possible counter-argument is to question the extent to which the *High Trees* principle can be used to circumvent the House of Lords' decision in *Foakes v Beer*. While the principle of promissory estoppel was subsequently accepted by the House of Lords (eg *Tool Metal Manufacturing Co. Ltd v Tungsten Electric Co. Ltd* [1955] 1 WLR 761) the extent to which the principle can be relied upon to protect a straightforward part-payment of debt issue remains unclear, although the preliminary ruling in *Collier v P and MJ Wright (Holdings) Ltd* [2007] EWCA Civ 1329, [2008] 1 WLR 643 suggests courts may be prepared to employ estoppel in this way. Indeed in *Rock Advertising Ltd* Kitchin LJ stated:

> I do not for my part think that it can be said, consistently with the authorities, including … *Foakes v Beer* and … *Selectmove*, that in every case where a creditor agrees to accept payment of a debt by instalments, and the debtor acts upon that agreement by paying one of the instalments, and the creditor accepts that instalment, then it will necessarily be inequitable for the creditor later to go back upon the agreement and insist on payment of the balance.

LOOKING FOR EXTRA MARKS?

- Apply the legal rules to the issues and come to conclusions on each issue. Be selective to ensure that your answer is relevant to the question.

- Remember: 'Consideration must be sufficient but need not be adequate'. Cases such as **Thomas v Thomas (1842) 2 QB 851** demonstrate that even though the respective contributions of the parties may be grossly disproportionate, provided both have supplied value recognized by the law the contract will be enforced.

- You could outline the requirements to establish economic duress, but do so only briefly to avoid straying too far from the main points raised by the question.

TAKING THINGS FURTHER

- Atiyah, P.S., 'Consideration: A Restatement' in *Essays on Contract* (Oxford: Oxford University Press 1986), Ch. 8.
  A critique of the modern doctrine of consideration as a requirement for formation of contracts.

- Capper, D., 'Consideration in the Modification of Contracts' in Merkin, R. and Devenney, J., *Essays in Memory of Professor Jill Poole: Coherence, Modernisation and Integration in Contract, Commercial and Corporate Laws* (Oxford: Routledge 2018), Ch.7.
  Explores recent case law in this area.

- Chen-Wishart, M., 'Consideration: Practical Benefit and the Emperor's New Clothes' in Beatson, J., and Friedman, D., *Good Faith and Fault in Contract Law* (Oxford: Oxford University Press 1995), Ch. 5.
  *A critique of the 'illusory' notion of practical benefit in **Williams v Roffey Bros & Nicholls (Contractors) Ltd** [1991] 1 QB 1.*

- Nolan, D., 'Following in their Footsteps: Equitable Estoppel in Australia and the United States' (2000) 11(2) *King's College Law Journal* 201.
  Offers a non-UK viewpoint.

- Treitel, G.H., 'Consideration: A Critical Analysis of Professor Atiyah's Fundamental Restatement' (1976) 50 ALJ 439.
  Explores the flexibility of the doctrine of consideration in response to Atiyah's criticism.

4 Terms of the Contract

In order to attempt the questions in this chapter you must have covered the following areas in your revision:

- Express terms and how to distinguish such terms from mere representations;
- The rules relating to the interpretation of contractual terms;
- The implication of terms into a contract and the different bases for implication; that is, terms implied in fact, terms implied in law and terms implied by custom;
- Terms implied by the **Sale of Goods Act 1979**, terms implied by the **Supply of Goods and Services Act 1982**, and an understanding of the ambit of the **Consumer Rights Act 2015**;
- The classification of contractual terms into conditions, warranties, and/or innominate terms.

KEY DEBATES

Debate: on what basis do the courts imply terms into contracts?

Terms implied in fact by the courts are based upon the intention of the parties, whereas terms implied in law by the courts appear to be based on policy reasons. Both processes give rise to issues of clarity and certainty.

Debate: how courts approach the classification of terms highlights a tension in the law between certainty and justice.

The traditional classification of terms as either conditions or warranties concentrates on the nature of the term as determining the available remedies for breach. This arguably promotes certainty although it is not always easy to decide whether a particular term is a condition or a warranty. One possible drawback of such an approach is that it may allow the non-breaching party to terminate a contract for a trivial breach of a condition. By contrast, if a term is classified as an innominate term, then the courts focus on the seriousness of the breach to determine the remedy. Thus 'justice' may be achieved but certainty is sacrificed. What factors should a court take into account in classifying a term?

It is illogical and unjust for the law to classify contractual obligations as either conditions or warranties at the time of contract formation as this prevents the remedies for a breach of contract from properly reflecting the actual consequences of that breach.

Discuss.

CAUTION!

- This essay question requires a *critical* examination of conditions and warranties, the consequences of their breach, and the development of the innominate term. In particular, you must be able to make a close analysis of the leading cases and display a critical awareness of the problems which have shaped the new developments in the law.

- An appraisal should be undertaken of the relative merits of orthodox conditions/warranties dichotomy as compared with an approach which includes innominate terms.

DIAGRAM ANSWER PLAN

What is the difference between a condition and a warranty?

What type of breach entitles the innocent party to terminate the contract?

How do the intentions of the parties affect the classification of terms?

Has the use of innominate terms introduced much-needed flexibility?

What role does statute perform in this area?

In what circumstances, if at all, should one adopt the condition/warranty approach?

Conclusion.

The promissory obligations of a contract are contained in its terms, and are traditionally classified as either conditions or warranties.[1] Broadly conditions are the important and fundamental obligations, whereas warranties are less important, subsidiary promises. In the nineteenth century, 'warranty' was often used by the judges to encompass all contract terms and the strict, twofold demarcation is relatively recent, having been originally expedited by a definition of these phrases in the **Sale of Goods Act 1893**. Importantly, a breach of condition allows the innocent party to terminate and/or claim damages whereas a breach of warranty allows only a claim in damages. The overriding notion of freedom of contract means that the court assesses the parties' intentions in order to decide whether a particular statement or clause is a condition or a warranty. Alternatively, statute may dictate that certain implied terms are conditions (eg the **Sale of Goods Act 1979 (SGA 1979), ss. 12–15**, although this terminology is singularly absent in the **Consumer Rights Act 2015 (CRA 2015)** which, instead, provides a menu of remedies for particular breaches of the provisions therein). The distinction is a crucial one as the right to terminate is of such importance and an opportunistic party may use a breach of condition as a way of enabling evasion of contractual obligations with the concomitant opportunity of entering into a more profitable contract with a third party. It is vital to establish how the two types of term are distinguished and whether the courts will always pay paramount attention to the parties' intentions.

The orthodox theory is that conditions and warranties are identifiable at the date the contract was formed. This approach has two peculiarities.[2] First, it is based upon the assumption that there is some essential substance which defines these obligations in the abstract and, secondly, it takes no account of the seriousness of the breach and its consequences. It is arguable that the only reason which should justify one party's termination of the contract is a breach by the other party which goes to the root of the contract, meaning that further performance is futile. Nevertheless, many undertakings have become definitive conditions by virtue of commercial usage, the operation of the doctrine of precedent and some statutory implied terms which are expressly declared to be conditions. In *Arcos Ltd v EA Ronaasen & Son* **[1933] AC 470**, the contract was to sell wooden staves of half an inch thickness for making cement barrels. Only a small percentage conformed to the specification but the remainder were nearly all less than nine-sixteenths of an inch thick. Although this made no

[1] The opening paragraph explains the traditional classification of conditions and warranties and indicates any potential injustice that may arise from such classification.

[2] This paragraph starts by making a point about conditions and warranties and then uses case law and statute as evidence.

difference to the manufacture of cement barrels (ie the goods were merchantable and fit for their purpose), it was held that the buyer was entitled to reject the entire consignment for breach of the implied condition of description in **s. 13 of the Sale of Goods Act 1893** (now **1979**), even though there was evidence that the motive for the buyer's rejection was that the market price of timber had fallen. A similar conclusion was reached regarding a breach of condition occasioning no loss in **Re Moore & Co. and Landauer & Co.** [1921] **2 KB 519**, where Scrutton LJ pointed out that the breach *might* have had drastic consequences. With respect, such a hypothesis did nothing to justify the repudiation where there was no loss on the facts. This tunnel vision has little to commend it and developments in recent years are arguably preferable.[3]

First, where the contract labels its terms as conditions or warranties the court must attempt to implement the parties' intentions, but it is clear that the form of the contract should not be allowed to dictate its substance or injustice may follow.[4] *Schuler (L) AG v Wickman Machine Tool Sales Ltd* [1974] AC 235 concerned a 'condition' in a four-and-a-half-year distributorship agreement that the distributor, Wickman, should visit six named customers once a week to solicit orders. This entailed an approximate total of 1,400 visits during the subsistence of the contract. Clause 11 of the contract provided that either party might terminate the contract if the other committed 'a material breach' of its obligations. The House of Lords refused to accept the contention that a single failure to make a visit should allow Schuler to terminate the entire contract, although Lord Wilberforce dissented.[5] Lord Reid said that the House was trying to discover intention as disclosed by the contract as a whole and while the use of 'condition' was a strong indication of intention, it was not conclusive. He considered that 'the fact that a particular construction leads to a very unreasonable result must be a relevant consideration. The more unreasonable the result the more unlikely it is that the parties can have intended it.'

Secondly, the development of the innominate or intermediate term[6] arguably introduces a more logical flexibility to this area of law. In *Hong Kong Fir Shipping Co. Ltd v Kawasaki Kisen Kaisha Ltd* [1962] 2 QB 26, the Court of Appeal emphasized that the orthodox division of conditions and warranties could be rigid and inflexible in operation, meaning that a negligible breach of condition might allow repudiation while only damages would be available for a catastrophic breach of warranty. The condition that a ship should be seaworthy could thus be breached across a spectrum of possibilities from inconsequential inconveniences at one extreme to calamities involving

[3] The paragraph analyses the evidence in relation to the question, concluding that the classification may give rise to injustice. Interestingly *Arcos* was recently applied in *Local Boy'z Ltd v Malu NV* [2021] EWHC 2439 (Comm).

[4] The injustice of the condition/warranty classification is ameliorated by developments in the law. The first is the court's search for the intention of the parties.

[5] When using a case as evidence, note any lack of unanimity among the judges. *Schuler* highlights the tension in the law.

[6] Discussion of innominate terms is a key point in answering the question. Three paragraphs are devoted to an explanation and exploration of innominate terms.

[7] The flexibility inherent in the use of innominate terms is explained.

substantial loss at the other. Diplock LJ held that such undertakings could not be categorized as conditions or warranties but that the legal consequences of the breach should 'depend upon the nature of the event to which the breach gives rise and . . . not . . . from a prior classification.'[7]

The *Hong Kong* reasoning has been endorsed in subsequent decisions. In *Cehave NV v Bremer Handelsgesellschaft mbH, The Hansa Nord* **[1976] QB 44**, the contract was for the sale of citrus pulp pellets for use in animal food. The contract price was £100,000, an express term being that the goods should be shipped 'in good condition'. The buyer sought to reject the goods for a relatively minor breach. In fact, the market in such goods had fallen dramatically at the delivery date and the buyer eventually bought the same goods from a third party for £30,000 *and* used the pellets for cattle food. The buyer argued that rejection was permissible under both the statutory implied condition of merchantability and the express condition relating to quality. The court held that the **Sale of Goods Act 1893** (now 1979) did not exhaustively define all obligations in a sale of goods contract as either conditions or warranties and that the express provision was an innominate term, breach of which, on the facts, did not permit rejection of the goods. The court assumed that merchantability was an immutable statutory condition but that, on the facts, the sellers were not in breach of that condition. The notion of the innominate term was similarly approved by the House of Lords in *Reardon Smith Line Ltd v Yngvar Hansen-Tangen* **[1976] 1 WLR 989** with Lord Wilberforce casting doubt upon the decisions in *Arcos* and *Re Moore* (although interestingly *Arcos* was recently applied in *Local Boy'z Ltd v Malu NV[2021] EWHC 2439 (Comm)*). More recently in *Ark Shipping Co LLC v Silverburn Shipping (IoM) Ltd (The Arctic)* [2019] EWCA Civ 1161 the Court of Appeal, in the context of a charterparty, held that, unless it is clear that a term is intended to be a condition (or indeed a warranty), it would be treated as an innominate term if the consequences of breach could be trivial or very serious.

[8] The limits of innominate terms are noted and the tension in the law is once again highlighted.

Although the innominate term is arguably an attractively logical proposition, there may nevertheless be instances where the necessity for commercial certainty and predictability demand that the parties should be able to classify a term of the contract at the time of its formation.[8] This is particularly so if there is no disparity of bargaining strength between them. Provisions relating to *time* are often crucial as are the precise descriptions of unascertained, future goods, such as a sale of commodities. In *The Mihalis Angelos* **[1971] 1 QB 164**, for example, a stipulation as to when a ship should be 'expected ready to load' under a charterparty was held to be a condition and, likewise, a notice of readiness to load in ***Bunge Corp. v Tradax Export SA*** **[1981] 1 WLR 711** (compare ***Universal Bulk Carriers Pte Ltd v Andre et Cie SA* [2001] EWCA Civ 588, [2001] 2 Lloyd's Rep 65,** ***Grand China Logistics Holding (Group) Co. Ltd v Spar Shipping AS* [2016] EWCA Civ 982** and ***DD Classics Ltd v Chen*** **[2022] 3 WLUK 476**).

[9] An amendment to the **Sale of Goods Act 1979** has sought to address the arguable injustice seen in cases such as ***Arcos v Ronaasen.***

Thirdly, **s. 15A of the SGA 1979**[9] provides that where a non-consumer buyer would have the right to reject goods by reason of a breach of any of the implied conditions in **ss. 13–15** but the breach is 'so slight that it would be unreasonable for him to reject [the goods]', the breach 'is not to be treated as a breach of condition but may be treated as a breach of warranty'. The principal target of **s. 15A** is thus the decision in ***Arcos Ltd v EA Ronaasen & Son***, referred to earlier (see also the **SGA 1979, s. 30(2A)**) although **s. 15A(2)** does allow the parties to exclude expressly the operation of **s. 15A**. (Note that the **CRA 2015** does not affect this analysis as the **CRA 2015** focuses exclusively on 'consumer' contracts, ie those between traders and consumers, leaving the **SGA 1979** in this respect to apply as between businesses.)

[10] The overall conclusion addresses the tension in the law between certainty and the need to achieve a just result.

In conclusion,[10] there is still room to implement the definitive intentions of the parties expressed as conditions and warranties. Lord Wilberforce dissented vigorously in ***Schuler*** and would not assume 'contrary to the evidence, that both parties to this contract adopted a standard of easy-going tolerance rather than one of aggressive, insistent punctuality and efficiency'. Such tensions will always be present where freedom of contract meets policy-interventionism but combining innominate terms with the orthodox classification of conditions and warranties allows the courts to tread a middle path between rigid, and sometimes unjust, rules on one side, and indeterminate flexibility on the other.

LOOKING FOR EXTRA MARKS?

■ Ensure that you show your appreciation of the uncertainties in the classifications set out in the suggested answer for Question 1. For example, what constitutes a *serious* breach of an innominate term allowing termination of obligations under a contract?

■ In **s. 15A of the SGA 1979** the use of the words 'slight' and 'unreasonable' create uncertainties. A critical exploration of the section illuminates the tension in the law of promoting certainty or achieving justice.

QUESTION | 2

The distinction between terms implied by the courts in fact and terms implied by the courts in law is clear, but the processes of implication are uncertain in operation.

Discuss.

CAUTION!

- This question focuses upon implied terms and the bases for implication. A clear structure based on PEA will help you organize the material you choose to use.

- As the question is broad you will have to ensure you cover the points raised but may not have time to write in detail about all of the relevant case law.

DIAGRAM ANSWER PLAN

Outline the differences between implied terms in fact and implied terms in law.

▼

Terms implied in fact are based upon presumed intention of the parties—traditionally two tests used: business efficacy test and the officious bystander test.

▼

Tests considered in *Belize* case: the real question is one of construction of a contract.

▼

Approach in *Belize* case doubted in *Marks & Spencer* case.

▼

Terms implied in law based upon different considerations—not necessarily based on search for presumed intention of the parties—*Liverpool CC v Irwin* as explained in *Crossley v Faithful & Gould*.

▼

Consideration of wider policy issues.

▼

Conclusion.

An important source of contractual terms is the process of implication whereby the law supplements those terms expressly agreed by the parties. Broadly, a court may imply a term as a matter of *fact* or as a matter of *law*. It is clear that the processes of implication *in fact*, which seeks to identify terms based upon the intention of the parties, and implication *in law*, which is based on wider considerations, are theoretically distinct.[1] The operation of the processes of implication raises questions of, first, how is the intention of the parties to be found and, secondly, what is meant by wider considerations?

Terms implied in fact are an attempt by the courts to give effect to the unexpressed common intentions (objectively assessed) of the parties.[2] Broadly in such circumstances the court is concluding that the parties have reached an agreement but have failed to fully state the terms of the agreement (objectively assessed). The courts, however, must not write/rewrite the contract for the parties—and certainly, the reasonableness of a term is not sufficient to permit implication (***Liverpool City Council v Irwin* [1977] AC 239**); the role of the courts is to give effect to that unexpressed intention, objectively assessed (***J N Hipwell & Son v Szurek* [2018] EWCA Civ 674**). Traditionally, the courts have employed two different tests that both seek to identify the intention of the parties: the business efficacy test and the officious bystander test.[3] The business efficacy test considers whether a contract needs a term to make the contract work as the parties would usually have included such a term had they thought about the issue: ***The Moorcock* (1889) 14 PD 64**. The officious bystander test requires the courts to consider whether a term is so obvious that it must have been intended by the parties to be a term of the contract, as its inclusion goes without saying. In ***Shirlaw v Southern Foundries (1926) Ltd* [1939] 2 KB 206** MacKinnon LJ said the test is if, while the parties are contracting, an officious bystander were to suggest an express provision for their agreement, they would 'testily suppress him with a common, "Oh, of course!"' The tests have the same purpose—that is, finding the intention of the parties—but reflect different ways of identifying that intention;[4] under the business efficacy test the term must be necessary to make the contract work as intended, whereas the officious bystander test focuses on the term being so obvious that there is no need for it to be expressed. The exact relationship of the tests was not always clear,[5] although Lord Simon in ***BP Refinery (Westernport) Pty Ltd v Shire of Hastings* (1977) 180 CLR 266** appeared to suggest that the tests were cumulative but overlapping. These tests were reviewed by the Privy Council in ***AG of Belize v Belize Telecom Ltd* [2009] UKPC 10**. Lord Hoffmann

[1] Note the question refers to terms implied by the courts. Terms may be implied by statute, eg the **Sale of Goods Act 1979** and the **Supply of Goods and Services Act 1982**. The question does not require a consideration of such terms.

[2] This is the point of discussion in the paragraph.

[3] The point is then developed by explaining what tests have been employed to discover the intention of the parties.

[4] As part of the evidence an explanation is needed of how the intention of the parties is to be determined.

[5] The analysis links to the question.

[6] The *Belize* case was significant and the uncertainties it created must be explored.

said that the implication of terms in fact was part of the process of construction of a contract.[6] His Lordship said that if 'some provision ought to be implied in an instrument, the question for the court is whether such a provision would spell out in express words what the instrument, read against the relevant background, would reasonably be understood to mean' and viewed the traditional tests not as independent tests to be satisfied but different ways of 'expressing the central idea that implied terms must spell out what the contract actually means'. This analysis, of subsuming the process of implication within the process of interpretation of a contract, caused controversy among academic writers and some uncertainty in the courts; for example, see Arden LJ's comments in *Stena Line Ltd v Merchant Navy Ratings Pension Fund Trustees Ltd* [2011] EWCA Civ 543. Hooley (2014)[7]

[7] Introducing a relevant academic comment not only evidences breadth of reading but adds to the analysis presented in an answer.

welcomed Lord Hoffmann's analysis but commented that the traditional tests existing alongside Lord Hoffmann's restatement of the law caused uncertainty and that further reference to the tests should be avoided. Lord Hoffmann's approach has now been considered by

[8] The *Marks & Spencer* case now explains the impact of the *Belize* case and must be discussed. See also *Yoo Design Services Ltd v Iliv Realty PTE Ltd* [2021] EWCA Civ 560.

the Supreme Court in *Marks & Spencer plc v BNP Paribas Services Trust Co. (Jersey) Ltd* [2015] UKSC 72.[8] Lord Neuberger, giving the view of the majority, stated that while the express terms of a contract have to be interpreted before implication of terms may be considered, the processes of interpretation and implication are different. He limited the impact of Lord Hoffmann's approach by saying it should be viewed as 'inspired discussion' not as 'authoritative guidance on the law of implied terms'. His Lordship added that the law on the implication of terms remained unchanged following the *Belize* case and was based on the application of the tests of 'business necessity' and 'obviousness'. Some clarification was given to the relationship between the tests in that they are to be viewed as alternatives as only one needs to be satisfied for a term to be implied in fact (see also *Wigan BC v Scullindale Global Ltd [2021]* EWHC 779 (Ch) for a rare example of where only one of these tests was satisfied). Lord Carnwath was more favourable towards the *Belize* case, but accepted that the case did not relax the 'traditional, highly restrictive approach to implication of terms'. It is still a strict process requiring a proposed implied term to be necessary, not merely reasonable, and the evidence must suggest that both parties intended the same term and it must not be inconsistent with the express terms of the contract.

[9] The answer considers the basis for the courts implying terms in law.

The process of implying terms *in law* is not based on a search for the intention of the parties (although the parties may seek to exclude the operation of such terms, subject to, for example, legislative controls) but on the courts identifying terms to be implied into contracts of a particular type:[9] for example, employment contracts, building contracts, and landlord and tenant contracts. The concern here is that the courts are deciding what should be terms of a contract, in effect writing the contract in part. The leading case on this process of implication is *Liverpool CC v Irwin*. This case concerned responsibility for common areas in a block of flats in a contract between a local authority landlord and a tenant of a flat. The House of Lords implied a term into the contract that the landlord would take reasonable care to maintain the common areas of the block of flats in reasonable repair. The majority said the term was to be implied into contracts of that type as a matter of 'necessity', although it is to be noted that Lord Cross used 'reasonableness' as the basis for implication in law.[10] What the House of Lords did not articulate in *Liverpool CC v Irwin* was the ambit of necessity or the meaning of reasonableness (although there has been some oscillation in tests, see *Agbeze v Barnet Enfield and Haringey Mental Health NHS Trust* [2022] I.R.L.R. 115). Lord Bridge in *Scally v Southern Health and Social Services Board* [1992] 1 AC 294 said that terms implied in law were based on 'wider considerations'. In *Crossley v Faithful & Gould Holdings Ltd* [2004] EWCA Civ 293, Dyson LJ said that the test of necessity was 'elusive' and 'protean', acknowledging the uncertainty of the test.[11] (It may be added that the use of 'necessary' in relation to terms implied in fact also creates some terminological confusion.) His Lordship then stated that rather than focusing on 'the elusive concept of necessity', it was better to recognize that in part 'the existence and scope of standardised implied terms raise questions of reasonableness, fairness and balancing competing policy considerations'. This acknowledges that the courts are looking at issues of policy in deciding whether a particular type of contract should be subject to a particular term. Peden (2001) suggests a number of policy considerations underpin this process of implication, such as which party is better able to bear the loss, the parties' bargaining positions, the size of the burden, and the effect on society. She further suggests that the courts are involved in a weighing process, but to maintain flexibility the list of policies is not exhaustive and the weight attaching to them is not fixed. An illustration of the impact of wider considerations may be seen in *Crossley v Faithful & Gould Holdings Ltd*, where the Court of Appeal refused to imply a term in law that employers will take care for employee's economic well-being. Two reasons given for this decision were, first, the House of Lords had refused to imply such a broad term in *Scally v Southern Health and Social Services Board* and, secondly, such a term would create an 'unfair and unreasonable burden on employers'.

A final point to consider is that while in *Scally* a term was implied in law requiring an employer to inform its employees of a valuable right within a contract (an amendment to the contract that had been agreed by an employer's representatives and trade unions on behalf of the employees) the decision was limited. The House of Lords said that the term was not to apply to employment contracts in general, but only in limited circumstances.[12]

[10] Pointing to differences in the reasoning of the judges further demonstrates that the process of implication is not without its problems.

[11] More uncertainties are highlighted, again addressing the issue raised by the question.

[12] This approach leads Phang (1993) to argue that the difference between the terms implied in law and terms implied in fact are becoming less distinct.

In conclusion,[13] it can be seen that the courts are involved in two reasonably distinct processes, one is a search for the intention of the parties, terms implied in fact, and the other is a search for terms to be implied into all contracts of a particular type based on necessity and wider considerations, terms implied in law. Although some House of Lords authority perhaps suggests that the distinction is not wholly distinct in effect. While the basis of each process may be identified, the application of each gives rise to significant uncertainty. This is seen in the terminological problems, a lack of clarity in relation to the tests to determine the intention of the parties, and the failure of the courts to articulate clear grounds for terms to be implied in law.

LOOKING FOR EXTRA MARKS?

- This question may be approached in a variety of ways. You could use specific cases to illustrate the points made in further depth at the expense of breadth.

- There is a significant academic literature which may be used in answering Question 2. For example, Richard Hooley in 'Implied Terms After *Belize Telecom*' (2014) 73 CLJ 315 counters the point that Lord Hoffmann's approach in **Belize** creates uncertainty as it is stated at too high a level of abstraction to be useful, by arguing that the 'business efficacy' and 'officious bystander' tests are also beset by problems of certainty.

QUESTION | 3

Steven, an antiques dealer, advertises in an antiques journal that he has an aeroplane for sale. The advertisement appears on 1 March and reads:

A rare opportunity to acquire a special collectable item. A biplane which belonged to the early flying ace, Sir George Ditcher, has come on the market for the first time. Sir George was an early member of the Royal Flying Corps and was the person upon whom Wiggles, the fictional flying hero, was based. £85,000, or nearest offer.

Boris, the owner of a museum dedicated to items connected with the First World War, contacts Steven on 15 March to discuss the sale. Steven shows Boris a large collection of letters written by Sir George Ditcher which describe an aeroplane, of the same type as the one offered for sale, as 'my little buzz-bomb'. Steven also points out numerous letters written to Sir George Ditcher by the author of the Wiggles books. On 10 April, Boris agrees to buy the aeroplane for £85,000 and a brief written contract is entered into which makes no mention of Sir George Ditcher or Wiggles.

Boris displays the biplane at his museum describing it as 'previously owned by Sir George Ditcher, the real-life Wiggles'. It has now been established that, although he did fly it, the aeroplane never belonged to Sir George Ditcher and that there were ten other people who had as strong a claim as Sir George Ditcher to be the basis of the Wiggles character. Boris claims that Steven is in breach of contract.

Advise Boris.

CAUTION!

- A clear structure is essential. Three broad questions should be answered. First, where is the contract to be found? Secondly, what are its terms? Thirdly, what remedies exist if the seller is in breach of a term of the contract? Use this chronological progression to ensure a logical and readable answer.

- There is a large amount of material to include in an answer to this question and not all points can be given equal weight—for example, to provide context, reference should be made to misrepresentation but only briefly.

DIAGRAM ANSWER PLAN

Identify the issues	■ What are the terms of the contract? ■ In outline what remedies are available for a breach of contract? ■ What is the relevance of the law of misrepresentation?
Relevant law	■ Where are the terms of this contract of sale of goods to be found? What are the tests for deciding if a statement is a term of the contract? ■ Once the terms of the contract have been located, it must be decided whether they are conditions, warranties, or innominate terms. How is this achieved? ■ As this is a contract for the sale of goods, might the implied terms of the **Sale of Goods Act 1979 (SGA 1979)** provide the most desirable remedy for Boris or should he seek to establish breach of an express term of the contract?
Apply the law	■ Statements made might be terms as guidelines suggest such an intention, although the specialist knowledge of Boris might be significant; ■ Consideration must be given to classification of the terms as conditions, warranties, or innominate terms; ■ The SGA 1979 appears to be of limited assistance.
Conclude	■ If terms are established, then the remedies in relation to breach of an innominate term may be available.

[1] The subject matter of the question is clearly identified in the opening sentence.

This question concerns the terms of a contract and the remedies for breach of any such term.[1] Not all statements made in connection to a contract are contractual in nature; some may be mere representations and some may be commendatory 'puffs' which lack any legal value. A seller of goods must be able to praise them *within a certain latitude* without legal consequence but if his/her statements are untrue statements of fact which induce the buyer to enter into the contract, an action may lie in misrepresentation. If the parties have a contract, it is natural to think of contractual remedies first and misrepresentation second; and that was certainly the position prior to the **Misrepresentation Act 1967**.[2] However, **s. 2(1)** of that Act introduced potent remedies for (essentially) negligent misrepresentation and placed the burden of proof on the representor to show that there was not negligence. This is therefore an attractive remedy but there are still advantages in proving a term.[3] First, if the contract is in writing, a term may be easier to prove than a misrepresentation (although it seems that, in some circumstances, a particular statement can be *both* a term and a misrepresentation). Secondly, it is not an essential requirement that a proposed term *induced* the buyer, and, thirdly, although a statement constituting a term is usually one of fact, there is no requirement that it *must* be. Where is the contract between Steven and Boris to be found and what are its terms?

[2] Indicates that the same facts may give rise to different legal consequences, ie a statement made may be a term and/or a representation.

[3] Advantages of pursuing an action for breach of contract over one for misrepresentation are considered.

It was established in **Heilbut, Symons & Co. v Buckleton [1913] AC 30** that the *intention* of the parties is the key to determining whether or not a statement is a term of the contract.[4] Sometimes it is suggested that the key is the intent of the *maker of the statement* (did he/she warrant its truth and accuracy rather than merely expressing an opinion?) but this is criticizable in that it does not sufficiently accentuate the effect of the statement on the other party and his/her justifiable *reliance* upon it. More recent cases have tended to emphasize these factors and in **Evans (J) & Son (Portsmouth) Ltd v Andrea Merzario Ltd [1976] 1 WLR 1078**, Lord Denning, referring to **Heilbut**, said that 'much of what was said in that case is entirely out of date'. Guidelines on determining the intention of the parties can be found in the relevant case law.

[4] How to determine whether a statement is a term or not is explained.

First, a lengthy interval between the making of the relevant statement (in the advertisement) and the conclusion of the contract *may* indicate that the statement does not have contractual force.[5] In **Routledge v McKay [1954] 1 WLR 615** an interval of one week between statement and contract was sufficient to deny any contractual intent to the statement. There it was the sale of a motorcycle but

[5] This paragraph shows a clear application of IRAC, as do the following paragraphs.

much depends on the facts, and if the contract and its subject matter are complicated, longer time may be allowed in order to verify statements. The interval of some five weeks between advertisement and contract is thus not necessarily fatal to Boris's claim.

[6] In searching for the intention of the parties note that a guideline may indicate an outcome which conflicts with the outcome of another guideline.

Secondly, the courts are influenced in their decision by any special knowledge that the maker of the statement may possess.[6] It is presumed that an owner of goods knows their condition and consequent weight attaches to his/her statements (see *Harling v Eddy* **[1951] 2 KB 739**—owner of a heifer who 'absolutely guaranteed' her sound condition) but it is possible that Boris, as an expert on the First World War, knows more than Steven and should have verified the statements in the five weeks before contract. This reasoning was influential in the decision in *Oscar Chess Ltd v Williams* **[1957] 1 WLR 370**, where it was held that the statement of a car's age made by its owner (the defendant) was not a term of the contract as the plaintiff car dealer had specialist knowledge and could/should have verified the statement. This test may therefore militate against Boris.

Thirdly, it is important to assess the overall importance of the statement in the light of the contract and its effect on the other party. Is the statement both crucial and pivotal in the contract's formation? In *Schawel v Reade* **[1913] 2 IR 64** and *Bannerman v White* **(1861) 10 CB (NS) 844** this test meant that the statements were terms. In *Schawel* the buyer stopped his examination of a horse when he was told that it was sound, and in *Bannerman* a buyer of hops asked whether they had been treated with sulphur, adding that he would not bother to ask the price if they had been so treated. Similarly, in *Esso Petroleum Co. Ltd v Mardon* **[1976] QB 801** the defendant's doubts as to the plaintiff's forecasted 'throughput' of petrol were quelled by the latter, and the statement was thus held to be a term. It is arguable that the provenance of the aeroplane is the dominant factor in this contract, as evidenced by the fact that it is displayed with its history at Boris's museum.

Finally, the presence of a written contract might indicate that the parties' intentions are crystallized therein. The parol evidence rule is surrounded by countless exceptions and it is quite possible to have a contract which is partly written and partly oral *if the parties so intend* (*Couchman v Hill* **[1947] KB 554**—oral assurance dominated the written sale catalogue). Alternatively, the court might construe the statements regarding the aeroplane's history as a collateral contract, thereby avoiding the parol evidence rule. In *Andrews v Hopkinson* **[1957] 1 QB 229**, for example, the plaintiff had a primary contract with a finance company to take a car on hire purchase and a collateral contract with the defendant car dealer that it was 'a good little bus'.

It is suggested that Boris may succeed in establishing a term but subject to the caveat that he is a specialist/expert buyer who did not provide for his requirements in a written contract.[7] As some prominent decisions show a distinct tendency to revert to nineteenth-century principles of laissez-faire (eg *Photo Production Ltd v Securicor Transport Ltd* [1980] AC 827), a court might thus castigate Boris's laxity.

[8] Once the terms of the contract have been established, the classification of the terms must be explored.

If the statements are terms of the contract it must be decided whether they are conditions, warranties, or innominate terms.[8] A condition is a major stipulation which allows the innocent party to terminate and/or claim damages, whereas a warranty sounds only in damages. Again, the distinction between these two types of term depends upon the parties' intentions (objectively assessed) at the date of contract. As the statements are not in the written contract they cannot be *labelled* as either conditions or warranties, and the contract is not one of an established commercial type where precedent may suggest that certain undertakings are conditions. It may be that the court would consider the statements regarding the aeroplane to be innominate terms which means that, instead of a prior classification of contract terms, the effects of the breach will provide the necessary yardstick for the court's decision. In *Reardon Smith Line Ltd v Yngvar Hansen-Tangen* [1976] 1 WLR 989, for example, it was held that a different numbering of a ship (showing the yard where it was built) from the one specified in the contract was insufficient to allow rejection of the vessel when it was up to specification in every other respect. It is arguable that the statements regarding the aeroplane cause a serious breach which goes to the root of the obligation, thereby allowing Boris to repudiate the contract. On the facts of the problem, damages alone may not 'remedy' this breach.

[9] This paragraph briefly explains that the identification of an express term is vital as statutorily implied terms may be inapplicable.

It is imperative that Boris attempts to establish an express term of the contract as it would appear that the implied terms of the **Sale of Goods Act 1979** will be of little avail.[9] The implied conditions in **s. 14** relating to satisfactory quality and fitness for purpose may not assist here; for example, in *Harlingdon and Leinster Enterprises Ltd v Christopher Hull Fine Art Ltd* [1991] 1 QB 564, a forged painting was held to be of 'merchantable quality' (the predecessor of 'satisfactory quality'). Moreover, **s. 13** relating to the description of the goods would seem to be ineffective on the facts of the problem. The reason for this is that, apart from commercial sales of future, unascertained goods where description is crucial, the courts have restricted **s. 13** to descriptive words which *identify the subject matter* of the contract. This involves a metaphysical distinction between the subject matter of the contract and its attributes but, as defective food was still held to be food in *Ashington Piggeries Ltd v Christopher Hill Ltd* [1972] AC 441, it seems indisputable that, although the aeroplane lacks many of the professed attributes, it is nevertheless an aeroplane, there being compliance with the essence of the bargain within **s. 13**.

[10] A general conclusion then pulls together the arguments completing the analysis of the question.

In conclusion,[10] while Boris may be able to pursue an action for misrepresentation, the focus of this advice, in accordance with Boris' explicit claim, is on a possible breach of contract. In order to be successful, he probably must establish that the statement made is an express term of the contract, any statutorily implied terms seem of little assistance on the facts. The guidelines to establish the intention of the parties on this point, as discussed earlier, may point to a term. The term established may be innominate, and given that the breach of the term by Steven is serious, Boris may repudiate the contract and claim damages.

LOOKING FOR EXTRA MARKS?

- A good student will show the examiner an overall knowledge of the area and be able to put the law in perspective when delineating the options available to the disgruntled buyer.

- Ensure you cover the main points raised by the facts of the question; concentrate on analysing the facts stated. For example, there are a number of facts that invite discussion of the existence of a term, but little factual context for discussing the remedies available to Boris in great detail.

TAKING THINGS FURTHER

- Courtney, W. and Carter, J.W., 'Implied Terms: What *Is* the Role of Construction?' (2014) 31 JCL 151.
  *Critically considers Lord Hoffmann's classification of factual implication, in **Attorney General of Belize v Belize Telecom Ltd** [2009] **UKPC 10**, as an exercise in the construction of the contract.*

- Peden, E., 'Policy Concerns Behind Implication of Terms in Law' (2001) 117 LQR 459.
  Explores the factors that the courts will take into account when deciding whether to imply terms in law.

- Peel, E., 'Terms implied in fact' (2016) 132 LQR 531.
  *Explores recent developments in this area including **Marks & Spencer plc v BNP Paribas Services Trust Co. (Jersey) Ltd** [2015] **UKSC 72**.*

- Phang, A., 'Implied Terms in English Law—Some Recent Developments' [1993] JBL 242.
  *Reviews the distinction between implied terms in fact and in law in the light of recent case law, including **Scally v Southern Health and Social Services Board** [1992] 1 AC 294.*

- Phang, A., 'Implied Terms, Business Efficacy and the Officious Bystander—A Modern History' [1998] JBL 1.
  Examines the development of the tests, the business efficacy test and officious bystander test, for implying terms in fact.

5 Exemption Clauses and Unfair Terms

ARE YOU READY?

In order to attempt the questions in this chapter you must have covered the following areas in your revision:

- The purpose of exemption clauses;
- The types of exemption clause, particularly exclusion and limitation clauses;
- How exemption clauses are incorporated into a contract—particularly through signature, notice, and a previous course of dealings;
- Common law rules on the interpretation of exemption clauses;
- The impact of legislation on exemption clauses—eg the Unfair Contract Terms Act 1977;
- Protection of consumers from unfair terms—Part 2 of the Consumer Rights Act 2015.

KEY DEBATES

Debate: what is the nature of an exemption clause?

Does an exemption clause act as a defence to liability for a breach of contract or does an exemption clause define obligations under the contract and thus determine if there is liability in the first place (compare *Impact Funding Solutions Ltd v Barrington Support Services Ltd (formerly Lawyers at Work Ltd)* [2016] UKSC 57)?

Debate: freedom of contract versus judicial intervention.

Why does the law seek to control the use of exemption clauses in consumer contracts (eg the Consumer Rights Act 2015)? Should the law seek to control the use of exemption clauses in contracts where both parties are businesses? This debate is of particular significance in the application of the test of reasonableness under the Unfair Contract Terms Act 1977.

Harvey, a businessman, buys a country hotel in Gloucestershire and decides to have the gardens landscaped. He contacts Capability Ltd after seeing their advertisement in the local newspaper stating: 'Paths, fencing and garden maintenance our speciality—also quotations given for larger jobs.' Before concluding any contract, Harvey discovers that there is a local builder, Scrapitt, who offers to do the work at '5 per cent less than whatever price Capability quotes'. Harvey has little confidence in Scrapitt and he therefore decides to enter into a contract with Capability Ltd.

A price of £10,000 is agreed and Harvey is given a document headed 'Memorandum of Terms'. This document sets out the job specification, price, and date of completion. The reverse has the following clauses added by rubber stamp:

Clause 1: The company accepts no responsibility for personal injury to the customer during performance of the contract.

Clause 2: Liability for any damage to the customer's property is limited to the sum of £500, and no liability can be accepted for loss of, or damage to, the customer's goods.

Reckless, employed by Capability Ltd, drives a dumper truck through the wall of Harvey's hotel. As Harvey returns in his car that night, he collides with the dumper truck which Reckless has left in the middle of the driveway. The car is completely ruined and Harvey is injured.

Advise Harvey.

CAUTION!

- Address the issue of liability: for example, has there been a breach of contract and/or has a party been negligent? The facts of the question will determine how much you can say about the issue of liability.

- There are two main areas for evaluation in this problem; first, the common law controls over the use of exemption clauses and, secondly, the relevant sections of the Unfair Contract Terms Act 1977 (UCTA 1977).

DIAGRAM ANSWER PLAN

Identify the issues	■ The question relates to the terms of a contract and exemption clauses.
Relevant law	■ Liability of Capability Ltd—look at express and implied terms. ■ Exemption clause—is it incorporated; does it cover the relevant liability; is it controlled by the **Unfair Contract Terms Act 1977**?
Apply the law	■ As no signature, rules of notice might suggest incorporation. ■ Interpretation—consideration of the traditional *contra proferentem* rule and the rule in *Canada Steamship Lines Ltd v The King*. ■ Application of Unfair Contract Terms Act 1977, ss. 1(3), 2(1), 2(2), and 11.
Conclude	■ There appears to be liability. While the exemption clause may be part of the contract it may not cover the liability or pass the reasonableness test.

 SUGGESTED ANSWER

This question concerns the extent to which Harvey (H) is bound by the attempted exemption of Capability Ltd's (C's) liability. A first issue to consider is that of C's liability[1] in relation to the damaged wall, damaged car, and the personal injuries suffered by H. While the facts of the question do not fully explain the circumstances of the events, it may be argued that there has been a failure by C to exercise reasonable care and skill either under the contract (see **Supply of Goods and Services Act 1982, s. 13**, which implies such a term) or by arguing negligence at common law. Should such liability exist, then C may seek to rely on the exemption clauses in the contract.

For an exemption clause to be effective as a matter of contract law it must be incorporated into the contract.[2] There are various ways in which an exemption clause can be incorporated into a contract. In the absence of a signature,[3] the exemption may be incorporated by notice; H must be given reasonable notice of the terms.[4] It was emphasized in *Parker v South Eastern Ry* (1877) 2 CPD 416 that it is notice of the terms which is important, not their actual reading or

[1] The issue of liability is considered first, but only briefly.

[2] Here one of the major issues raised by the question is identified.

[3] In explaining the rules of incorporation concentrate on the method of incorporation relevant to the facts, ie notice.

[4] This paragraph shows the rules and application part of IRAC; state the rule and immediately apply it to the facts.

understanding, and it follows that if the notice is illegible or obscured by a date stamp as in *Richardson, Spence & Co. v Rowntree* **[1894] AC 217**, it will be ineffective. The clauses in the problem appear to be quite legible but they are on the reverse of the document and there may be no notice such as 'See over for conditions' on its face. This may well be fatal to C, for in *Henderson v Stevenson* **(1875) LR 2 HL (Sc) 470** the court held that the absence of a notice on the front of a ticket referring to clauses printed on its back rendered the clauses invalid. Moreover, in *Interfoto Picture Library Ltd v Stiletto Visual Programmes Ltd* **[1989] QB 433**, the court emphasized that if the clause is particularly unusual, or onerous, extra care must be taken to draw its attention to the other party. On the facts it may be argued that the terms are neither unusual nor onerous (and in *Goodlife Foods Ltd v Hall Fire Protection Ltd* **[2018] EWCA Civ 1371** the Court of Appeal stressed that an exemption clause is not per se onerous or unusual) but, if they were, it would seem that C has not taken any further steps to draw the terms to H's attention. Furthermore, the notice that is given must be, at the latest, contemporaneous with the contract's formation (see *Olley v Marlborough Court Ltd* **[1949] 1 KB 532**). It is not entirely clear when the exclusion clauses in the problem are presented to H and so there is some uncertainty over whether or not this requirement is satisfied.

Additionally, the document containing the clauses must be a contractual document; that is, one which a reasonable person would expect to contain the conditions of the contract. In *Chapelton v Barry Urban District Council* **[1940] 1 KB 532**, a receipt which was given for the hire of a deckchair was not such a contractual document. The courts preserve great flexibility when deciding this question (see *McCutcheon v MacBrayne (David) Ltd* **[1964] 1 WLR 125**) and it may be that the 'Memorandum of Terms' in the problem will suffice. However, there might be a full, written contract elsewhere which would mean that the court could strike down this 'Memorandum'.

[5] In conclusion, the argument as to incorporation by notice seems to particularly turn on whether or not steps had been taken to draw H's attention to the clauses at the time of contracting. The lack of an indication that H should turn to the reverse of the document may be fatal to C's reliance on the exemption clauses.

Before leaving the common law, it must be emphasized that, should the clauses be successfully incorporated in the contract, the question then becomes one of interpretation[6]—does the exemption clause cover the liability that has arisen? A traditional rule of construction was that any ambiguity in a clause would be construed against C (ie *contra proferentem*). Similarly, clauses attempting to exclude all liability for negligence needed to be clear and the law traditionally

[5] A short conclusion highlights the main point of the argument in relation to incorporation.

[6] Another issue is identified, that of interpretation of the exemption clause, followed by an explanation and application of the rules.

preserved this head of liability wherever possible (see *Alderslade v Hendon Laundry Ltd* **[1945] 1 KB 189**; *White v John Warwick & Co. Ltd* **[1953] 1 WLR 1285**). The question is ultimately one of construction of the contract, but if the defendant disclaims liability for 'any loss' the court may consider that he is attempting to exclude all *types* of loss without being sufficiently specific as to their *cause* (see *Price v Union Lighterage Co.* **[1904] 1 KB 412**) and in commercial contracts, between parties of comparable strength, it seems the *contra proferentem* rule is now of limited use (see *Persimmon Homes Ltd v Ove Arup & Partners Ltd* **[2017] EWCA Civ 373**). The clauses in the problem make no express reference to negligence and, as such, they would traditionally have been construed against C following the tests laid down by Lord Morton in *Canada Steamship Lines Ltd v The King* **[1952] AC 192**. However, the common law's powers to circumvent clauses by deft interpretation are now of less significance in the light of the **Unfair Contract Terms Act 1977 (UCTA 1977)** and in *Persimmon Homes Ltd v Ove Arup & Partners Ltd* **[2017] EWCA Civ 373** Jackson LJ was of the opinion that Lord Morton's test is much less relevant today (see also in a similar vein *The Federal Republic of Nigeria v JP Morgan Chase Bank, N.A.* [2019] EWHC 347 (Comm) at [64]).

[7] It is important to explain when the **UCTA 1977** applies.

The UCTA 1977[7] seeks to control the use of exemption clauses and generally applies where there is 'business liability'. **Section 1(3)** defines 'business liability' as 'liability for breach of obligations or duties . . . arising from things done or to be done by a person in the course of a business (whether his own or another's)'. As C's liability arises from their undertaking landscaping work in the course of his business the 1977 Act would apply.

[8] Some exemptions are rendered ineffective by the **Unfair Contract Terms Act 1977**.

Section 2(1) of the UCTA 1977[8] invalidates any attempt by a contract term or notice to exclude or restrict liability for death or bodily injury *resulting from negligence*. It is clearly arguable that it was negligent to leave the dumper truck in the driveway and, if the basis of H's claim is negligence, clause 1 of the contract would be ineffective as regards H's claim for his injuries.

Section 2(2) further provides that in the case of 'other loss or damage' a person cannot exclude or restrict his/her liability *for negligence* except insofar as the term or notice satisfies the test of reasonableness. This seems applicable to C, as liability seems to have arisen due to negligence (including an implied term to take reasonable care). It must be decided whether clause 2 can pass the reasonableness

[9] The test of reasonableness requires detailed consideration.

test. Section 11(1) provides that the time for determining whether the clause is reasonable is the time at which the contract is made.[9] Thus the seriousness of the loss or damage caused should not be considered except to the extent to which it was, or ought reasonably to have been, in the contemplation of the parties at the time of contract. Following the interpretation given to **s. 11** in *Stewart Gill Ltd v Horatio Myer & Co. Ltd* [1992] 1 QB 600, it seems unlikely that C could justify the insertion of the exclusion clause in the contract. *Stewart Gill* also decides that the *whole* clause must be reasonable, not merely the part relied upon by the defendant: clause 2 may therefore fail in its entirety (see also *Watford Electronics Ltd v Sanderson CFL Ltd* [2001] EWCA Civ 317, which would clearly support the view that clauses 1 and 2 were separate for the purposes of applying s. 11 of the UCTA 1977, and compare *Goodlife Foods Ltd v Hall Fire Protection Ltd* [2017] EWHC 767, affirmed on appeal [2018] EWCA Civ 1371). Section 11(4) provides that if the defendant limits liability to a specific sum of money, regard shall be had, in assessing reasonableness, to the resources which he/she could expect to be available to him for meeting the liability and how far it was open to him/her to cover himself by insurance. This provision was designed to alleviate undue hardship to small businesses but it is arguable that C could and should have insured against the risk in question and this would certainly be the case if C could insure without any material increase to H in the contract price.

It is also vital to consider the guidelines for assessing reasonableness in Sch. 2 to the Act. Particularly relevant to this problem is the question of whether the customer was given any inducement to agree to the clause or had the opportunity of doing business elsewhere without having to accept the clause. As C charges more than one of its competitors (Scrapitt would give a 5 per cent discount on C's prices), it is legitimate to ask whether Scrapitt would use any exclusion clauses and, if so, whether they are more or less onerous than C's. C's exclusion clause might, therefore, be condemned using such a comparative assessment.

In *Watford Electronics Ltd v Sanderson CFL Ltd* it was said that where commercial parties of equal bargaining power negotiate and arrive at a bargain, then the courts should not interfere. Both H and C are in business. However, it would seem that there was no negotiation in relation to the terms and, indeed, even if at common law the exemptions had been incorporated, the facts do not suggest that H was aware of the clause before contracting (see Sch. 2, guideline (c)). In these circumstances, on balance, it is suggested that C's clause might not be regarded as a reasonable one. Indeed, by **s. 11(5)** the burden of proof lies on C to show that the clause is reasonable.

LOOKING FOR EXTRA MARKS?

■ Few questions in this area can be answered simply by reference to common law principles: allocate a reasonable proportion of your answer to the law contained in the UCTA 1977, citing and applying specific subsections wherever possible. Consider whether clauses which define obligations can be covered by UCTA 1977 (see ***Avrora Fine Arts Investment Ltd v Christie, Manson & Woods Ltd* [2012] EWHC 2198** and ***McClean v Thornhill* [2022] EWHC 457 (Ch)**).

■ The question of reasonableness under the UCTA 1977 is a matter for the discretion of a trial court. While the law has identified a number of factors that may be taken into account in assessing reasonableness, ultimately the weight to be attached to the factors in an individual case is for the trial court to assess. In consequence, it is difficult to predict if an exemption clause will satisfy the test of reasonableness.

QUESTION | 2

Patrick, a director of Dartsma Ltd, which manufactures computers, decided that the company should purchase a prestigious car which could be used principally for entertaining the company's customers but which would also be suitable for private use by Patrick and the other directors. Accordingly, the company bought a second-hand 'Lynx' car from Dependable Motors Ltd (DM), a motor dealership. Patrick managed to negotiate a 15 per cent 'trade discount' on the price of the car. The lengthy contract for the sale of the car, which Patrick signed, contained the following clause on p. 10:

DM Ltd will refund the price of any defective goods provided that such defects are communicated to the company in writing no later than 3 days after the contract of sale is concluded but the Company shall not otherwise be liable for any loss or damage caused by defects in the goods.

Before leaving DM's premises, Patrick noticed that the car's windscreen wiper blades needed replacing. He therefore purchased two new blades from the parts department of DM Ltd, fitting them himself. The sales invoice contained the same exclusion clause as that in the contract for the sale of the car and was also signed by Patrick. After using the car for two weeks, Patrick had a minor accident while driving the car in wet weather and the car was damaged. He discovered that the rubber wiper blades had perished and had consequently failed to clear the windscreen of rain. In the third week of using the car, its gearbox seized up and was ruined. DM Ltd had failed to refill the gearbox with oil during the pre-delivery service of the car.

a   Advise Patrick.
    (Ignore any issues relating to acceptance of breach and remedies.)

b   Would your answer differ, and if so how, if Patrick bought the car from Chemcall plc, a chemical processing manufacturer, that had a car which was surplus to requirements, and the car had serious mechanical problems?

CAUTION!

- Consider the extent to which the implied terms emanating from the Sale of Goods Act 1979 can be excluded in business sales. Section 6 of the Unfair Contract Terms Act 1977 (UCTA 1977) must be considered.

- Note that the UCTA 1977 does not create liability. To establish liability, you must look to the terms of a contract and breach. Should liability exist then the 1977 Act may regulate attempts to exempt liability.

DIAGRAM ANSWER PLAN

Identify the issues	■ The question relates to the terms of sale of goods contracts, including exemption clauses.
Relevant law	■ Is DM in breach of an express term or an implied term—eg Sale of Goods Act 1979, s. 14? ■ Note part (b) of question raises the issue of whether the sale takes place 'in the course of a business'. ■ Exclusion clause—is it incorporated; does it cover the relevant liability; how is such an exclusion controlled by the Unfair Contract Terms Act 1977?
Apply the law	■ As there is signature incorporation possible, no problem with interpretation. ■ Application of Unfair Contract Terms Act 1977, ss. 1(3), 6(1A), and 11. ■ Part (b) of question, sale does occur in course of business— *Stevenson v Rogers*.
Conclude	■ There appears to be liability under **Sale of Goods Act 1979**. While the exclusion clause may be part of the contract, it arguably does not satisfy the reasonableness test. ■ Part (b): **Sale of Goods Act 1979**, s. 14 implies a term which has been broken and potentially there would be liability.

[1] The opening sentence indicates the areas of law raised by the question.

[2] The logic of this question requires that the terms of the contract and possible breach are considered to establish potential liability.

[3] The answer considers whether the requirement of s. 14 of the SGA 1979 that the goods are sold in the course of a business is satisfied.

[4] Once liability is established the effectiveness of the exemption clauses must be considered, starting with whether or not the clauses are incorporated in the contract.

(a) This problem raises issues concerning implied terms, breach of contract, and the operation of exemption clauses.[1] The answer will address whether the exemption clause in issue protects Dependable Motors from any breach of the implied terms of s. 14 of the Sale of Goods Act 1979 (SGA 1979), which covers the quality and fitness for any particular purpose of the goods sold.

First, what are the terms of the contract[2] between Patrick (P) and Dependable Motors (DM)? The question does not indicate that express terms provide for the events that have occurred, in consequence it is necessary to consider the potential implied terms contained in s. 14 of the SGA 1979. This section implies, in some situations, conditions that the goods sold are of satisfactory quality and, where relevant, fit for any particular purpose. By s. 14(2A) of the SGA 1979 goods are of satisfactory quality if they meet the standard that a reasonable person would regard as satisfactory, taking into account any description, price, and other relevant circumstances (see also the SGA 1979, s. 14(2B)). However, for the terms to be implied the goods must be sold 'in the course of a business'.[3] As DM is a motor dealer, both the car and the wiper blades were sold 'in the course of a business' by DM and the goods seem to be both unsatisfactory and unfit for their purpose. It is arguable that DM is in breach of s. 14 of the SGA 1979.

Secondly, DM will seek to rely upon the exemption clauses in answer to any claim by P.[4] For such clauses to be effective as a matter of contract law, they must be incorporated in the contracts. There can scarcely be any dispute regarding the incorporation of these exemption clauses. The terms in the contracts of sale seem to be advanced by DM at the moment of the formation of both contracts (compare *Olley v Marlborough Court Ltd* **[1949] 1 KB 532**, where an exclusion clause was only notified after the formation of the contract and was therefore ineffective). Also, both documents are probably contractual in nature (see *Chapelton v Barry Urban District Council* **[1940] 1 KB 532**, where an exclusion clause contained in a receipt was not incorporated in a contract as the receipt was not intended to be contractual in nature). The lengthy document signed by P in relation to the purchase of the car appears to be contractual and certainly would so appear to a reasonable person (*Thompson v LM & S Ry* **[1930] 1 KB 41**). There might only be some doubt in this respect regarding the 'sales invoice' for the wiper blades (see *Grogan v Robin Meredith Plant Hire* **[1996] CLC 1127**, where signature of a time sheet, containing terms, did not incorporate the terms because the document was not contractual) but the problem does not provide enough information to decide the issue. More importantly, as both documents are signed[5] by P and, in the absence of any misrepresentation or duress and irrespective of whether or not P has read the documents, the exemption clauses may be incorporated as terms of the contract (see *L'Estrange v F Graucob Ltd* [1934] 2 KB 394). It is arguable, therefore, that at common law these exemption clauses would bind P.

At common law it may be argued that an exemption clause is ineffective as its wording does not cover the liability that has arisen. On the facts of the problem this interpretation question does not appear to be an issue.

However, the Unfair Contract Terms Act 1977 (UCTA 1977) seeks to control the use of exemption clauses between businesses.[6] By s. 1(3) the 1977 Act applies (subject to s.6(4)) where there is 'business liability'; that is, 'liability for breach of obligations … arising from things done or to be done by a person in the course of a business'. As DM is a motor dealership the sale of the car and liability is in the course of a business. Although the clause on page 10 arguably does not directly exclude or limit liability, the 1977 Act nonetheless applies as by s. 13 an exemption clause includes an attempt to 'make the liability or its enforcement subject to restrictive or onerous conditions'.[7] DM, by making liability subject to communication in writing to them of any defects in the goods within three days, seeks to impose a restrictive condition. Section 6(1A) of the UCTA 1977 restricts the extent to which ss. 13–15 of the SGA 1979 may be excluded. Section 6(1A) provides that liability for breach of obligations arising from ss. 13–15 of the SGA 1979 can be excluded but only 'in so far as the term satisfies the requirement of reasonableness'.[8] The exclusions will be subject to the test of reasonableness. By s. 11(1) of the UCTA 1977 it is provided that in relation to a contract term reasonableness is assessed at the time *the contract is made*, having regard to the circumstances which were, or ought reasonably to have been, known to or in the contemplation of the parties at that time. By s. 11(2) of the UCTA 1977 guidelines concerning reasonableness are found in Sch. 2 to the UCTA 1977. It will be for DM to establish that the exemptions are reasonable as s. 11(5) of the UCTA 1977 places the burden of proof on the party who claims the clause is reasonable.[9] So, will the exemptions relied upon by DM be able to pass the 'reasonableness' test? Having regard to the Sch. 2 guidelines concerning reasonableness,[10] the parties have roughly equal bargaining power and P has been given a 15 per cent discount, both of which favour DM, pointing to the reasonableness of the clause. However, is it likely that P could have bought the same model of car elsewhere without such

[5] While there are three methods of incorporation, the answer concentrates on the method of incorporation raised by the question, that of signature.

[6] An indication is given of the scope of the UCTA 1977.

[7] The answer refers to the definition of such clauses in s. 13 to ensure that the clauses in the question are within the ambit of the 1977 Act.

[8] Section 6(1A) provides that the clause, in its attempt to exempt liability for breach of contract, will be subject to the test of reasonableness.

[9] How the test of reasonableness applies is to be explored in some detail. Note also on whom the burden of proof is placed.

[10] By considering the matters relevant to the facts of the question, and explanatory case law, the answer analyses how reasonableness is to be determined.

a restrictive clause but with as generous a discount? Schedule 2(c) provides that for the purposes of assessing reasonableness, regard is to be had as to whether the customer knew or ought reasonably to have known of the existence and extent of the term and (d) where the term excludes or restricts any relevant liability if some condition is not complied with, whether it was reasonable at the time of the contract to expect that compliance with that condition would be practicable. It may be argued that perhaps P ought not reasonably to have known of the existence of the term in this lengthy document at page 10 and it seems that the time limit of three days for notifying defects could not be justified at the date the contract was entered into, this being the time that an evaluation is made under s. 11 of the UCTA 1977. It is quite unreasonable to expect defects to manifest themselves and then be notified within three days (see *RW Green Ltd v Cade Bros Farms* [1978] 1 Lloyd's Rep 602). Furthermore, in *Rees Hough Ltd v Redland Reinforced Plastics Ltd* (1984) 1 Const LJ 67, a clause in a contract between two businesses was held to be unreasonable because it provided that the sellers of piping excluded all liability unless notified of complaints within three months.

More generous protection exists under the Consumer Rights Act 2015 (CRA 2015)[11] against exclusion of liability in relation to the (essentially implied) terms of satisfactory quality or fitness for purpose of goods. By **s. 31(1)** an attempt to exclude such liability is not binding on a consumer. However, as P is contracting on behalf of Dartsma Ltd, a company, the transaction will not be a 'consumer contract' as only individuals, not companies, fall within the definition of a 'consumer' (see the **CRA 2015, s. 2** where a consumer is defined as 'an individual acting for purposes that are wholly or mainly outside that individual's trade, business, craft or profession').

(b) As Chemcall plc's business is chemical manufacturing, not selling cars, would the terms in s. 14 of the SGA 1979 be implied in the contract between P and Chemcall plc?[12] In *Stevenson v Rogers* [1999] QB 1028, the Court of Appeal held that the phrase 'sells goods in the course of a business' in s. 14(2) of the SGA 1979 must be given a literal interpretation. In the case, the defendant had an established business as a fisherman and he sold a fishing vessel which he used in the course of his business, replacing that vessel with a new one. The defendant's business was thus not that of buying and selling ships or boats. The Court of Appeal ruled that, having regard to the legislative history of the SGA 1979, the wording in s. 14(2) of the Act had been deliberately changed to widen the protection conferred upon a buyer of goods from a business seller. Thus, it was held that s. 14(2) must be construed at face value and the sale of the fishing vessel was in the course of a business: the wording of the section did not demand

[11] A brief paragraph explains why Dartsma cannot claim the protections contained in the CRA 2015.

[12] The alteration of the facts allows further consideration of the statutory phrase 'in the course of a business'.

any element of regularity of dealing and so there was no reason 'to re-introduce some implied qualification, difficult to define, in order to narrow what appears to be the wide scope and apparent purpose of the words' (at 623 per Potter LJ). This reasoning would clearly apply to the sale of the car by Chemcall to P and the terms of **s. 14 of the SGA 1979** would be implied in the contract. Liability arises if the serious mechanical problems breach the implied term of satisfactory quality.

LOOKING FOR EXTRA MARKS?

- As the question raises issues concerning legislation it is essential that you explain the circumstances in which the legislation applies. This is true of both the SGA 1979 and the **UCTA 1977**. The question requires you to explain the meaning of the legislation. In so doing, appropriate reference to the aids to interpretation, for example, the literal rule, the purposive approach, and so on, would strengthen your answer.

QUESTION | 3

The statutory framework for policing the enforceability of exemption clauses and unfair terms in contracts has been thoroughly overhauled by the **Consumer Rights Act 2015** to provide clear, effective, and comprehensive protection for consumers.

Discuss.

CAUTION!

- You must have a reasonable knowledge of the main provisions contained in the UCTA 1977 and the (now repealed) Unfair Terms in Consumer Contracts Regulations 1999 (UTCCR 1999), as well as the changes made by the CRA 2015.

- The ambit of the question is wide so you will need to consider the major issues by sacrificing some detail. Clearly, given the constraints of time in an examination, examples cannot be used in relation to every point made.

DIAGRAM ANSWER PLAN

Does the **Consumer Rights Act 2015** provide clear, effective, and comprehensive protection for consumers, particularly when compared with the previous law concerning the control of exemption clause and unfair terms?

▼

Outline of protection offered by previous law in **Unfair Contract Terms Act 1977** and the **Unfair Terms in Consumer Contracts Regulations 1999**.

▼

How wide-ranging was the **UCTA 1977** in proscribing the use of unfair contract terms?

▼

In what ways did the **UTCCR 1999** provide greater protection for consumers in entering contracts?

▼

Give examples of how the **UCTA 1977** and the **UTCCR 1999** treated the same set of facts differently.

▼

Does the **CRA 2015** clarify and simplify the existing legal position of consumers? How effective is the **CRA 2015**?

▼

Conclusion.

SUGGESTED ANSWER

The previous statutory framework for regulating the enforceability of exemption clauses and unfair terms within contracts was primarily contained in the Unfair Contract Terms Act 1977 (UCTA 1977) **and the** Unfair Terms in Consumer Contracts Regulations 1999 (UTCCR 1999).[1] Both operated independently of one another but their provisions overlapped considerably. The potential for conflict and confusion was exacerbated by their different styles and approaches. Whilst the UCTA 1977 acknowledged and built upon the heritage of the common law, using tests which would clearly be part of the vocabulary of any English contract lawyer (eg the 'reasonableness' test contained in s. 11), the UTCCR 1999 adopted a much more European approach, placing (some would argue) alien concepts such as 'good faith' at the heart of its regulatory design. The Consumer Rights Act 2015 (CRA 2015) amended the UCTA 1977, so that the 1977 Act focuses on contracts between businesses. The CRA 2015 also revoked the UTCCR

[1] The previous law affecting consumers is stated and will form the basis for comparison with the new law.

[2] The relationship between the old and new law is outlined.

1999 and replaced them with a unified scheme of protection for consumers from the use by traders of particular exemption clauses and unfair terms.[2]

The types of contracts covered by the UCTA 1977,[3] prior to the CRA 2015, included consumer, business, and employment contracts, albeit with numerous limitations; for example, where businesses contracted with each other, the general section on breach of contract (s. 3) only applied to the extent that one party dealt on the other's 'standard terms'. More importantly, the title of the UCTA 1977 was and is misleading insofar as it suggests that the reasonableness or validity of *any* term can be the subject of litigation. The reality was that the UCTA 1977 focused on a relatively narrow range of clauses, for example those seeking to exclude or limit common law or statutory liability for negligence (see s. 2) or breach of contract (see ss. 3, 6, and 7), or which assert a right to 'render a contractual performance substantially different from that which was reasonably expected' (see s. 3). Where the Act was applicable, the relevant term either would be automatically unenforceable (eg s. 2(1)) or would only be adjudged valid if found to be fair and reasonable (see s. 11 for the applicable test). Finally, the UCTA 1977 was written in a dense style that makes its understanding by lawyers, let alone the average consumer, somewhat problematic. As the Law Commission noted: 'Pity the poor adviser who has to work out that s. 6 applies to exemption clauses in two types of contract (sale and hire-purchase) in four possible patterns: business to consumer, consumer to business, business to business, and "private" contracts where neither party acts in the course of a business.'

The UTCCR 1999, on the other hand, applied to consumer contracts made with a business seller or supplier, but not to business to business or purely private contracts.[4] Apart from the main subject matter or the price (and some other exceptions), UTCCR 1999 covered all terms that had not been individually negotiated. Any term found to contravene the requirement of 'good faith' and which created a significant imbalance between the parties was unfair and not binding on the consumer. The UTCCR 1999 contained an indicative list of terms that were potentially considered unfair but, unlike the UCTA 1977, generally terms were not automatically considered invalid (compare former reg 5(5)). Finally, the Competition and Markets Authority and other bodies were empowered to prevent unfair terms from being used by businesses against consumers, unlike the provisions of the UCTA 1977 which applied only as between the parties.

The overlap between the UCTA 1977 and the UTCCR 1999 was confusing, especially where similar words or concepts were being used.[5] For example, in both the UCTA 1977 and the UTCCR 1999, to qualify as a 'consumer' a party to the contract must not have been acting in the course of his/her business, yet the case law suggested that the meaning of 'consumer' differed in important respects. As regards the UCTA 1977, in *R & B Customs Brokers Co. Ltd v United Dominions Trust Ltd* **[1988] 1 WLR 321** it was recognized that a company might be treated as a 'consumer'[6] where the contract (to purchase a car for the personal and business use of its directors) was incidental to the main activity of that business. However, the UTCCR 1999 only recognized a 'natural person' as being consumers, narrowing the meaning of consumer. Nevertheless, as the 'person' was still to be 'acting for purposes which are outside his trade, business or profession', similar difficulties were encountered when dealing with the activities of sole traders. Did the accountant who bought a computer primarily for personal entertainment, but then used it for business purposes when working from home, act as a consumer under the UTCCR 1999?[7]

There were also major differences in the way the UCTA 1977 and the UTCCR 1999 approached the use of 'standard terms' in consumer contracts. The latter applied only to terms that had 'not been individually negotiated' (reg. 5); thereby distinguishing those terms that have been drafted in advance from those where their substance had been influenced by the consumer. These two examples are symptomatic of a range of linguistic and interpretational differences that existed between the UCTA 1977 and the UTCCR 1999. Even the burden of proof was arguably different: the UCTA 1977 either rendered a clause totally unenforceable or required the party seeking to rely upon it to establish its reasonableness, whereas under the UTCCR 1999 it is arguable that it was for the consumer to prove the term was 'unfair'.

After much consideration the UK government introduced a Bill to create a single, unifying Act covering all exemption clauses and unfair terms contained in trader-to-consumer contracts (T2C) which led to the passing of the CRA 2015. The UTCCR 1999 was revoked (with most of its provisions being transferred to the CRA 2015), while the UCTA 1977 was amended so as not to apply to T2C contracts but to focus on exemption clauses in business-to-business (B2B) contracts.

In principle, this separation of T2C and B2B is welcome. The skills and expectations of consumers and businesses when contracting are often very different, so any legal rules impacting on the content and enforceability of the resultant contracts need to reflect such variances.[8] The new CRA 2015 applies irrespective of whether those terms were pre-formulated or negotiated. Only 'individuals' acting for purposes wholly or mainly outside that individual's trade, business, craft, or profession, will fall within the definition of consumers. In consequence, companies and partnerships cannot be consumers, thereby avoiding the problem raised in *R & B Customs Brokers Co.*

[6] Examples are given of the different definitions used by the legislation and associated problems.

[7] A problem in the application of the law is highlighted.

[8] This point lies at the heart of the question that the law must address the needs of two very different audiences—businesses and consumers.

Ltd v United Dominions Trust Ltd [1988] **1 WLR 321**. Provisions in the UCTA 1977 which *automatically* prohibited certain exclusion clauses from being enforced, such as s. 2(1) (death or personal injury caused negligently) or **s. 6** (excluding liability for breach of the standard implied terms in the Sale of Goods Act 1979), are transferred across (in respect of T2C contracts) to the CRA 2015 (s. 65(1) and s. 31, respectively)—automatic prohibitions that were surprisingly not included in the UTCCR 1999. Moreover, by s. 57 a trader supplying a service now cannot exclude liability for a failure to take reasonable care and skill (previously subject to a test of reasonableness) or for information provided about the trader or service. Also, a trader cannot limit liability: (a) as to reasonable care and skill; (b) information about trader or service; (c) reasonable time; or (d) price, to a sum less than the contract price. If a trader otherwise limits liability, for example, liability beyond the contract price, then this may be subject to the control of unfair terms under the CRA 2015. Lastly, any clause will need to be 'legible' (CRA 2015, s. 64(3)), a requirement that was missing in the UTCCR 1999.

The previous paragraph gives a flavour of the greater rights consumers enjoy as well as acknowledging that the new framework, with its separation of B2B and T2C contracts, should aid clarification and better understanding by consumers.[9] However, some changes are not so clear (and indeed some of the drafting has been criticized— see *Salt v Stratstone Specialist Ltd* [2015] **EWCA Civ 745**).[10] For example, a term specifying the main subject matter of a contract or price will not be assessed for fairness (CRA 2015, s. 64(1)). The exclusion of such terms caused problems under the **UTCCR 1999** and it does not appear that the CRA 2015 has changed this position (see also *Casehub Ltd v Wolf Cola Ltd* [2017] **EWHC 1169 (Ch)**). This exclusion only operates so long as such terms are 'transparent and prominent': s. 64(2). In s. 64(4) a term is 'prominent' where it has been 'brought to the consumer's attention in such a way that an average consumer would be aware of the term'. In s. 64(5) such a consumer is described as 'reasonably well-informed, observant and circumspect'. It is therefore quite possible that the common law would find notice of an exclusion clause unreasonable (see generally *Thornton v Shoe Lane Parking Ltd* [1971] **2 QB 163**) whilst under s. 64(4) and (5) notice of the clause is considered reasonable as the consumer 'ought' to have seen it if 'observant and circumspect'.

In conclusion, the previous law on unfair contract terms, which affected ordinary people in their everyday lives, was unnecessarily complicated and difficult to understand. It led to widespread confusion among consumers, businesses, and their advisers. The passing of the CRA 2015 has simplified the existing legal framework for consumers, and enhanced their rights to some extent, for instance, the regime of control applies to pre-formulated and negotiated contract terms, but some of

[9] In the light of changes made by the **CRA 2015** the answer states that consumers are better protected and some clarification of the law has resulted.

[10] The issue of clarity is considered. PEA is apparent in the remainder of the paragraph, highlighting some uncertainties that the new law may have created.

its provisions will require judicial clarification. Moreover, in relation to establishing the reasonableness of an exemption clause, the burden of proof under the UCTA 1977 was more advantageous to consumers than is possibly the case under the CRA 2015 (where it may be on the consumer although a court has a duty, in certain circumstances, to consider the question of unfairness of its own motion: see s. 71).

LOOKING FOR EXTRA MARKS?

- Consider whether the CRA 2015 addresses the deficiencies in the pre-existing law or simply substitutes one set of problems with another.

- As the question is broad you may focus on different examples by way of comparison. For example, the issue of s. 64 of the CRA 2015 and the exclusion of terms defining subject matter and price from an assessment of fairness might be explored. Note the criticisms made of the decision in *Office of Fair Trading v Abbey National plc* **[2009] UKSC 6**; consideration may be given to the question 'has the CRA 2015 addressed these criticisms'?

QUESTION | 4

The Smiths want to hold a party in a marquee to be erected in their garden. After contacting a number of companies, they decide to sign a contract with Christent Ltd for the supply and erection of a marquee.

It is agreed that for a sum of £2,000 the marquee will be erected by Friday evening, so as to allow for decoration by the Smiths in time for the party on Saturday. The marquee will be dismantled and removed by Christent Ltd on Sunday. As part of the agreement Christent Ltd will also supply 30 tables and 100 chairs. The contract which the Smiths sign is a standard form contract produced by Christent Ltd. The terms of the contract are in general use within the trade.

The contract signed by the Smiths includes the following terms:

5. The contractor accepts no liability for damage to trees, garden ornaments, walls and other garden features, howsoever caused …

9. The contractor accepts no liability for harm or injury to the customer, his family or his guests, howsoever caused . .

15. The contractor reserves the right to alter the times of erection and dismantling of the marquee.

16. The quantity of goods supplied for use in marquees is wholly at the discretion of Christent Ltd.

Christent Ltd fail to erect the marquee on Friday as agreed and arrive on Saturday morning to erect the marquee. The van driver delivering the marquee approaches the Smiths' lawn too fast and skids into a greenhouse, destroying it.

The marquee is erected by early afternoon leaving the Smiths insufficient time to decorate the tent as they had planned. Also, Christent Ltd delivers an insufficient number of tables and chairs.

On Sunday Christent Ltd fail to dismantle the marquee.

Christent Ltd arrives on Monday to dismantle the marquee. Mr Smith complains to the Christent Ltd foreman of the service provided, but while doing so Mr Smith is hit by a tent pole thrown by a Christent Ltd worker.

Mr Smith wants to claim against Christent Ltd. Christent Ltd refuses to accept any claim, relying on the terms of the agreement.

Advise Mr Smith.

 CAUTION!

- An answer to this type of question needs to be carefully planned as there are a number of issues raised by the question.
- The type of terms must be identified and their effect considered. Some of the terms are exemption clauses, others may have an unfair effect.

 DIAGRAM ANSWER PLAN

Identify the issues	■ The question relates to exemption clauses and unfair terms.
Relevant law	■ Express and 'included' terms in contract—**Consumer Rights Act 2015**, applies between a trader and a consumer. ■ Common law—incorporation and interpretation. ■ Exemption clauses and unfair terms—Consumer Rights Act 2015, ss. 57, 62, 64, 65, 67, and Sch. 2.
Apply the law	■ As signature incorporation possible but possible issues with interpretation. ■ Application of **Consumer Rights Act 2015**. Exemption of liability for failing to take reasonable care not binding; cannot exclude liability for personal injury caused by negligence. Other terms may be subject to a test of unfairness.
Conclude	■ Liabilities arise under contract and while arguably the exemption clauses and other relevant terms are part of the contract and might cover potential liabilities, such clauses are subject to the Consumer Rights Act 2015. ■ The exemption clauses and some of the other terms are unlikely to survive judicial scrutiny.

[1]Outlines the subject matter raised by the question.

This question raises issues relating to exemption clauses and unfair terms.[1] In advising Mr Smith consideration must be given, first, to the potential liabilities of Christent Ltd and, secondly, to the effectiveness of the relevant terms of the agreement in protecting Christent Ltd against such liabilities. Assessment of the effectiveness of the terms requires explanation of the common law controls on the use of such terms and, more importantly, the legislative controls to be found in the Consumer Rights Act 2015 (CRA 2015).

[2]It is necessary to establish the terms of the contract, both express and implied (although the CRA 2015 does not use the phrase 'implied terms'), in order to discuss any liability on the part of Christent Ltd.

The contract between Mr Smith and Christent Ltd is to provide a service (or a "mixed contract—see **s 1(4)**) and consists of express terms and terms to be included in the contract under the CRA 2015.[2] The express terms include the dates for the erection and dismantling of the marquee, and the number of tables and chairs to be supplied; these terms appear to have been broken by Christent Ltd. For any additional terms to be included in the contract by virtue of the CRA 2015, it must be established that the Act applies. The Act applies as between a trader and a consumer.[3] By s. 2 a trader is a person acting for purposes relating to that person's trade, business, craft, or profession: this definition clearly applies to Christent Ltd. A consumer is defined as an individual acting for purposes that are wholly or mainly outside that individual's trade, business, craft, or profession: this would apply to Mr Smith hiring a marquee in a domestic capacity. By s. 49 of the CRA 2015 Christent Ltd is under a duty to perform the service with reasonable care and skill. It may be argued that there has been a breach of the duty in both driving too fast and destroying the greenhouse and during the dismantling of the marquee by throwing a tent pole causing personal injury to Mr Smith.

[3]You must establish that the CRA 2015 applies, in the first instance to identify which terms are included in a contract.

[4]Having established liability, the impact of clauses 5, 9, 15, and 16 on such liability must be explored.

Should liability be established, the effectiveness of the terms in Christent Ltd's standard terms needs to be addressed. Clauses 5 and 9 seek to exempt liability and clauses 14 and 15 permit Christent Ltd to alter, at its discretion, performance under the contract and may be viewed as potentially unfair terms.[4] The common law controls[5] on such clauses may be considered first.

[5]The common law controls, in spite of legislative controls, remain as additional arguments in relation to the validity of exclusions and other potentially unfair terms.

Christent Ltd would have to establish that their standard terms have been incorporated into the contract with Mr Smith.[6] A clause may become a term of a contract, regardless of whether the document has been read or not, if it is in a contractual document which has been signed: *L'Estrange v Graucob* **[1934] 2 QB 394**. Mr Smith has assented to the clauses by signature and is thereby bound.

[6]This paragraph relating to incorporation is an illustration of IRAC.

[7]The second common law control of interpretation of terms of a contract is considered here.

The next common law control is that of interpretation, do the words of the clause cover the liability that has arisen?[7] The first question to be asked is do the words of clause 5, 'damage to trees, garden orna-ments, walls and other garden features' exempt liability for the de-struction of the greenhouse? The greenhouse does not fall within the specific words used—that is, trees, ornaments, and walls—but is it a garden feature and might these words have to be read using the *ejus-dem generis* rule of construction? As trees, ornaments, and walls do not seem to create a class which gives meaning to the words 'garden features', the words may be given an ordinary meaning; a greenhouse is a feature of a garden. However, if there is any doubt over the mean-ing of these words, the *contra proferentem* rule traditionally provides such doubt is to be resolved against the party seeking to rely on the clause; that is, Christent Ltd. In *Persimmon Homes Ltd v Ove Arup & Partners Ltd* [2017] EWCA Civ 373 the Court of Appeal expressed doubts about the modern usefulness of such a rule although that was in the context of a purely commercial contract (and see **s. 69 of the CRA 2015,** and *Earl of Plymouth v Rees* [2019] EWHC 1008 (Ch) at [56] for the view that the rule is rational in cases on ambiguity). Additionally, as Christent Ltd is arguably liable for negligence, is the use of 'howsoever caused' in clauses 5 and 9 apt to cover such li-ability? The courts have traditionally taken a strict approach as is seen in *Canada Steamship Lines Ltd v The King* [1952] AC 192 (although, at least in a commercial context, some doubt was expressed about the approach in that case in *Persimmon Homes Ltd v Ove Arup & Partners Ltd* [2017] EWCA Civ 373 (compare *The Federal Republic of Nigeria v JP Morgan Chase Bank, N.A.* [2019] EWHC 347 (Comm) at [64] where the 'test' in Canada Steamships was re-garded as a flexible guide rather than a rigid rule)). In the absence of an express reference to negligence or the use of a synonym for neg-ligence, as is the case in this scenario, the words must be sufficiently wide to cover negligence. 'Howsoever caused' are wide words and may cover negligence so long as there is no liability other than neg-ligence. If there is an alternative source of liability the courts might construe the clause as only applying to that other liability and not to negligence: *White v John Warwick & Co. Ltd* [1953] 1 WLR 1285.

The CRA 2015 offers extensive protection to consumers as against traders. By s. 57(1), a term seeking to exclude a trader's liability under s. 49(1) for a failure to take reasonable care and skill in the performance of a contract is not binding. In consequence, clause 5 would not be binding on Mr Smith. The attempt by Christent Ltd to exclude liability for personal injury resulting from negligence would also fail as s. 65 provides that such liability cannot be excluded. However, clauses 15 and 16 would be subject to a test of unfairness. By s. 62(4) a term is unfair if, contrary to the requirement of good faith, it causes a significant imbalance in the rights and obligations

[8] The test of unfairness is a key provision which must be stated and then its elements identified, explained, and applied to the facts of the question.

of the parties to the detriment of the consumer.[8] In determining the fairness of a term, account is to be taken of the nature of the subject matter of the contract, and all the circumstances existing when the term was agreed and to all of the other terms of the contract and any other contract on which it depends: s. 62(5). As the CRA 2015 replaces and, to some extent, replicates the Unfair Terms in Consumer Contracts Regulations 1999, it would seem that the previous case law may still be used in interpreting the Act.

[9]Good faith is an important concept that must be explained using relevant case law.

The first part of the test requires an absence of good faith.[9] This appears to relate primarily to how the contract is formed. In *Director General of Fair Trading v First National Bank* **[2001] UKHL 52**, the House of Lords said that 'good faith' requires fair and open dealing. Lord Bingham said openness requires that 'the terms should be expressed fully, clearly and legibly, containing no pitfalls or traps'. There should be no unfair surprises, so prominence should be given to terms disadvantageous to the consumer. Also, fair dealing requires that the trader does not take advantage of a consumer by using a superior bargaining position, exploiting a consumer's lack of experience, or by failing to take into account the consumer's legitimate interests. An absence of choice is also indicative of a lack of good faith. It may be argued there is an absence of good faith, as Christent did not draw Smith's attention to clauses 15 and 16, the clauses were not prominent, Smith was given no choice, and the contract terms are one-sided; that is, in favour of Christent, in their operation.

[10]This requirement allows reference to be made to the indicative but non-exhaustive list of potentially unfair terms in Sch. 2, which may aid a consumer in establishing a term to be unfair.

Next it must be established that the term causes a significant imbalance in the rights and obligations of the parties.[10] This inquiry considers the substance of the term. The imbalance in favour of the trader must be 'significant', *Office of Fair Trading v Ashbourne Management Services Ltd* **[2011] EWHC 1237 (Ch)**. The indicative but non-exhaustive list of potentially unfair terms in Part 1 of Sch. 2 to the 2015 Act may be used to help establish unfairness. Terms which permit a trader to unilaterally vary the terms of a contract in the absence of a valid reason in the contract are considered potentially unfair. As clauses 15 and 16 allow Christent Ltd to unilaterally alter the contract, and there is no counterbalancing provision in Smith's favour, it may be argued that there is a significant imbalance in the rights and obligations of the parties.

Finally, the term must be to the detriment of the consumer. Clearly clauses 15 and 16 are to the detriment to Smith.

[11]This issue gives rise to difficulties of interpretation. The answer acknowledges the issue but as the facts do not raise it as an issue it is dealt with briefly.

The CRA 2015 does not allocate the burden of proof for establishing the fairness of a term. It will arguably be for Mr Smith to present a case arguing that clauses 15 and 16 are unfair.

It ought to be noted that the test of unfairness does not apply to terms that define the main subject matter of the contract or the appropriateness of the price payable: s. 64(1).[11] On the facts it would seem that the express terms stating dates for the erection and dismantling of the marquee and the number of tables and chairs defined the main subject matter of the contract. However, it may be argued that clauses 15 and 16 do not define the main subject matter of the contract and are therefore not excluded from an assessment of fairness. Note also that such a term only avoids an assessment of fairness to the extent it is transparent and prominent: s. 64(2).

Having argued that clauses 15 and 16 are unfair, the consequence of such a finding is that the terms will not be binding on Mr Smith (s. 62(1)) but the remainder of the contract will continue to have effect, so far as is practicable (s. 67). As clauses 15 and 16 are not essential to the existence of the contract, it would seem that the contract could continue to have effect.

In conclusion, Mr Smith has a strong claim in respect of the damage to the greenhouse and the personal injury sustained, and the exemptions in clauses 5 and 9 will have no effect. In relation to the delayed erection and dismantling of the marquee and the reduced number of tables and chairs, again there appears to be a good claim. However, clauses 15 and 16 could prevent liability if the terms are fair, but there is a strong argument for challenging the clauses as unfair under the CRA 2015.

 ## LOOKING FOR EXTRA MARKS?

■ The case law decided under the UTCCR 1999 may be used where the words of the CRA 2015 are similar. Being aware of these similarities and differences gives scope for developing arguments relating to the interpretation of the 2015 Act.

■ As the CRA 2015 implemented the EC Council Directive 93/13/EEC on Unfair Terms in Consumer Contracts, decisions of the Court of Justice of the European Union (CJEU) could be used to interpret the relevant sections in Part 2 **of the 2015 Act**. See, for example, *Aziz v Caixa d'Estalvis de Catalunya, Tarragona, i Manresa (Catalunyacaixa)* **(C-415/11) [2013] 3 CMLR 5**. Does Brexit affect this position (see **European Union (Withdrawal) Act 2018, s 6(3)**)?

 ## TAKING THINGS FURTHER

■ Adams, J. and Brownsword, A., 'The Unfair Contract Terms Act: A Decade of Discretion' (1988) 104 LQR 94.
*Considers the test of reasonableness and the approach of intervention and non-intervention apparent in the cases of **Photo Production Ltd v Securicor Transport Ltd** [1980] AC 827 and **George Mitchell (Chesterhall) Ltd v Finney Lock Seeds Ltd** [1983] 2 AC 803, respectively.*

▪ Davies, P., 'Bank Charges in the Supreme Court' (2010) 69 CLJ 21.

Considers the decision of the Supreme Court in **Office of Fair Trading v Abbey National plc [2009] UKSC 6, [2009] 3 WLR 1215** *where the court interpreted* **reg. 6 of UTCCR 1999** *based on consumer choice rather than consumer protection.*

▪ Dean, M., 'Defining Unfair Terms in Consumer Contracts—Crystal Ball Gazing?' (2002) 65 MLR 773.

Reviews the case of the **Director General of Fair Trading v First National Bank plc [2001] UKHL 52** *which was the first House of Lords decision on the* **UTCCR 1994** *and an opportunity to consider the test of unfairness.*

▪ Devenney, J., 'The Legacy of the Cameron-Clegg Coalition Programme of Reform of the Law on the Supply of Goods, Digital Content and Services to Consumers' [2018] JBL 485.

Reflects on some of the reforms introduced by the Consumer Rights Act 2015.

▪ Peel, E., 'Reasonable Exemption Clauses' (2001) 117 LQR 545.

Reviews the case of **Watford Electronics Ltd v Sanderson CFL Ltd [2001] EWCA Civ 317** *which concerns the application of the test of reasonableness under the* **UCTA 1977** *and concludes that the court struck the correct balance in promoting freedom of contract and the parties' allocation of risk.*

Misrepresentation 6

In order to attempt the questions in this chapter you must have covered the following areas in your revision:

- The development of the concept of misrepresentation;

- The interaction of the law of misrepresentation with remedies for breach of contract;

- The definition of an actionable misrepresentation as an unambiguous (incorrect) statement of fact/law addressed to the party misled and which induces that party to enter into a contract;

- What constitutes a statement of fact;

- When statements of opinion and statements of intention might constitute actionable misrepresentations;

- When silence or conduct may constitute actionable misrepresentation;

- Meaning of inducement;

- The types of misrepresentation and the available remedies. Remedies derive from both statute and common law in this area, so you will usually need to address both.

KEY DEBATES

Debate: whether the law of England and Wales should adopt a general duty of disclosure.

The law of England and Wales generally does not recognize a duty of disclosure in contractual negotiations; however, might it be preferable to follow those European systems which impose, for example, a pre-contractual duty of good faith (note also the **Consumer Protection from Unfair Trading Regulations 2008** which, to some extent, now regulate misleading omissions)?

(▷)

Debate: whether the complex situation regarding the remedy of damages for misrepresentation needs reform.

The overlap between misrepresentation and breach of contract means it can be worth considering these two areas together, for while damages in contract often focus on loss of bargain, damages for misrepresentation are usually based on reliance losses (and it depends on the precise facts as to which measure will yield the greatest damages). In addition, there are advantages to suing under s. 2(1) of the Misrepresentation Act 1967, where applicable, as opposed to pursuing a breach of contract action.

Q

QUESTION | **1**

Watson Summers, a well-known singer, decides to use the Biztek Concert Hall (BCH) as the first venue in his 'Round UK Music Tour'. During negotiations the BCH Manager, Jim, informs Watson that 'the hall will hold 3,000 people . . . [and] . . . the acoustics are suitable for the performance of your musical repertoire'.

Watson's concert is sold out. However, only 2,500 are admitted on the instructions of the local police, and the acoustics are so bad that a large percentage of the audience demands its money back.

The adverse media publicity affects ticket sales for the remainder of Watson's UK tour.

Advise the parties.

CAUTION!

- Use the IRAC method to demonstrate the relevant law and how it applies to the facts.
- If any statements arguably constitute contractual terms, consider remedies for breach of contract.
- When asked to 'advise the parties', advise *all* parties.
- Be selective: the examiner does not want you to write everything you know about misrepresentation; ensure your answer is relevant to the question.

DIAGRAM ANSWER PLAN

Identify the issues	▪ Identify the legal issues; ▪ Two possible remedies: for misrepresentation and for breach of contract.
Relevant law	▪ Outline the elements of misrepresentation; ▪ In particular, the important concepts of statements of fact/law and reliance; ▪ **Misrepresentation Act 1967;** ▪ Remedies for breach of contract.
Apply the law	▪ Outline the elements of misrepresentation present in the problem facts; ▪ Explain the possible problems with its application; ▪ Requirements for remedy for misrepresentation under **Misrepresentation Act 1967, s. 2(1);** ▪ Availability of remedies for breach of contract on the problem facts.
Conclude	▪ Advisability of pursuing a claim for misrepresentation and/or breach of contract; ▪ Conclusion.

 SUGGESTED ANSWER

[1] Answers to problem questions do not need the same type of formal introduction as for an essay answer. Following the IRAC method, your opening paragraph should analyse the facts to identify the legal issues raised.

[2] Outline the principal elements of an actionable misrepresentation.

Watson will need advice on any possible remedies in misrepresentation and/or for breach of contract.[1] Misrepresentation can be broadly defined[2] as a false statement of fact/law made pre-contractually by one party (the representor) with a view to inducing the other party (the representee) to enter into the contract. The statement must, it seems, have been intended to be acted upon and must *actually* induce the other party to enter the contract.

Did any of the pre-contractual statements made by Jim constitute statements of fact/law (as opposed to, for example, statements of

[3] Apply the law to the facts of the specific question throughout.

[4] *Esso Petroleum Ltd v Mardon* [1976] QB 801 could also be considered here.

opinion which are not generally actionable)? The first statement concerned the capacity of the hall.[3] It does not appear that the statement was phrased as an opinion (see *Bisset v Wilkinson* [1927] AC 177 which presumes that opinions which prove to be unfounded are not considered false statements of 'fact'); even if that was the case, it would be possible to argue that Jim is an expert and that the figure is presumably based upon facts known to him. For example, in *Smith v Land and House Property Corp.* (1884) 28 Ch D 7,[4] the vendor described the sitting tenant as 'desirable and a first class investment'. This constituted a misrepresentation as the only facts known to the vendor directly contradicted this statement.

There is, however, a further difficulty. Technically, the capacity of the hall seems to be 3,000. Did Jim realize that this figure would be limited by the local police? If this was a common occurrence when concerts were held, Jim's silence regarding the safety feature effectively distorts his original statement, conveying the wrong impression to Watson. One could argue that the statement constitutes a half-truth and, therefore, amounts to a misstatement of fact (eg *Nottingham Patent & Brick Tile Co. v Butler* (1889) 16 QBD 778).

Jim also states that the 'acoustics are suitable' for the intended performance; a relatively vague and ambiguous comment. In *Scott v Hanson* (1829) 1 Russ & M 128, the description of land as being 'uncommonly rich water meadow' was held only to constitute a misrepresentation with reference to non-meadow land, rather than meadow that was of poor quality. Perhaps, as in the previous paragraph, Watson will need to show that Jim had no facts upon which to base his statement (eg *Smith v Land and House Property*) in which case he is misrepresenting the state of his mind. As Bowen LJ put it in *Edgington v Fitzmaurice* (1885) 29 Ch D 459 at 483: 'The state of a man's mind is as much a fact as the state of his digestion.'[5] There is also some precedent for suggesting that an actionable misrepresentation may lie where an opinion is stated and the representor is the only person to be in a position to know the true facts (*Brown v Raphael* [1958] Ch 636).

[5] Quotations are not essential to this answer, but can attract additional marks if relevant to the points you make.

[6] Explain the legal rules relating to the concepts of materiality and reliance and apply to the question.

Assuming that a false statement of fact is established, was it intended to induce Watson to enter into the contract and was it material? If so, did Watson actually rely upon it in this way?[6] It seems, although it is not without controversy, that there is an objective element to inducement (see *Sharland v Sharland* [2015] UKSC 60): would a reasonable person have considered the statement to be a *material* factor? Here, the answer is yes. The capacity of the hall will influence the hire charge. The standard of acoustics will determine suitability for its intended use.

[7] Addresses one of the essential
questions raised in relation to
misrepresentation.

The next important question is whether Watson *actually* relied upon the statement in entering into the contract.[7] The facts suggest that Watson had already decided to hire the concert hall before negotiations began. However, if Jim had proposed a much greater hire charge or the capacity of the hall was embarrassingly low or the acoustics were only considered suitable for the performance of classical opera, Watson would have presumably withdrawn. In such a case, arguably Watson can demonstrate some form of potential reliance (although care must be exercised as in *BV Nederlandse Industrie Van Eiprodukten v Rembrandt Enterprises Inc* **[2019] EWCA Civ 596** the view was expressed that in cases of non-fraudulent misrepresentation the 'but for' test still needs to be satisfied).

[8] To determine an appropriate
remedy, first establish the type of
misrepresentation in question.

The remedies for misrepresentation will be determined by the state of mind of the misrepresentor at the time of the misrepresentation.[8] Traditionally, fraud has attracted the widest remedies for the representee but the burden of proof is a heavy one to discharge (eg *Derry v Peek* **(1889) 14 App Cas 337**). Also, in the light of case law concerning **s. 2(1) of the Misrepresentation Act 1967 (MA 1967)**,[9] it is unlikely that Watson would be advised to pursue a claim in fraud unless he had firm evidence that Jim was intentionally lying.

[9] Spell out the name of a statute the
first time you use it in your answer;
you can then use abbreviations like
MA 1967.

Alternatively, if a duty of care exists between the parties (and this will depend on whether there was an assumption of responsibility by Jim, see *Steel v NRAM Ltd (formerly NRAM Plc)* **[2018] UKSC 13**) Watson might consider suing in the tort of negligent misstatement (eg *Esso Petroleum Co. Ltd v Mardon* **[1976] QB 801**). Here, Watson must affirmatively establish negligence on the part of Jim in making those pre-contractual statements. However, as we shall see, in view of **s. 2(1)** of the 1967 Act, it seems pointless to pursue this line of argument.[10]

Section 2(1) of the MA 1967 reverses the burden of proof, requiring Jim to prove that he had 'reasonable grounds' for his belief. This may be difficult to establish, especially in the light of *Howard Marine & Dredging Co. Ltd v A Ogden & Sons (Excavations) Ltd* **[1978] QB 574**, where the Court of Appeal stated that a party had an 'absolute obligation' not to state facts which he had no reasonable grounds for believing were true. As honest belief is insufficient, it may be difficult for Jim to argue that, for example, he was not expected to know of the theatre's capacity when negotiating the hire charge. Perhaps his only escape route would be if the capacity of the hall had never previously been restricted by police measures and the acoustics had always been found to be suitable at previous concerts of a similar nature. If not, the possibility of innocent misrepresentation is unlikely, as it generally refers to false statements made without provable fault.

Rescission is the principal remedy for misrepresentation,[11] subject to the standard bars such as *restitutio in integrum* being impossible.

As the concert has already been performed, it may be that rescission is no longer available.

[12] Do not assume that there will be only one possible remedy available on the facts. Explain the possibility of an alternative remedy, apply the law and draw a conclusion.

Regarding the remedy of damages for misrepresentation,[12] Watson would be best advised to pursue his claim under **s. 2(1)** of the 1967 Act. Case law indicates that damages will be assessed in the tort of deceit (eg *Royscot Trust Ltd v Rogerson* **[1991] 2 QB 297**). Watson will be entitled to reclaim all those damages which directly flow from his reliance upon the misrepresentation, such as the losses sustained in returning money to dissatisfied customers. This might also include any subsequent losses incurred on the remainder of the tour, resulting from the adverse media publicity, as well as any personal distress and anxiety suffered by Watson (see, generally, *Doyle v Olby (Ironmongers) Ltd* **[1969] 2 QB 158**; *Archer v Brown*).

[13] Discuss this alternative briefly: keep the focus of your answer on the law relating to misrepresentation.

Watson could consider the alternative possibility of claiming damages for breach of contract.[13] The test for determining whether a pre-contractual statement has become part of the contract is one of objective intent (eg *Heilbut, Symons & Co. v Buckleton* **[1913] AC 30**). The courts have developed a variety of guidelines as aids to identifying the requisite degree of contractual intent. For example, Watson could argue that Jim possessed specialist knowledge (eg *Oscar Chess Ltd v Williams* **[1957] 1 WLR 370**), that he (Watson) attached considerable importance to the statement (eg *Bannerman v White* **(1861) 10 CB (NS) 844**), and that he was not encouraged by Jim to verify the statement. Jim would point out that the statement was not incorporated into the written contract (eg *Birch v Paramount Estates (Liverpool) Ltd* **(1956) 16 EG 396**), that Watson's previous experience of arranging musical venues should be taken into account as it created an equality of expertise between the parties (see generally *Bentley (Dick) Productions Ltd v Harold Smith (Motors) Ltd* **[1965] 1 WLR 623**), and, finally, that there was no evidence of a collateral contract as Watson did not place any specific emphasis on Jim's statement during the negotiations (unlike in *City and Westminster Properties (1934) Ltd v Mudd* **[1959] Ch 129**). The decision could go either way but it does seem that the statement lies at the heart of the hire contract and therefore would be intended to have some legal effect, especially with regard to the hall's capacity which is couched in a clear and definite manner.

LOOKING FOR EXTRA MARKS?

■ When discussing rescission, additional marks could be gained by noting that there may be a trend to introduce more flexibility in the *restitutio in integrum* principle (see, for example, *Halpern v Halpern* **[2007] EWCA Civ 291**).

■ It is unlikely that an examiner would expect an extended analysis of damages for breach of contract in a problem question so clearly based on misrepresentation, but a brief explanation may achieve extra marks.

QUESTION | 2

Case law suggests that, where there is a choice, litigants are generally better advised to pursue a claim in misrepresentation rather than an action for breach of contract.

Discuss.

CAUTION!

- Use the PEA structure for essays: introduce the Point (this can be your opinion); add the Evidence to support your point (e.g. indicate from what/where you have drawn your opinion); offer your Analysis (explain how and why this evidence supports your point). Do not forget to explain how the point helps to answer the question.

- The general remedies for breach of contract are termination and/or damages, whereas in misrepresentation the general remedies are rescission and/or damages. Your answer should compare: (a) the availability of rescission and termination; and (b) the basis upon which damages are assessed in misrepresentation and for breach of contract.

DIAGRAM ANSWER PLAN

Outline the general remedies for breach of contract and for misrepresentation.

▼

Compare the availability of rescission and termination.

▼

Compare the basis upon which damages are assessed for misrepresentation and breach of contract.

▼

Address the impact of the **Misrepresentation Act 1967**.

▼

Retain a focus on case law in the explanation and analysis.

▼

Consider whether the evidence in the essay points to a preferable course of action for claimants.

▼

Conclusion.

This question requires a general comparison of the remedies available for misrepresentation and for breach of contract, especially with a specific focus upon the decisions in which damages under **s. 2(1) of the Misrepresentation Act 1967 (MA 1967)** have been equated with the expansive damages available for an action in deceit. The general remedies for breach of contract are termination and/or damages, whereas in misrepresentation the general remedies are rescission and/or damages. This essay will therefore compare[1] the availability of rescission and termination, and the basis upon which damages are assessed in misrepresentation and for breach of contract, to reach a conclusion on which course of action litigants could best be advised to pursue.[2]

Rescission v Repudiation

In relation to rescission as opposed to termination,[3] a victim of a breach of contract does not have an automatic right to terminate the contract. The right of termination generally arises only in two circumstances. First, where it is established that the term which has been broken constitutes either a condition or, following the decision in *Hongkong Fir Shipping Co. Ltd v Kawasaki Kisen Kaisha Ltd* **[1962] 2 QB 26**, an innominate term, breach of which has deprived the victim of a substantial part of the intended benefit under the contract. Secondly, where a party commits an anticipatory breach by, for example, intimating by words or conduct his/her refusal to perform particular contractual obligations when they fall due (see, generally, *Woodar Investment Development Ltd v Wimpey Construction (UK) Ltd* **[1980] 1 WLR 277**). If neither of these situations applies, the victim of a breach will be left with a remedy in damages.[4]

The law on misrepresentation does not really consider the relative importance of pre-contractual statements. Provided a false statement of fact/law has been made, the representee will usually have the right to claim rescission and thereby avoid the contract. The representee need only establish that the statement induced him/her to enter the contract; and it need not be the only factor (see *Edgington v Fitzmaurice* **(1885) 29 Ch D 459**). This right is available for all types of misrepresentation—innocent, negligent, and fraudulent. However, the right to rescission can be lost on certain grounds: by affirmation of the contract (see *Long v Lloyd* **[1958] 1 WLR 753**); by lapse of time (see *Leaf v International Galleries* **[1950] 2 KB 86** although note *Salt v Stratstone Specialist Limited T/A Stratstone Cadillac Newcastle* **[2015] EWCA Civ 745**); where third parties

Sidenotes:

[1] Introduces the PEA structure, showing awareness that the question calls for a general comparison of the remedies available for misrepresentation and for breach of contract.

[2] Clear focus upon decisions in which damages under **s. 2(1) of the MA 1967** have been equated with those available for an action in deceit.

[3] First address the difference between repudiation and rescission. Some examiners dislike subheadings in essays, so you might choose to avoid this style.

[4] This sentence clearly sets out the relationship between termination and damages.

have acquired rights in the subject matter prior to avoidance of the contract (see *White v Garden* **(1851) 10 CB 919**); and where the parties cannot be restored substantially to their original positions (see *Clarke v Dickson* **(1858) EB & E 148**).

Damages

Whereas some contractual remedies depend upon whether the term which the defendant has broken is a condition, innominate term or a warranty, in misrepresentation it is the culpability of the defendant which will determine some of the claimant's remedies. In misrepresentation, generally damages[5] will be assessed on a tortious basis, the aim broadly being to place the victim in the position he/she would have occupied had the wrong (the actionable misrepresentation) not taken place. This normally means that the court will seek to place the victim in the position they occupied before entering into the contract by, for example, compensating the victim for losses incurred as a result of entering into the contract. This 'compensation for reliance losses' does not take account of the profit which the victim was expecting to derive from a proper performance of the contract in question. Conversely, damages for breach of contract may include such profits and, indeed, incorporate wasted expenditure under the heading of 'loss of bargain' (where the claimant made a 'good' bargain in the sense that they would have recouped this expenditure if the contract had been duly performed). Here, the usual purpose of damages is to put the claimant, so far as possible, in the position he/she would have occupied had the contract in question been properly performed (see *Robinson v Harman* **(1848) 1 Ex 850** at 855), although a court, in appropriate circumstances, may just focus on a victim's reliance or restitution interests (see *Anglia Television Ltd v Reed* **[1972] 1 QB 60**).

Prior to the passing of the **MA 1967** damages were generally only available for a fraudulent misrepresentation—and allegations of fraud are extremely difficult to substantiate. Damages were based on the tort of deceit, the representor being liable for *all* the losses flowing directly from his/her fraud even though such losses might not have been reasonably foreseeable (see *Doyle v Olby (Ironmongers) Ltd* **[1969] 2 QB 158**; *Smith New Court Securities Ltd v Scrimgeour Vickers (Asset Management) Ltd* **[1996] 4 All ER 769**). Moreover, apart from pecuniary loss the courts have permitted the recovery of various types of non-pecuniary losses, including damages for pain and suffering (see *Burrows v Rhodes* **[1899] 1 QB 816**), physical inconvenience, and discomfort (see *Mafo v Adams* **[1970] 1 QB 548**) and mental disquiet (see *Archer v Brown* **[1985] QB 401**; *Kinch v Rosling* **[2009] EWHC 286 (QB), [2009] All ER (D) 54**). Contrast

[5] Address the basis for awarding damages for breach of contract and for misrepresentation.

this with the pre-1967 position for non-fraudulent misrepresentations where rescission was the primary remedy, if available, and available monetary awards took the very limited form of an 'indemnity' (see *Whittington v Seale-Hayne* **(1900) 82 LT 49**). At that time, an action for breach of contract contrasted favourably with that in misrepresentation. However, the passing of the **MA 1967** has changed this in at least four ways.[6]

[6] This point makes clear that evidence will be offered to show the advantages of suing under **s. 2(1) of the MA 1967.**

First, damages are now available for all non-innocent misrepresentations, innocence in this context proving difficult to establish (see *Howard Marine & Dredging Co. Ltd v A Ogden & Sons (Excavations) Ltd* **[1978] QB 574**). In particular, the burden of proof is reversed under **s. 2(1)** of the 1967 Act, requiring the representor to prove that he/she had reasonable grounds to believe, and did believe up to the time the contract was made, that the facts represented were true.

Secondly, it is currently assumed that the measure of damages under **s. 2(1)** is based on the tort of deceit. This results from the peculiarity of the wording employed in the subsection (although certain *obiter* comments in **Smith New Court** might suggest a level of disquiet with this conclusion as do the more recent comments in *Hodgson v Creative Consumer Finance Ltd* **[2021] EWHC 2167 (Comm)**). Specifically, if the representor would have been liable in damages had the misrepresentation been made fraudulently, 'that person shall be so liable notwithstanding that the misrepresentation was not made fraudulently' provided objective 'innocence' cannot be proven. Thus, unlike damages for breach of contract which are limited by the reasonable contemplation of the parties (see *Hadley v Baxendale* **(1854) 9 Exch 341**), damages under **s. 2(1)** follow the test laid down in *Doyle v Olby (Ironmongers) Ltd* **[1969] 2 QB 158**. These damages are based on a direct consequence test in which reasonable foreseeability seems to have no application, an approach adopted in such cases as *Naughton v O'Callaghan* **[1990] 3 All ER 191**; *Royscot Trust Ltd v Rogerson* **[1991] 2 QB 297**; and *Cemp v Dentsply R&D Corp. (No. 2)* **[1991] 34 EG 62**.

Thirdly, a further effect of this is that many types of non-pecuniary loss which are not normally available for breach of contract can be recovered in the tort of deceit and also by using **s. 2(1)** of the 1967 Act (eg anxiety and stress although compare at *Hodgson v Creative Consumer Finance Ltd* **[2021] EWHC 2167 (Comm)** at **[159]**).

[7] The essay title requires a focus on case law.

Fourthly, two Court of Appeal decisions have arguably even blurred the distinction between loss of bargain damages in contract and reliance losses in tort.[7] In *East v Maurer* **[1991] 1 WLR 461** M owned two successful hairdressing salons. E bought one of them in 1979, being induced by M's representation that M had no intention of working in the other salon. In fact, M continued to work in the other salon, enticing many customers away from E's salon. After several abortive attempts, E sold out several years later at a considerable loss. The court held that a fraudulent misrepresentation had been made and, among other things, awarded E a sum in respect of lost profits. More specifically, this sum reflected the profits which E would have derived from the purchase of a *different* salon if she had not been induced to buy M's salon. This measure seems very similar to awarding damages for loss of bargain (although see *McCullagh v Lane Fox & Partners* [1994] 1 EGLR 48 and [1996] PNLR 205) and reinforces the attraction of bringing an action under **s. 2(1) of the MA 1967**, which employs the same measure of damages, as opposed to suing for breach of contract. In *Clef Aquitaine Sarl v Laporte Materials (Barrow) Ltd* [2000] 3 All ER 493, the claimant was allowed to argue that a different and more favourable transaction would have been entered into but for the fraud, with his recoverable loss being measured on that basis (see also *Parabola Investments Ltd v Browallia* [2010] EWCA Civ 486, [2011] QB 477; *4 Eng Ltd v Harper* [2009] EWHC 901 (Ch), [2009] Ch 91). Against this must be contrasted the problems of recovering any damages for purely innocent misrepresentations, the possible bars to the remedy of rescission, including the exercise of judicial discretion under **s. 2(2)** of the 1967 Act (see *William Sindall plc v Cambridgeshire County Council* [1994] 1 WLR 1016) and the general emphasis on reliance losses in tort.

[8]Offer your own opinion when writing a conclusion. Conclusions can reinforce how your points answer the essay question.

In conclusion,[8] case law has suggested that the representee must think carefully before choosing which action to pursue where a pre-contractual statement constitutes *both* a breach of a contract and a misrepresentation. The use of a deceit measure for all non-innocent misrepresentations, with its disregard of any foreseeability criterion, the potentially enhanced recovery of non-pecuniary losses, and even the award of quasi 'loss of bargain' damages, is clearly advantageous in many situations.

LOOKING FOR EXTRA MARKS?

Additional marks might be gained for addressing the right to rescind for misrepresentation in more detail:

- **s. 1(a)** of the 1967 Act permits the right of rescission if the representation became part of the contract (prior to the 1967 Act a representee lost the right to rescind in such circumstances).

- **s. 2(2)** of the 1967 Act gives the court discretion, with non-fraudulent misrepresentations, to award damages in lieu of rescission, taking account of the equitable considerations affecting *both* parties (see also *SK Shipping Europe Limited v Capital VLCC 3 Corp* [2022] EWCA Civ 231).

- A misrepresentation renders a contract voidable (provided the representee elects to rescind) so the parties are restored to the positions they occupied before the contract was entered into (see *Abram SS Co. v Westville Shipping Co. Ltd* [1923] AC 773).

Edward decides to invest his savings in the purchase of a small post office. He consults *Postman's Gazette* and is particularly interested in one advertisement which reads: 'Post office to the community—the only lifeline for the elderly. Net profits for the current year = £25,000. A steal at £100,000.' Edward speaks to the owner, Cameron, and is offered the opportunity to view the current accounts, which he politely declines. Still uncertain as to whether he should purchase the business, he is convinced when Cameron says: 'I'm finally retiring to sunny Spain.'

Two months after purchasing the post office, Edward discovers that it had only made a profit of £25,000 in the previous year owing to a one-off 'Rural Aid Grant' of £15,000 from the district council, while a nearby grocery store has recently opened up a small post office counter and is proving particularly attractive to the more elderly members of the local community. Finally, Cameron has decided to stay in the village and set up a small corner shop after being informed by his doctor that he is displaying early signs of skin cancer, which can only be aggravated by living in a hot climate.

Edward tries to make a success of the post office, even building a small extension so that he could sell local handicrafts. Unfortunately, this new venture turns out to be a disaster and Edward loses all his savings.

Advise Edward.

CAUTION!

- As in Question 1, address whether or not there is a false statement of fact and inducement, as well as the type of misrepresentation and remedies. Think also whether rescission may be barred and what method will be used to assess damages.

- Remember: if any pre-contractual statements were incorporated into the contract, you may have to consider the possibility of breach of contract. Keep a focus on misrepresentation by indicating that you are aware of this possibility without going into much detail.

DIAGRAM ANSWER PLAN

Identify the issues	▨ Identify the legal issues; ▨ Two possible claims: for misrepresentation and for breach of contract.
Relevant law	▨ Outline the elements of misrepresentation: false statement of fact/law, materiality, and reliance; ▨ **Misrepresentation Act 1967;** ▨ Remedies for breach of contract.
Apply the law	▨ Outline the elements of misrepresentation present in the problem facts; ▨ Explain the possible problems with its application; ▨ Requirements for remedies for misrepresentation under **Misrepresentation Act 1967, s. 2(1);** ▨ Availability of remedies for breach of contract on the problem facts?
Conclude	▨ Advisability of pursuing a claim for misrepresentation and/or breach of contract; ▨ Conclusion.

A **SUGGESTED ANSWER**

Edward's first possible course of action is to claim that the contract is voidable for misrepresentation. For our purposes, an actionable misrepresentation can be defined as a false statement of fact/law, made pre-contractually by one party (representor), with a view to inducing the other party (representee) to enter into the contract. The statement must be intended, it seems, to be acted upon and must *actually* induce the other party to enter the contract.

In deciding whether any pre-contractual false statements of fact/law have been made it is probably best to separate out Cameron's comments[1] as follows: 'Post office to the community—the only life-line for the elderly' . . . 'Net profits for the current year = £25,000. A steal at £100,000' . . . 'I'm finally retiring to sunny Spain.' With regard

 [1] Address whether, during the preliminary negotiations, Cameron made any false statements of fact, or were all his comments mere puffs/opinions?

to the first of those comments, how clear is this statement? For example, what is the meaning of 'lifeline'? On the one hand, it is arguable that the statement is sufficiently vague to make the establishment of an underlying 'fact' problematic (see eg *Dimmock v Hallett* (1866) 2 Ch App 21 where use of the words 'fertile' and 'improvable' was considered too vague to constitute 'statements of fact'). On the other hand, Edward might counter this by drawing the court's attention to the post-office conversion within the other village shop as this seems to represent an alternative 'lifeline'. If the statement was accurate at the time of purchase Edward will probably fail, whereas, if the conversion took place before Edward bought the post office (or if Cameron became aware of the planned conversion prior to the sale), Cameron may have a duty to alert Edward to this change of circumstances (see *With v O'Flanagan* [1936] Ch 575). On the facts stated it appears that Edward will struggle to convince a court on this point.

Edward's next argument concerns the profit achieved by the post office in the previous year. Here, again, the statement appears accurate, but Edward will argue that it constituted a half-truth[2] as it gave the impression that the post office generated that level of profit through normal retailing activity, rather than relying on a 'one-off' grant. Reference might be made to *Atlantic Estates plc v Ezekiel* [1991] 35 EG 118 where the impression given in auction particulars was that a wine bar (for sale) was a thriving business, whereas its alcohol licence had recently been revoked. On balance, Edward's argument appears reasonably persuasive.

Finally, Cameron informed Edward of his plans to retire to 'sunny Spain'. This represents a statement of future conduct which is rarely actionable unless the representor knew at the time that he had no intention of carrying out his plans (see *Edgington v Fitzmaurice* (1885) 29 Ch D 459). On the facts, this is difficult to prove unless Cameron was already aware of his skin cancer before he sold his post office to Edward.

Assuming Edward succeeds in establishing a false statement of fact (eg a half-truth regarding last year's profit), he must convince a court that it induced him to purchase the post office,[3] which on the facts he should be able to achieve. All of Cameron's statements were communicated to Edward, there is no evidence that Edward ignored any of those statements, and each of those statements had the capacity to influence the judgement of a reasonable person when purchasing the business (especially the previous level of profitability and/or existence of local competition). It is true that Edward was given the opportunity to scrutinize the accounts but, as he did not view them, this simply represents constructive knowledge of the true position which is

[2] Where Cameron remained 'silent' on particular issues, could Edward claim misrepresentation based on a 'half-truth' or a 'change of circumstances'?

[3] Apply the law: establish whether any 'statements of fact' have induced Edward to enter into the contract.

insufficient to disprove Edward's reliance on Cameron's statement(s) (see *Redgrave v Hurd* **(1881) 20 Ch D 1**).

The next question is what type of misrepresentation Cameron has made.[4] Focusing on Cameron's failure to explain fully the constituents of last year's profit figure, Edward would presumably argue that Cameron had been guilty of fraudulent misrepresentation. Fraud was defined in *Derry v Peek* **(1889) 14 App Cas 337** as making a 'false statement': (a) knowingly; or (b) without belief in its truth; or (c) recklessly, careless whether it be true or false. The litmus test is that of an absence of honest belief, subjectively assessed (see *Akerhielm v Rolf De Mare* **[1959] AC 789**). Cameron will presumably plead his innocence by arguing that he had no *intention* to mislead Edward (although an 'intention to deceive' is not an additional requirement of the tort of deceit, see *Ludsin Overseas Ltd v Eco3 Capital Ltd* **[2013] EWCA Civ 413**), and that his statement of last year's profit was accurate. The court may need some convincing on this point but, if Cameron was successful, it would simply transfer judicial attention on to **s. 2(1)** of the **Misrepresentation Act 1967 (MA 1967)**. That subsection primarily affords Edward the same level of damages by treating any misrepresentation by Cameron 'as if' it had been made fraudulently, unless the misrepresentor had 'reasonable' grounds for making that statement. Under **s. 2(1)** the onus of proof rests with Cameron. The Court of Appeal decision in *Howard Marine & Dredging Co. Ltd v Ogden & Sons Ltd* **[1978] QB 574** demonstrates the difficulty that Cameron may face in rebutting the statutory presumption as it interpreted **s. 2(1)** as imposing an 'absolute obligation' on the misrepresentor not to state facts of which he had no reasonable grounds for believing were true. Cameron will struggle on this point. Nor will his task necessarily be easier with regard to the other possible misrepresentations; for example, if he knew of local competition, then he would have no 'reasonable grounds' for using the words 'only lifeline'.

If successful,[5] the remedies available to Edward will be rescission and/or damages. Common law bars to rescission include: lapse of time, affirmation, impossibility to restore the parties to their original positions (ie *restitutio in integrum*), and third-party rights acquired over the subject matter of the contract prior to any attempted rescission. Here, as Edward continued to run the business after discovering the true state of affairs, a court might refuse rescission on grounds of affirmation (see also *Leeds City Council v Barclays Bank Plc* **[2021] EWHC 363 (Comm)** at **[165]**). Failing that, rescission is likely to be refused as it will be difficult to return the parties to their original positions in the light of the physical structure of the post office having been altered by the building extension (and presumably the

---

[4] Identify what type of misrepresentation, if any, Cameron was guilty of making.

[5] Note how this concluding section encompasses IRAC in one paragraph.

diversification into the sale of local handicraft products) as well as tax considerations, etc. (see *Thomas Witter Ltd v TBP Industries Ltd* [1996] 2 All E.R. 573). It therefore seems that Edward must settle for damages only.

[6] Identify the types of losses for which Edward can be compensated.

[7] Explain the rule.

Damages under **s. 2(1) of the MA 1967** are based on those awarded in the tort of deceit.[6] The standard test of 'reasonable foreseeability' gives way to the 'direct consequence' test (see *Royscot Trust Ltd v Rogerson* [1991] 2 QB 297) whereby a court awards the claimant all losses *directly* flowing from the misrepresentation, however unforeseeable those losses proved to be.[7] Edward could receive damages under the following headings:[8] (a) diminution in value (the difference between the contract price and the true value of the business)—whether the true value is estimated at the date of purchase or at a later date is subject to the guidance proffered by the House of Lords in *Smith New Court Securities v Scrimgeour Vickers* [1996] 4 All ER 769; and (b) consequential losses generated by reliance on the misrepresentation (eg Edward's loss of personal savings, subject to the rules on double recovery). Edward may also consider the possibility of claiming 'lost opportunity costs' (see *East v Maurer* [1991] 2 QB 297) as he was deprived of the opportunity to use his original start-up capital to invest in a more profitable business. Indeed, following *4 Eng Ltd v Harper* [2008] EWHC 915 (Ch), [2009] Ch 91, it seems Edward will not even need to prove that there *was* some other profitable business that he was actively considering purchasing, in substitution for the post office.

[8] Apply the rule by explaining the measure of damages Edward could recover.

[9] Indicates awareness of this possibility without going into much detail on the point.

Edward's alternative course of action is to sue Cameron for breach of contract,[9] requiring proof that one of Cameron's pre-contractual statements constituted a term of the contract that had subsequently been broken. However, this is unlikely on the facts. Cameron's statements mainly appear in an advertisement, which, following *Partridge v Crittenden* [1968] 1 WLR 1204, are unlikely to form part of any 'offer' that Edward accepted when agreeing to purchase the post office. Also, it would be difficult for Edward to prove that the relevant statements—for example, 'a steal' or 'a lifeline'—contained a sufficient degree of objective intent to imbue them with a contractual status (see *Heilbut, Symons & Co. v Buckleton* [1913] AC 30). On that basis, it may be unlikely that a court will identify a specific breach of contract. However, if Edward was successful, his primary remedy would lie in damages. Termination of the contract, assuming the relevant term was viewed as a condition, would be unlikely as Edward continued trading after he had discovered the full extent of his problems and even extended the premises.

LOOKING FOR EXTRA MARKS?

- When considering the possibility of claiming 'lost opportunity costs', although following *4 Eng Ltd v Harper* **[2008] EWHC 915 (Ch), [2009] Ch 91**, it seems Edward would not need to prove that there was another profitable business that he was actively considering purchasing, additional marks may be awarded for noting that under **s. 2(1) of the MA 1967**, as opposed to fraud, damages may be reduced by the court if it is of the opinion that the claimant had been contributorily negligent—see *Gran Gelato v Richcliff* **[1992] 1 All ER 865**.

TAKING THINGS FURTHER

- Atiyah, P.S. and Treitel, G., 'Misrepresentation Act 1967' (1967) 30 MLR 369.
  Addresses the effects of the **Misrepresentation Act 1967**.

- O'Sullivan, J., 'Rescission as a Self-Help Remedy: A Critical Analysis' (2000) 59 CLJ 509.
  Questions whether rescission should be a court-ordered remedy rather than an act of the rescinding party.

- Poole, J. and Devenney, J., 'Reforming Damages for Misrepresentation: The Case for Coherent Aims and Principles' [2007] JBL 269.
  Considers whether damages in cases under **s. 2(1) of the Misrepresentation Act 1967** *should be limited to losses resulting from the specific misrepresentation.*

7 Improper Pressure

KEY DEBATES

Debate: what must be shown for economic duress to be established?

At times, inconsistent language used by the courts has created uncertainty. Has this been improved by the Supreme Court in *Pakistan International Airline Corporation v Times Travel (UK) Ltd* [2021] **UKSC 40** (for example, by focusing on finding 'highly reprehensible' behaviour by one party – see [4])?

Debate: lack of clarity on the meaning of 'undue influence'.

The majority view is that undue influence is based on a defendant's wrongdoing; however, a view has also been put forward that undue influence is a 'claimant-sided' doctrine.

Debate: relationship between the doctrines of undue influence and duress.

There is a division in the law between undue influence and duress. Would it be better to merge these two doctrines (in *Pakistan International Airline Corporation v Times Travel (UK) Ltd*

[2021] UKSC 40 at [19] Lord Hodge noted the influence of equity on the development of the common law concept of duress)?

Debate: how far protection of consumers is or should be the subject of specific legislation. See, for example, the **Consumer Rights Act 2015** and the **Consumer Protection from Unfair Trading Regulations 2008**.

QUESTION | 1

Marjorie, a firm believer in psychic phenomena, was recently devastated by the sudden death of her husband. She was left a sizeable amount of money in her husband's will, as well as his business, Ghosthunters & Co. She decides to communicate with the spirit of her husband through her long-standing medium, Spook. Spook tells Marjorie that her husband wishes her to donate £25,000 to the Spirit Appreciation Society Ltd (SAS), a company which publishes a journal entitled *Supernatural Monthly*. Marjorie donates the money by gift under seal.

Meanwhile, Ghosthunters & Co. is facing financial collapse because its main creditor, Banshee, is threatening to call in an overdue loan of £50,000. In return for an extra six weeks to repay the loan, Marjorie agrees to transfer a 33 per cent shareholding in Ghosthunters & Co. to Banshee.

Three months later, Marjorie finds out that Spook is a director of SAS. Moreover, she is becoming worried about the way in which Banshee is using his shareholding to redirect the policy of the business.

Advise Marjorie whether she can avoid either transaction on grounds of improper pressure. (Ignore any potential application of the Consumer Protection from Unfair Trading Regulations 2008, SI No. 1277.)

CAUTION!

- Although there is a considerable degree of overlap between the doctrines of duress and undue influence (see, for example, *Pakistan International Airline Corporation v Times Travel (UK) Ltd* [2021] UKSC 40, particularly at [19]), you should be careful not to confuse the requirements/terminology of undue influence—which often refers to trust, confidence, etc.—and economic duress, which emphasizes illegitimate pressure, the effect of the pressure, and calculated threats of damage.

- Marjorie acts in two capacities: undue influence is arguably more relevant when Marjorie deals with Spook as a private client; economic duress is arguably more relevant to the arm's-length business transaction between Marjorie and Banshee.

DIAGRAM ANSWER PLAN

Identify the issues
- Identify legal issues: undue influence and economic duress;
- Identify two possible claims by Marjorie: against Spook and against Banshee.

Relevant law
- Outline the relevant law for the claim of undue influence;
- Outline the relevant law for the claim under doctrine of economic duress.

Apply the law
- Identify how undue influence might be established;
- Effect of a finding of undue influence: contract/deed prima facie voidable;
- For economic duress, outline the need for illegitimate pressure and the effect of the pressure.

Conclude
- Available remedies for undue influence;
- Available remedies in cases of economic duress;
- Conclusion.

SUGGESTED ANSWER

[1]Identify the two issues affecting Marjorie and address each separately.

There are two main issues affecting Marjorie and each will be addressed separately.[1]

Marjorie v Spook

Marjorie's dealings with Spook are as a private client and raise the possibility of undue influence. Marjorie might argue that her deed of donation to SAS is voidable for undue influence. Undue influence can be established in two ways: by affirmative proof of undue influence, or by raising a presumption of undue influence which is not rebutted.

[2]Having identified the types of undue influence, then note the effect on the burden of proof.

This distinction emphasizes a shifting onus of proof[2] resulting from, for example, the proximity of the parties' relationship and the nature of the transaction.

Dealing first with affirmative proof of undue influence, the Court of Appeal in *Allcard v Skinner* **(1887) 36 Ch D 145** defined undue influence as:

some unfair and improper conduct, some coercion from outside, some overreaching, some form of cheating and generally, though not always, some personal advantage gained.

[3] State and apply the law.

As Spook arguably tricked Marjorie for the purposes of personal gain, it would seem to fall within this definition.[3] In particular, Marjorie's recent bereavement and her belief in psychic phenomena are presumably known to Spook, and are likely to make her susceptible to Spook's suggestions (see *Lyon v Home* **(1868) LR 6 Eq 655** and *Nottidge v Prince* **(1860) 2 Giff 246**). If Spook was unaware of Marjorie's belief in psychic phenomena the difficulty of proof might be increased, at least on a defendant-sided analysis of undue influence.

[4] This paragraph demonstrates using IRAC for each issue, not just for a complete answer. This sentence identifies the issue.

[5] State the legal rule.

[6] Apply the law.

[7] Reach a conclusion on the point.

If undue influence is established, the deed is prima facie voidable although the right to rescind may be lost if the victim waits too long before seeking relief.[4] If fraud is involved, it is generally thought that time runs from discovery of the fraud (eg *Leaf v International Galleries* **[1950] 2 KB 86**); an alternative opinion suggests that time runs from when the pressure ceases to operate on the mind of the victim.[5] On the present facts[6], these tests are effectively contemporaneous as both would require Marjorie to unearth Spook's underhand dealing. However, if SAS has spent the donation in the meantime, Marjorie may be unable to recover her money (see *Allcard v Skinner*) and damages are generally not available in this area (although compare *Mahoney v Purnell* **[1996] 3 All ER 61**).[7]

[8] Address all of the alternatives raised by the facts.

Marjorie might alternatively claim that a presumption of undue influence has arisen.[8] Marjorie could argue that her relationship with Spook fell into a category which *automatically* assumes that the requisite degree of trust and confidence existed between the parties, as the first step in generating a presumption of influence. However, it might be unlikely that a medium would be expected to put the interests of his/her client first in such a relationship. Marjorie may draw an analogy with *Allcard v Skinner* where the relationship of religious leader and 'disciple' fell into this category, but the decision in *Nottidge v Prince* suggests that this argument is unlikely to succeed for a medium–client relationship. Marjorie's second argument is that, de facto, the level of trust and confidence that she placed in Spook should raise a presumption of *influence*. On the facts, given Marjorie's fragile emotional state and firm belief in psychic phenomena, she may well have placed great reliance on the guidance of Spook, her longstanding medium. In such circumstances, Marjorie could argue that Spook occupied a clear position of dominance that would *presumably* enable him to *influence* the will of his client.

[9] To this point the presumption is of *influence only*, so it must be established that the transaction is one that 'calls for explanation' to establish a presumption of *undue* influence.

If Marjorie can establish either such relationship, the court will apply the test set out by the House of Lords in *Royal Bank of Scotland v Etridge (No. 2)* [2001] UKHL 44, [2001] 4 All ER 449 to determine whether there should be a presumption of *undue* influence.[9] The court will need to be convinced that the resulting transaction was in some way 'wrongful', not readily explicable by the relationship of the parties. Does the gift of £25,000 raise such suspicions? Alternatively, does Spook's undisclosed directorship at SAS suggest an element of underhand dealing which, if known, *might* have dissuaded Marjorie from making the gift (see *UCB Corporate Services Ltd v Williams*

[10] Reach a conclusion on how the law will be applied on the facts of your question.

[2002] EWCA Civ 555, [2003] 1 P & CR 12)? These arguments appear likely to succeed on the facts,[10] so a presumption of undue influence will be levelled against Spook as regards Marjorie's gift to SAS.

[11] These two sentences involve Identifying the legal issue, stating the relevant Rule and Applying the law, dealing with the third element of presumed undue influence, ie can the presumption be rebutted?

To rebut this presumption, essentially Spook must prove that Marjorie's actions were 'voluntary'. This can take two forms: spontaneity of action or proper independent advice. Here there is no evidence of any independent advice.[11] That Spook's true role in the transaction was concealed suggests that Marjorie was unable to make a full, free, and informed estimate of the expediency of the transaction (see *Inche Noriah v Sheik Allie Bin Omar* [1929] AC 127). Alternatively, Spook might argue that Marjorie acted *spontaneously*, free of any undue pressures at that moment. The majority decision in *Re Brocklehurst's Estate, Hall v Roberts* [1978] Ch 14 suggests that people should be free to do as they wish with their money and property, that friendship and eccentricity are human characteristics, meaning that courts should not interfere with such transactions in the absence of fraud or trickery (see also *R v Attorney-General for England and Wales* [2003] UKPC 22, [2003] EMLR 24). Here, as Marjorie appears to have been deceived, Spook will struggle to rebut the presumption of undue influence in the absence of proof that Marjorie made the gift with full knowledge of the facts.

[12] When advising a party, do not forget to address possible remedies.

If Marjorie successfully establishes undue influence her primary remedy is that of rescission.[12] She must not delay unduly in seeking legal redress. However, if the money has been spent there may be an issue (see *Allcard v Skinner*, although see also the more relaxed approach adopted in *Cheese v Thomas* [1994] 1 All ER 35; *Halpern v Halpern (No. 2)* [2007] EWCA Civ 291, [2007] 3 All ER 478).

Marjorie v Banshee

[13] Address the second issue, which requires consideration of the doctrine of duress.

In relation to Banshee,[13] Marjorie is attempting to avoid the contract in her capacity as proprietor of Ghosthunters Ltd As the transaction involves arm's-length commercial dealing, the doctrine of economic duress is particularly appropriate.

Courts will not lightly infer economic duress. The *type* of pressure exerted is usually key: even when acting under overwhelming pressure, an absence of choice will not negate consent in law unless it is of a kind that is regarded as illegitimate (see **Barton v Armstrong [1976] AC 104** at 121). Illegitimate pressure[14] often involves an unlawful threat by the dominant party to cause damage to the economic interests of the other party. In **Universe Tankships Inc. of Monrovia v ITWF [1983] 1 AC 366**, Lord Scarman identified two aspects of illegitimate pressure: the nature of the pressure and the nature of the demand which the pressure was applied to support. So, pressure which appears lawful might still be considered illegitimate if exerted for unconscionable reasons.

Did Banshee apply illegitimate pressure to Marjorie (as in, for example, **Atlas Express Ltd v Kafco (Importers and Distributors) Ltd [1989] QB 833**) by threatening to do something which may be construed as unconscionable, knowing the severe consequences which this will visit upon Marjorie's business (eg **ITWF**)? The question whether Banshee is threatening to break an existing contract (eg **North Ocean Shipping Co. Ltd v Hyundai Construction Co. Ltd [1979] QB 705**) deserves closer attention.[15] There is nothing to suggest that Banshee does not have the right to call in the debt. If so, it is doubtful whether the doctrine of economic duress is applicable. Thus in **Pakistan International Airline Corporation v Times Travel (UK) Ltd [2021] UKSC 40** at [29] Lord Hodge was of the opinion that it is generally not duress to threaten to do something which is lawful. In that case Times Travel (UK) Ltd (TTL) was a small family-owned travel agency based in Birmingham. Its business consisted almost entirely of the sale to the Pakistani community in Birmingham of flight tickets to Pakistan. At the relevant time, Pakistan International Airlines Corp (PIAC) was the only airline offering direct flights to Pakistan from the UK. The contractual arrangements between the parties, particularly as to commission, was not straightforward. Ultimately disputes arose between PAIC and its agents (including TTL) over commission. A trade association, APTA, was formed to represent the agents in these disputes and some of the agents brought legal action. In September 2012, PAIC lawfully gave notice to terminate all of its contracts with agents in the UK. In September 2012, PIAC also lawfully reduced TTL's ticket allocation from 300 to 60 tickets. This reduction had a major negative impact of TTL, one which could ultimately put it out of business. However, PIAC offered its agents (including TTL) a new, revised agreement. Indeed counsel for PIAC accepted that the termination notices were designed to get agents to agree to the new contracts. The new agreement changed the terms as to commission but crucially for present purposes required agents to release PIAC from claims for commission calculated on the old basis. Ultimately TTL signed this

[14] The requirement of illegitimate pressure must be identified, explained, and applied.

[15] Expand upon matters most relevant to the facts of the question.

new agreement as, unless it did so, it would no longer be able to sell PIAC tickets and would almost inevitably would go out of business. Subsequently, TTL sought to avoid this agreement on the ground that it was procured by economic duress but the Supreme Court ultimately held that there was no economic duress not least as PIAC genuinely believed it was not liable to the commission claimed under the earlier agreement.

Conversely, if Banshee is wrongfully calling in the loan (eg prematurely) this may amount to illegitimate pressure, especially if he knows of Marjorie's plight and/or the court is willing to regard his acquisition of a 33 per cent shareholding as being morally reprehensible (see *D & C Builders v Rees* **[1966] 2 QB 617** and *CTN Cash and Carry Ltd v Gallaher Ltd* **[1994] 4 All ER 715**), although the precise relevance of whether or not a claim was made bona fide by the creditor is unclear following *Pakistan International Airline Corporation v Times Travel (UK) Ltd* **[2021] UKSC 40** (see, for example, Lord Burrows at **[133]**).

In conclusion, although exercising an existing contractual right to call in an overdue loan seems reasonable, Lord Scarman in the *ITWF* case suggested that a lawful demand coupled with an 'illegitimate motive' *might* be illegitimate. Here, for instance, is Banshee's real motive the procurement of a 33 per cent shareholding? Such a situation does not come within the two categories of cases, identified by Lord Hodge in *Pakistan International Airline Corporation v Times Travel (UK) Ltd* **[2021] UKSC 40**, where lawful act duress has to-date been found.

[16] Consider all of the elements of the doctrine, ie look at the effect of the illegitimate pressure.

Assuming illegitimate pressure has been identified, was Marjorie coerced by this pressure?[16] Did it cause Marjorie to enter the contract? Did she have any reasonable options other than to transfer her shareholding to Banshee? Could she have brought an action for breach of contract and would her business have survived in the meantime? Did she enter voluntarily into a compromise agreement; that is, extending the time for repayment in return for a 33 per cent shareholding? Could she have refinanced the debt from another source? If not, her lack of any practicable available alternatives may suggest that the illegitimate pressure was a significant cause inducing her into the contract (in *Pakistan International Airline Corporation v Times Travel (UK) Ltd* **[2021] UKSC 40** causation and lack of reasonable alternatives were treated as separate requirements). Even though Marjorie seemed to accept the new arrangement, in *ITWF* Lord Scarman recognized that protest by the weaker party at the time the pressure was exerted is not always relevant if the pressure is so great as to make protest pointless.

LOOKING FOR EXTRA MARKS?

- Marjorie may have an action in misrepresentation (eg **Misrepresentation Act 1967, s. 2(1)**, or breach of a duty of care—***Cornish v Midland Bank plc* [1985] 3 All ER 513**), although difficulties in establishing the factual basis of any statements relying upon the interpretation of psychic phenomena may make this problematic unless she can establish actual fraud.

- ***North Ocean Shipping*** suggests that time runs quickly against a party seeking rescission on grounds of economic duress. Marjorie waited some time before seeking legal advice, but could retain her right to rescind if, for example, she felt unable to question the shareholding transfer until the existing debt repayment was resolved.

QUESTION | 2

Ron is a retired lorry driver who has set up his own distribution service. His first customer was Cottonvalue plc, a company with a nationwide network of retail outlets. Cottonvalue plc wanted to use Ron to deliver stationery to all its outlets in the north of England. A contract was signed for Ron to deliver a 'minimum 1,000 boxes of stationery' for Cottonvalue plc over a period of 12 months, beginning on 1 January. No maximum figure for deliveries was specified. The stationery was to be packed in specially selected boxes, of one size only, incurring a delivery charge of 50p per box irrespective of the distance travelled within the designated area. Both parties expected Ron to be called on to deliver far more than the 'minimum' specified in the contract.

Ron relied on the projected profits to take out a bank loan to upgrade his existing fleet of lorries. Unfortunately, midway through the contract, Cottonvalue expressed its wish to renegotiate the delivery charge, threatening immediate withdrawal unless the delivery charge was reduced to 40p. Ron agreed as the prospect of losing Cottonvalue's custom is unthinkable.

At the end of the year, Ron asks you for advice as to whether he can reclaim the lost 10p on every delivery he made on the ground that the contractual modification was voidable for improper pressure.

CAUTION!

- Economic duress cannot be established unless the stronger party has applied *illegitimate* pressure, that pressure caused the contract and the weaker party had no reasonable alternative but to submit. All of these aspects must be addressed in your answer.

- Your answer must show that, to succeed, Ron will need to establish that: (a) Cottonvalue plc exerted illegitimate pressure; (b) the pressure caused the contract modification; and (c) Ron had no reasonable alternative but to agree to the renegotiation.

DIAGRAM ANSWER PLAN

Identify the issues	■ Identify the legal issues in Ron's possible claim of economic duress against Cottonvalue plc.
Relevant law	■ Outline the relevant law: need to establish both that Cottonvalue applied illegitimate pressure, that such pressure caused the contract and that Ron had no real alternative course of action.
Apply the law	■ Outline the requirements to establish illegitimate pressure: Lord Scarman in *Universe Tankships Inc of Monrovia v ITWF*; ■ What impact did the illegitimate pressure have on Ron's decision to enter into the contract?
Conclude	■ Possible remedies for improper pressure; ■ Conclusion.

SUGGESTED ANSWER

[1] Identifying the cause of action and the elements that will need to be established sets out the structure of your answer.

Ron might try to avoid the modified contract on the ground of economic duress.[1] A court will not set aside a contract merely because 'normal commercial pressure' has been exerted by the dominant party (***Barton v Armstrong* [1976] AC 104**). Ron will have to provide evidence that the pressure which Cottonvalue exerted was of a type characterizable as 'illegitimate', that this caused Ron to agree to the contract renegotiation and that Ron had no real alternative but to agree to the new terms.

Illegitimate Pressure

In ***Universe Tankships Inc. of Monrovia v ITWF* [1983] 1 AC 366**, Lord Scarman identified two aspects of illegitimate pressure:[2] the nature of the pressure and the nature of the demand which the pressure was applied to support. This distinction demonstrates that pressure which appears lawful might still be considered illegitimate if exerted for unconscionable reasons. Therefore, *even if* Cottonvalue was contractually entitled to threaten withdrawal, Ron might try to argue that

[2] Make sure that your answer addresses both aspects.

the pressure was not legitimate. However, such an argument seems difficult to make following *Pakistan International Airline Corporation v Times Travel (UK) Ltd* **[2021] UKSC 40** at **[29]** where Lord Hodge started with the general proposition that it is usually not duress to threaten to do something which you have the right to do.

Illegitimate pressure usually involves a threat by the dominant party to do something which would cause damage to the economic interests of the other party unless some demand is met. One example might be a threatened breach of an *existing* contract. However, additional evidence would be required as such threats are not necessarily illegitimate per se. For instance, in *Atlas Express Ltd v Kafco (Importers & Distributors) Ltd* **[1989] QB 833**, it was the manner in which the plaintiff exerted the pressure which was crucial—in particular, compelling a renegotiation of an existing contract purely for the plaintiff's benefit, leaving the communication of the threat to an innocent third party, timing its communication to correspond with his own absence, and judging the precise moment when the pressure would be heightened by the defendant's realization that only the plaintiff was in the position to meet his needs (eg *Carillion Construction Ltd v Felix (UK) Ltd* **[2001] BLR 1**). In such situations, it is clear that the dominant party intends to apply the pressure and has sufficient knowledge of the weaker party's predicament to predict the impact of that pressure (eg *D & C Builders v Rees* **[1966] 2 QB 617**). Here, has Cottonvalue threatened to break an existing contract? Are there any facts which suggest that this threat is illegitimate? Does Cottonvalue recognize that Ron is relying upon the contract to service his existing indebtedness to his bank? Is Cottonvalue itself not in financial difficulty? If so, this might suggest that the pressure is illegitimate.[3]

Clearly, hard bargaining is an everyday incident of normal business relationships (see *Barton v Armstrong* **[1976] AC 104**). Ron was not obliged, it seems, to upgrade his existing fleet of lorries; that is, it does not seem to be a condition of his contract with Cottonvalue. It might be argued that a predicament of one's own making should not be used to label normal commercial pressure as something which is unconscionable, whereas if Cottonvalue was aware of Ron's financial state, and the serious economic consequences of withdrawing from the contract, this might suggest a contrary finding. Pressure might be regarded as illegitimate *because* it represents an intentional, bad-faith threat of damage to the other party's economic interest (see *B & S Contracts & Design Ltd v Victor Green Publications Ltd* **[1984] ICR 419** and *Al Nehayan v Kent* **[2018] EWHC 333**). Remove this intent and economic duress may become all the harder to establish. However, the relevance of good/bad faith is unclear following *Pakistan International Airline Corporation v Times Travel (UK) Ltd* **[2021] UKSC 40** (see, for example, Lord Burrows at **[133]**).

[3] Where there is insufficient detail in the question for you to speculate further, you can reach a tentative conclusion.

Effect of Illegitimate Pressure

[4] Dealing with the next element of your answer, as identified in your opening paragraph.

The next question is what impact any illegitimate pressure had on Ron's decision to enter into the contract.[4] In *The Evia Luck* [1992] 2 AC 152 Lord Goff said the illegitimate pressure must be a 'significant cause' in inducing a party to enter into a contract. Various factors have been identified as being of importance: the protest of the weaker party, the unavailability of any other course of action (eg legal remedy), the lack of independent advice, and the attempted subsequent avoidance of the contract by the weaker party (see, generally, *Pao On v Lau Yiu Long* [1980] AC 614 at 635). There has been some debate as to whether a lack of effective choice is a separate requirement or part of the test of causation.[5] In *Pakistan International Airline Corporation v Times Travel (UK) Ltd* [2021] UKSC 40 the Supreme Court regarded a lack of a reasonable choice as a separate requirement for cases of economic duress. In any case the unavoidable and serious consequence of non-submission forms a crucial part of the requirements for economic duress. For example, in *Vantage Navigation Corp. v Suhail & Saud Bahwan Building Materials, The Alev* [1989] 1 Lloyd's Rep 138, the plaintiffs implicitly threatened non-delivery of the defendants' cargo, perhaps even to jettison or sell it, unless a contribution was made towards paying the increased port and discharge costs. The cargo was aboard a ship thousands of miles away. The defendants needed the cargo to be delivered on time. A wait-and-see approach was not a realistic course of action, especially as other sources of purchase were out of the question. Economic duress was thereby established.

[5] Demonstrate knowledge of a debate about a possible third requirement.

What should Ron have done at the time of the threat? Perhaps he should have refused to renegotiate? The answer, in turn, might depend upon whether Ron had already delivered the 'minimum' quantity of goods specified in the contract. If this had occurred then Cottonvalue would have a contractual right to employ other transport agencies to deliver their goods, leaving Ron with no remedy (indeed, as suggested previously, it may be difficult to demonstrate illegitimate pressure in such a case). Conversely, if the 'minimum' had not yet been delivered Ron could, in theory, claim damages if Cottonvalue did not continue to employ his services until the minimum delivery had been fulfilled. But is this practical? The facts suggest that legal action is 'unthinkable'. Cottonvalue are threatening a complete withdrawal, with the clear implication that it might not employ Ron again. This would affect Ron when he considers his existing indebtedness to his bank.

[6] This complex point requires speculation; keep such discussions brief.

Moreover, how would damages have been assessed?[6] Would it include damages for the 'expectation' that more boxes would be delivered by Ron? In truth, an available remedy in damages does not seem to have unduly influenced the courts in duress cases (eg *Atlas Express Ltd v Kafco (Importers & Distributors) Ltd*). Perhaps this is because litigation is a protracted affair often requiring considerable financial resources over a long period of time—Ron appears devoid of spare cash and needs to negotiate a solution immediately.

[7] The advice here is clear.

Finally, if Ron can successfully plead economic duress he should be advised to proceed quickly.[7] Economic duress makes a contract voidable, allowing the victim the option of rescission. However, this right can be lost through lapse of time. The question is whether a court would have expected him to institute legal proceedings against Cottonvalue at an earlier date. The basic principle[8] as applied in *North Ocean*

[8] Explain the law.

Shipping Co. Ltd v Hyundai Construction Co. Ltd [1979] QB 705 is that a victim of duress must seek rescission as soon as possible after the original pressure has ceased to operate. In *North Ocean*, there was no evidence that, had the plaintiffs sought to reclaim their additional payment immediately, the defendants would have stopped the ship's construction. Here, was it appropriate for Ron to wait until the year has passed before seeking rescission of the modified payment schedule? He might argue that the pressure continued throughout the

[9] Your conclusion must answer the question set, offering advice to Ron in relation to the contract and improper pressure.

year. Without such evidence Ron's chances look bleak,[9] as Cottonvalue will presumably contend that *both* parties had a vested interest in ensuring the legality of the contract modification and would therefore welcome a clear ruling as quickly as possible. Whatever else, case law suggests that in business transactions *both* parties must be able to ascertain what their enforceable contractual rights are as quickly as possible so that they can take appropriate contingency measures in their subsequent dealings with each other. In Cottonvalue's situation, if the reduction in delivery charge had been unenforceable, alternative distributors might have been sought *after* Ron had fulfilled his minimum obligations but *before* the year had passed.

LOOKING FOR EXTRA MARKS?

- Additional marks might be gained in identifying factual similarities with *Atlas Express*.

- A very good answer might link the absence of consideration and the presence of duress, referring to *Williams v Roffey Bros & Nicholls (Contractors) Ltd* [1991] 1 QB 1. See also *South Caribbean Trading Ltd v Trafigura Beheer BV* [2004] EWHC 2676 (Comm), [2005] 1 Lloyd's Rep 128, and *Adam Opel GmbH v Mitras Automotive (UK) Ltd* [2008] EWHC 3205 (QB).

- To further explore the causation issue, see *Huyton SA v Peter Cremer GmbH* [1999] 1 Lloyd's Rep 620 and *Kolmar Group AG v Traxpo Enterprises Pty Ltd* [2010] EWHC 113 (Comm).

QUESTION | **3**

The decisions of the House of Lords in *Barclays Bank plc v O'Brien* [1994] 1 AC 180 and *Royal Bank of Scotland v Etridge (No. 2)* [2001] UKHL 44, [2001] 4 All ER 449, have established a clearer, more coherent set of rules that strike an appropriate balance between the rights of creditors and those of wives who have been unduly influenced by their spouses.

To what extent do you agree with this statement?

 CAUTION!

- Note that the House of Lords' decision in *O'Brien* was never intended to offer a definitive exposition of the law. Rather, it represented a framework of principle which lower courts should adapt and modify, in accordance with the facts presented to them. The unpredictability of subsequent case law suggested that greater clarity and specificity was required, culminating in the *Etridge (No. 2)* decision.

DIAGRAM ANSWER PLAN

Introduction—outline the legal issues to be addressed in your answer.

Point: what was the state of the law prior to the House of Lords' decision in *O'Brien*?

Evidence: what policy considerations influenced the House of Lords' decision in *O'Brien*?

Analysis: to what extent did subsequent case law depart from the spirit of *O'Brien*?

Analysis: to what extent did the House of Lords' decision in *Etridge (No. 2)* clarify any outstanding ambiguities in the relevant law?

Conclusion.

SUGGESTED ANSWER

The House of Lords' landmark decisions in *Barclays Bank plc v O'Brien* **[1994] 1 AC 180** and *Royal Bank of Scotland v Etridge (No. 2)* **[2001] UKHL 44, [2001] 4 All ER 449**, offer important guidance to banks and other financial institutions on how to deal, for example, with wives acting as sureties for their husbands' debts, as well as those who secure joint advances with their husbands. When a bank lends money to a debtor-husband who has exerted undue influence over his wife to get her, for example, to allow the use of the matrimonial home as security for the loan, the courts have always recognized the possibility that any ensuing transaction entered into between the wife and the bank (the surety transaction) might be voidable for undue influence. Until 1994, there was considerable confusion regarding the specific conditions that were needed to justify judicial intervention on behalf of a wife. In particular, the courts appeared to adopt any one of three possible approaches, making it very difficult to predict the outcome.[1]

[1] This introduces and contextualizes a discussion of the law pre-*O'Brien* and relates it directly to the essay question.

Pre-*O'Brien*

First, there was the 'special equity theory' (see *Turnbull & Co. v Duvall* **[1902] AC 429**), that seemed to reinforce the nineteenth-century attitude towards wives as well as their role and importance in marriage. Similarly, in *Yerkey v Jones* **(1939) 63 CLR 649** Dixon J emphasized the importance of the creditor actually proving that the wife understood the transaction she was entering into, effectively treating a wife more like a child than an independent-thinking adult. The second approach was termed the 'agency' theory: a bank that 'left everything to the husband' might be tainted by any undue influence exerted by the husband over his wife (eg *Barclays Bank plc v Kennedy* **[1989] 1 FLR 356**). However, the use of agency principles appears artificial: banks rarely appoint a husband formally as their agent. Finally, a line of Court of Appeal decisions from 1985 demonstrated a greater acceptance of notice as being pivotal to the determination of a creditor's liability (eg *Coldunell Ltd v Gallon* **[1986] QB 1184** and *Midland Bank plc v Shephard* **[1988] 3 All ER 17**). Briefly, if the creditor should have realized the possibility of the husband using unfair means to procure his wife's signature, the creditor might be tainted by such impropriety. This latter approach was eventually adopted by the House of Lords in *O'Brien*, specifically focusing attention on the *nature* of the transaction and the consequential risk of impropriety.[2]

[2] An effective summary of the position pre-*O'Brien* leads neatly into the discussion of the case law following that decision.

O'Brien and its Aftermath

In *O'Brien* the House of Lords stated that where the creditor had notice, actual or constructive, of possible impropriety between husband and wife, reasonable steps had to be taken to ensure that the wife's consent had been properly obtained. Two types of transactions were distinguished. First, if the wife acted as surety for her husband's business debts, it seemed the creditor would be put on notice if the transaction was financially disadvantageous and there was a substantial risk that the wife's signature had been inequitably procured by her husband. Secondly, where the transaction simply involved a joint advance to a husband and wife then, unless there were special circumstances known to the creditor, the creditor would not be fixed with constructive notice of any impropriety between the spouses.

The House of Lords also recommended that the husband and wife be interviewed separately, avoiding the problem faced by the interviewer in *Bank of Credit and Commerce International SA v Aboody* [1990] 1 QB 923 where the husband's hysterics at a joint meeting clearly affected the wife. It would be sufficient if the creditor insisted that the wife attend a private meeting (in the absence of her husband) with a representative of the creditor at which she was told of the extent of her liability, warned of the risk she was running, and urged to take independent advice.

Subsequent case law demonstrated a willingness to embrace the spirit of *O'Brien*, without being restricted by specific rules of interpretation. In *Goode Durrant Administration v Biddulph* (1994) 26 HLR 625 the creditor was put on notice in a simple joint advance transaction (the loan financing a joint venture) because of the significant disparity between the wife's potential gain and the scale of her liability. As the creditor had done nothing to advise the wife, the transaction was tainted by the husband's undue influence. Unfortunately, this broad approach was not always beneficial to the wronged wife. For example, in dealing with the actions of the bank, it seemed acceptable for the wife to be advised by the husband's solicitor (eg *Bank of Baroda v Rayarel* [1995] 27 HLR 387). The bank was entitled to rely on the professional integrity of the solicitor and his/her ability to resolve conflicts of interest properly (eg *Banco Exterior Internacional v Mann, Mann and Harris* [1995] 1 All ER 936). Case law reinforced the view that once advice had been given by a solicitor the bank was relieved of any further responsibilities, irrespective of whether the nature and type of advice that the wife received was appropriate to her needs and circumstances (see *Midland Bank plc v Massey* [1995] 1 All ER 929). It seemed that the best policy for banks to adopt was to leave everything to the solicitor; a state of affairs that was beneficial to the banks as it apparently exonerated them of any culpability in most circumstances.[3]

[3] Such sentences create a cohesive argument across an answer.

Etridge (No. 2)

[4] Address the second decision from the essay to deal with the requirements of the question.

The House of Lords' decision in *Etridge (No. 2)* attempted to address some of the deficiencies in the prevailing case law.[4] It discarded notions of financially disadvantageous transactions, set out much clearer guidelines on the procedures that banks and independent advisers should adopt, and, in particular, extended the principles to incorporate all 'non-commercial' debtor/surety relationships. Importantly, whilst accepting that the banks could rely upon the good sense and expertise of a solicitor, the Law Lords stressed that if the creditor withheld information from the solicitor or knew that no competent solicitor could ever advise the wife to enter such a transaction, the availability of legal advice would be insufficient for the creditor to avoid being fixed by constructive notice of any legal impropriety perpetrated by the husband-debtor upon his wife. Subsequently, the general need for the creditor to take reasonable steps to ensure that the nature of the risks arising from the transaction has been brought home to the wife by the independent adviser was re-emphasized by the Court of Appeal in *First National Bank plc v Achampong* [2003] EWCA Civ 487, [2004] 1 FCR 18, strongly suggesting that the creditor must actually confirm that the independent adviser covered all of the essential points.

An Appropriate Balance?

[5] Remember that the question requires some conclusion to be reached on this point.

In conclusion,[5] the House of Lords stressed the need to retain a sense of balance in this area. Courts need to ensure that people can access equity tied up in their matrimonial homes and that financial institutions are not too hindered by the law that they become unwilling to accept such security. Moreover, the law cannot operate in a social vacuum. Views that wives are subservient to their husbands are anachronistic today. However, there must be a clear legal safety net for circumstances where a husband possesses the business acumen and experience and the wife tends to follow her husband's advice in such matters. Courts recognize that some wives place confidence and trust in their husbands in relation to financial affairs, potentially raising the presumption of undue influence between spouses. Certainly, the House of Lords' decisions warn creditor institutions that, unless they follow the correct procedures, the ensuing financial transactions may become unenforceable as against wives.

However, the *Etridge* decision does have a sting in its tail. Their Lordships made clear that the standard surety transaction in which a wife agrees to act as guarantor for her husband's business debts does not necessarily create a presumption of undue influence that would taint the creditor. More evidence will be required to demonstrate that the husband used unfair means to procure his wife's agreement (eg some form of misrepresentation). Equally, a court will not be so quick to characterize the ensuing transaction as *wrongful*, and therefore voidable, as it is natural that a wife might support her husband's business; that is, in the absence of any suspicious facts, there is no presumption of undue influence (per Lord Nicholls in *Etridge*). This suggests that a wife will struggle without clear evidence that the disparity between the husband's gain and the wife's potential loss is disproportionately large. Such an approach may tend unfairly towards the protection of creditors in such circumstances. Consequently,[6] while it may be possible to argue that the decisions of the House of Lords in *O'Brien* and *Etridge*, among others, have established a clearer, more coherent set of rules, it is not necessarily the case that these strike an appropriate balance between the rights of creditors and of wives unduly influenced by their spouses.

[6] Conclusion is clear and concise in demonstrating how the answer addressed the question.

LOOKING FOR EXTRA MARKS?

- Interestingly, in both cases, the Law Lords did not merely direct their attention to wives but also to other types of relationship (eg unmarried cohabitees) whether heterosexual or homosexual, or any other relationship where the prospect of undue influence by the debtor was foreseeable (eg *Avon Finance Co. v Bridger* [1985] 2 All ER 281).

TAKING THINGS FURTHER

- Bigwood, R., 'Undue Influence in the House of Lords: Principles and Proof' (2002) 65 MLR 435.
  Examines Royal Bank of Scotland v Etridge (No. 2) [2001] UKHL 44, [2001] 4 All ER 449*, and requirements for a presumption of undue influence.*

- Chandler, A., 'Economic Duress: Confusion or Clarity' [1989] LMCLQ 270.
  Examines illegitimate pressure and coercion in relation to duress.

- Chen-Wishart, M., 'The O'Brien Principle and Substantive Unfairness' (1997) 56 CLJ 60.
  Considers Credit Lyonnais Bank Nederland NV v Burch [1997] 1 All ER 144*, and the concept of unfairness.*

- O'Sullivan, D., 'Developing O'Brien' (2002) 118 LQR 337.
  Considers the impact of Etridge for wives seeking to establish undue influence.

Mistake

8

 ## KEY DEBATES

Debate: should there be a doctrine of mistake at all?

Some have suggested that the problems which are addressed by the doctrine of mistake could be better addressed by using other doctrines, such as those relating to unconscionable behaviour.

Debate: should an operative common mistake always lead to the contract being void?

An alternative view would suggest a more flexible, discretionary approach to the consequences of a common mistake might be more appropriate in many cases.

Debate: what is the role of equity in mistake cases?

The role of equity in mistake cases was criticized by the Court of Appeal in *Great Peace Shipping Ltd v Tsavliris Salvage (International) Ltd* [2002] EWCA Civ 1407.

Simon, an antiques dealer, is negotiating with Bette the possible sale of a 'nursing chair' and an 'armchair' from the 'mid-Victorian era'. Bette offers to buy the nursing chair for £3,000, provided it is fully re-upholstered. Secretly Bette believes the armchair to be a valuable antique from the Jacobean era and she offers Simon the sum of £25,000 for it. Simon accepts both offers gladly, particularly as he has been trying, unsuccessfully, to sell the armchair for months at the much lower price of £1,000.

During the re-upholstering of the nursing chair, one of Simon's employees discovers that it is an extremely rare Sheraton chair worth at least £100,000. Simon decides not to sell the nursing chair to Bette. A week later Bette is informed that the armchair is a very good twentieth-century copy worth only £2,500. She decides to return the armchair to Simon and demand a full refund but Simon refuses.

Discuss the legal position of Simon and Bette in each of the two transactions.

CAUTION!

- Your answer must reflect the fact that several types of mistakes have potentially occurred.

- Where both parties, for example, make the same mistake (ie common), *always* consider first whether the contract allocated the risk of the 'mistake' to one or other party, or in some other way set out the consequences of the 'mistake' occurring, before considering any possible separate doctrine of common mistake.

DIAGRAM ANSWER PLAN

Identify the issues	■ Identify the legal issues; ■ Possible types of mistake: common mistake, mutual mistake, and unilateral mistake.
Relevant law	■ Outline the relevant law and the differences between the different types of mistake.
Apply the law	■ Any term (express or implied) in the contract allocating risk to either party? ■ Nursing chair: consider the possibility of common mistake; ■ Armchair: mutual mistake or did the parties reach an agreement? ■ Should Simon have realized Bette was making a unilateral mistake?
Conclude	■ If parties were clear on subject matter of their agreements (and price to be paid), should any potential gains/losses on the deal simply represent normal risks in sale transactions? ■ Availability of remedies? ■ Conclusion.

SUGGESTED ANSWER

[1] Keep introductions to problem questions brief. Here you identify the different categories of mistake which you will consider separately.

[2] In problem questions, the use of subheadings, if permitted, can help to structure your answer.

[3] Remember: *always* consider first whether the contract allocated the risk of the 'mistake' to one or other party, or in some other way set out the consequences of the 'mistake' occurring, before considering any possible separate doctrine of common mistake. For a discussion of some of the uncertainties in this area see also *John Lobb Ltd v John Lobb SAS* [2021] EWHC 1226 (Ch).

Simon and Bette seem to have entered into a contract for the sale of the two chairs but one or both of the parties have made certain mistakes regarding the subject matter. Regarding the nursing chair, both parties appear to have made the same 'common mistake' that it was manufactured in Victorian times. The sale of the armchair raises issues of mutual and unilateral mistake.[1]

The nursing chair

Both parties mistakenly believe that the nursing chair[2] was manufactured in Victorian times and therefore was worth £3,000, whereas in fact it is a rare Sheraton chair worth £100,000. Modern case law (see *Associated Japanese Bank (International) Ltd v Credit du Nord SA* [1989] 1 WLR 255 and *Great Peace Shipping Ltd v Tsavliris Salvage (International) Ltd* [2002] EWCA Civ 1407) clearly emphasizes that, before any independent notion of mistake can be considered, the court should first seek to identify any express or implied terms that might allocate the risk of such a mistake to one or other party.[3]

Here the express terms of the contract identify the subject matter ('nursing chair') and the price ('£3,000'), but it is not immediately clear whether or not the contract allocates the risk of the 'nursing chair' not being 'mid Victorian period' and/or being significantly more valuable than the parties had understood. The possibility of an implied term, through which the contract might be undone if the nursing chair was found to be significantly more valuable, must be considered. However, as the value of the chair is not *necessary* for the contract's performance (the chair can be physically transferred whatever its value), and it does not seem to represent the parties' *common* intention (those buying antiques often hope to acquire a 'hidden gem'), any implied term that favoured the seller would arguably undermine the entire notion of a bargain and its attendant risks. Therefore, in line with the principle of *caveat venditor*, it is probable that Simon will bear the risk of this mistake.

However, if the court remains uncertain as to who, if anyone, *took the risk* of the 'nursing chair' not being 'mid Victorian period' and/or being significantly more valuable than the parties had understood it might consider the doctrine of common mistake. In *Bell v Lever Bros Ltd* [1932] AC 161, the House of Lords seemingly admitted the existence of an independent doctrine of mistake.[4] Lord Atkin proposed at least two tests, based on the notion that only a fundamental mistake can invalidate a contract. The first was whether 'the state of the new facts destroy[s] the identity of the subject matter as it was in the original state of facts'. The second test focused on 'the existence of some quality which makes the thing without the quality essentially different from the thing as it was believed to be'.

Applying the tests in *Bell* here, it is unlikely that the contract would be declared void for common mistake.[5] The first test, destruction of the identity of the subject matter, does not seem to apply: the subject matter of the contract is and remains a chair. The second test, which relates to the subject matter being essentially different from what it was believed to be, appears equally fruitless: in *Bell* Lord Atkin suggested, *obiter*, that if A bought a picture from B which believed by both to be the work of an old master, with a commensurately high purchase price, whereas it was a worthless modern copy, A would have no remedy 'in the absence of representation or warranty'. Applying that to our facts, a chair that is less or more valuable than its contract price does not render that article *essentially* different from what it was believed to be: the chair remains a chair.

In *Great Peace* the Court of Appeal acknowledged that, while an independent doctrine of common mistake does exist, it has an extremely narrow ambit and the court must ask whether the fundamental, mistaken assumption renders performance of the contract 'impossible'. This requirement of 'impossibility' is arguably stricter than either of Lord Atkin's tests. The sale of the nursing chair is obviously capable

[4] Demonstrates awareness of uncertainties in the law.

[5] Apply the law: this is a clear statement of whether the common mistake is sufficient to render the contract void.

of performance and, even if a wider interpretation of 'impossibility' were adopted (as in *Chalcot Training Limited v Ralph* **[2020] EWHC 1054 (Ch)**) and it was asked whether the commercial purpose of the contract had ceased to exist, the answer would remain negative. The possibility of immense gain (or loss) *is* arguably the accepted, commercial purpose of this contract and so, rather than ceasing to exist, that purpose has been realized (compare *Pitt v Holt* **[2013] UKSC 26**).

[6] Applying the law to the question includes outlining available remedies.

Almost certainly, the contract in our facts is valid and binding at common law, so Simon would be in breach of contract if he withdrew from the sale.[6] Finally, where a contract is declared valid and enforceable under the ordinary principles of common law contract law, it is now reasonably clear that rescission cannot be granted in equity on the ground of common mistake (see *Great Peace* and *Pitt v Holt* **[2013] UKSC 26** although cf. *FII Group Litigation v Revenue and Customs Commissioners (formerly Inland Revenue Commissioners)* **[2020] UKSC 47** at **[109]** which suggests that the existence of an equitable jurisdiction in this area has not been finally resolved).

The armchair

[7] Clearly identifies the legal issues to be addressed in this part of the answer.

First, we must decide what categories of mistake, if any, might be engaged and then ascertain whether any mistake is an operative mistake rendering the contract void.[7] This might be classified as a mutual mistake in that Bette thinks the armchair is much older (and therefore more valuable), whereas Simon clearly believes that even the contract price overvalues it. It seems neither realizes the other's error as nothing is said. The facts of the problem resemble those in *Scott v Littledale* **(1858) 8 E & B 815**, where the defendants sold by sample 100 chests of tea but later discovered they had submitted a sample of poorer quality than the bulk. The contract was not declared void, allowing the buyer to profit from the transaction. This clearly shows that if the subject matter of a sale is ascertained precisely, a mistake as to quality may be immaterial, otherwise a buyer of goods who has made a bad bargain (as Bette has done) would be able to reopen contracts at will.

[8] Applies the law clearly and concisely.

In short, this mistake should not render the contract void as objectively there is an agreement in the same terms on the same subject matter: the parties are *ad idem*.[8]

[9] Identify the legal rule.

Alternatively, might it be argued that a unilateral mistake has occurred? This would assume that only Bette made a mistake. Here, again, objective appearances count and if Simon has done nothing to mislead Bette, the dominant principle is *caveat emptor*.[9] Following Lord Atkin in *Bell*, generally this would still be the position if Simon *knew* that Bette was labouring under a mistake. In this situation, Bette's mistake is arguably one of quality and judgement which is not induced by Simon: if Bette has poor judgement she should make provision for it in the terms of the contract.

[10] Address any exceptions to that rule which appear relevant on the facts.

However, this dominant principle can occasionally give way to evidence of subjective mistake.[10] It is usually said that the contract will be void if one party is mistaken as to the *promise itself* and this is known to the other party. Here Simon accepted Bette's offer but there is no suggestion that he even knew of Bette's mistaken assumption that the chair was more valuable. Moreover, although it appears sufficient that an operative mistake is one that a reasonable person *ought* to have been aware of (see ***Centrovincial Estates plc v Merchant Investors Assurance Co. Ltd* [1983] Com LR 158**), the decision in ***Bank of Credit and Commerce International v Ali* [1999] 4 All ER 83** makes clear that the doctrine of mistake should not be used to extricate parties from 'bad bargains'. Does Bette's offer of £25,000 for the armchair indicate that she is labouring under some sort of mistake that Simon ought to have realized? Given that the value of antiques is inherently subjective (it all depends on what the buyer is prepared to pay) and that often no two experts would agree on a fair value for an item, it is unlikely that a court would depart from the standard principle of *caveat emptor* unless there was clear evidence that Simon had led Bette to believe that the armchair was worth a lot more than its true value. This means that Bette will be unable to return the chair and demand a full refund.[11]

[11] Again, remember to apply the law.

LOOKING FOR EXTRA MARKS?

■ You could briefly mention that it is unlikely that cases involving *res extincta* (ie where goods have perished at the date of contract or never existed) would prove helpful here. Such cases generally involve a total failure of consideration (see ***Couturier v Hastie* (1856) 5 HL Cas 673**—the buyer did not have to pay for the goods as the seller could not deliver them), but in our facts the nursing chair does exist and does have value.

QUESTION 2

Albert owned three Rolls-Royce cars, manufactured in 1950, 1960, and 1970, respectively. He wanted to sell the 1970 model but he also wanted to ensure that the buyer was a private car collector. Accordingly, he advertised it for sale in his local newspaper as: 'For sale only to a private car collector.' Unfortunately, due to a printing error, the car advertised for sale was the 1960 model. Byron, a car dealer, wished to acquire the 1950 model and was informed, incorrectly, by a friend that Albert had the 1950 model advertised for sale in the newspaper.

Byron knew that, because he was a car dealer, Albert would not sell the car to him. He therefore telephoned Albert and said: 'Hello, I am Mr Jones. I should like to buy the car that you have advertised in the newspaper and will give the full asking price of £80,000 for it.' Albert replied: 'I am pleased to sell the car to you Mr Jones and I am glad it will have a good home.' When Albert delivered the 1970 model, he discovered the buyer's identity and refused to complete the sale but Byron wished to enforce the contract even though the car was not the 1950 model.

Discuss the legal position.

CAUTION!

- This is quite a difficult problem. It potentially involves mutual mistake and unilateral mistake which must be considered separately in the answer.

- In answering any exam question on mistake of identity, you will probably need to demonstrate some knowledge of the case law that predated the House of Lords' decision in *Shogun Finance Ltd v Hudson* **[2003] UKHL 62, [2004] 1 All ER 215**.

DIAGRAM ANSWER PLAN

Identify the issues
- Identify the legal issues;
- Possible types of mistake: mutual mistake, and unilateral mistake.

Relevant law
- Outline the relevant law and the differences between the different types of mistake;
- On the facts, focus on mutual mistake and unilateral mistake;
- Explain the overall effect of an operative mistake on the enforceability of a contract.

Apply the law
- Mutual mistake: will contract be enforceable where parties are at cross-purposes (on the car being sold)?
- Might contract be void for unilateral mistake of identity? Consider *Shogun Finance Ltd v Hudson* and the manner of the pre-contractual negotiations;
- If no mistake of identity, is there an operative unilateral mistake as to the terms of the contract?

Conclude
- Availability of remedies?
- Conclusion.

[1] Identify immediately an awareness that the problem involves mutual mistake and unilateral mistake, and that each will be considered separately in the answer.

[2] This is an important point to make in answers about mistake.

[3] As regards mutual mistake, it must be decided whether the parties are in agreement or sufficiently at cross-purposes to nullify any notion of contract.

[4] Think: does the fact that third parties (the newspaper and B's friend) induce the contracting parties' mistake make any difference?

Two different types of mistake arguably may arise here.[1] First, the misunderstanding between the parties regarding the year of manufacture of the car and, secondly, Albert's (A's) 'mistake' as to the identity of the other contracting party, Byron (B). Each mistake must be considered. It should be noted that although issues of mistake permeate this transaction, it does not necessarily follow that the contract will be affected. The key question relates to which mistakes the law regards as sufficiently fundamental to render a contract void.[2] In the interests of commercial certainty the courts are reluctant to invalidate contracts. As a general rule, if the parties objectively agree in the same terms on the same subject matter, the contract will be binding, even if both parties are subjectively mistaken; any potential gains/losses resulting from their deal arguably simply represent the normal risks associated with transacting.

There is, it seems, a mutual mistake in relation to which car is being sold, the parties therefore making different mistakes and being at cross-purposes but neither realizing the other's mistake at the date of contract.[3] Because of confusion caused by third parties, A intends to sell the 1970 model whereas B intends to buy the 1950 model.[4] To be operative, a mutual mistake must entail an absence of genuine agreement; offer, and acceptance thus failing to coincide. It is tempting to conclude that if the parties are at cross-purposes, there can be no agreement, but the test is an objective one and so real, subjective intentions may be dominated by ostensible objectivity, meaning that the contract is valid and binding. In *Wood v Scarth* (1858) 1 F & F 293, the defendant offered in writing to let a property to the plaintiff for £63 per annum. The plaintiff negotiated with the defendant's clerk and then accepted the offer by letter. The defendant intended that a premium of £500 would be payable as well as the rent and assumed that his clerk had made that clear but the plaintiff thought that the only liability was the £63 rent. The contract was held binding. Similarly, in *Scott v Littledale* (1858) 8 E & B 815 the defendants sold by sample to the plaintiff 100 chests of tea but later discovered that the sample was poorer in quality than the bulk. The defendants had made a bad bargain but the contract was held to be valid and the plaintiff's claim for non-delivery upheld. In both of these cases the reasonable man would see a coincidence between offer and acceptance but the opposite conclusion can be reached where the evidence is ambiguous and conflicting. In *Raffles v Wichelhaus* (1864) 2 H & C 906 the defendant agreed to buy from the plaintiff a cargo of cotton to arrive '*ex Peerless* from Bombay', but while the defendant meant a *Peerless* which sailed in October, the plaintiff meant a *Peerless* which sailed in December. The description of the goods covered either of the ships' cargoes. The court did not in fact decide whether there was a contract or not but upheld the defendant's refusal to accept the goods from the December shipment on the basis that he could show that the contract was ambiguous and that he intended the October ship. The buyer and seller were similarly at cross-purposes in *Scriven Bros & Co. v Hindley & Co.* **[1913] 3 KB 564** where the plaintiff intended to sell a quantity of tow and the defendant to buy hemp, the court holding that there was such ambiguity that the subject matter of the contract could not be established with certainty. No contract will exist if the parties arrive at fundamental cross-purposes because of the act of a third party (as in *Henkel v Pape* **(1870) LR 6 Ex 7**).[5]

It is arguable that these cases are not based upon an independent concept of mistake but, instead, are illustrations of lack of concurrence between offer and acceptance. In the problem, the parties are not (objectively) *ad idem* and there is nothing in the contract which could clarify the ambiguity. Indeed, the advertisement to which the parties refer advertises the 1960 model for sale and *neither* party wants to make that car the subject of a contract. It is therefore at least arguable that there is no contract on the facts of the problem.

There are further difficulties if A attempts to prove that he did not intend to contract with B. Until the House of Lords' decision in *Shogun Finance Ltd v Hudson* **[2003] UKHL 62, [2004] 1 All ER 215**, if A appeared to contract with B yet alleged mistaken identity, he had to meet four requirements: A intended to contract with some person other than B; identity was fundamental and material; B knew of A's mistake; and A took reasonable steps to verify B's identity. The mistake needed to be a fundamental mistake of substance, here a mistake of identity rather than one relating to the attributes or qualities of a person. However, the decision in *Shogun* reviewed the then-existing common law.[6] The facts involved a rogue who sought to purchase a car on hire-purchase terms, pretending to be a Mr Durlabh Patel. The rogue had stolen Mr Patel's driving licence and other personal documents. The car dealer faxed the information to the claimant, Shogun Finance, who carried out a full credit check on Mr Patel. Satisfied with the result, the claimant agreed to finance the purchase of the car by the rogue on standard hire-purchase terms, signed by both parties. The rogue took possession of the car and wrongfully sold it to the defendant. The House of Lords, by a simple majority, concluded that the parties to the hire-purchase contract could only be Mr Patel, as named in the contract, and the claimant finance company. The contract stated the name and address of Mr Patel and did not refer to the rogue. As no offer and acceptance had taken place between these two parties, no contract could come into existence and no title to the car could be transferred to the defendant. It remains unclear whether this was an alternative way of saying that the contract had become 'void for mistake of identity'.[7]

[5] Might this apply here, where third parties (the newspaper and B's friend) induced the contracting parties' mistake?

[6] An answer must include detailed analysis of this important case.

[7] Acknowledges uncertainties in the law.

The problem here involves an apparent exchange of offer and acceptance by telephone rather than in writing. If this is classed as face-to-face dealings, in line with *Shogun*, there will be an almost irrebuttable presumption that A intended to reach an agreement with B. However, the meaning of 'face-to-face' in *Shogun* is unclear. Lords Millett and Nicholls saw no logic in excluding televisual links and telephone conversations from any definition of the term. Lord Walker accepted that the face-to-face presumption might be extended to cover telephone conversations, although any presumption might be more easily rebutted. Lord Phillips saw no reason to depart from the standard meaning of face-to-face, while Lord Hobhouse offered no view on the matter. Clearly, it is open to a future court to view A and B's telephone call as being 'face-to-face', in which case it could conclude that A intended to deal with B, making the ensuing contract enforceable.

Conversely, if a telephone conversation is not an example of face-to-face dealings (ie the dealings are considered to be *inter absentes*) then it is difficult to find any clear test in *Shogun* that would resolve the matter. The intent test advocated by Lords Phillips and Walker suggests that A did not intend to contract with B or, put another way, he did not intend to accept the offer from B. A might argue that his advertisement clearly evidenced a desire to receive offers only from private car collectors and therefore explicitly or implicitly excluded B. If so, A could successfully argue that he had not displayed any objectively verifiable intention of accepting an offer from B and, thus, no contract could arise. The alternative dealing test proposed by Lords Nicholls and Millett (dissenting) in *Shogun* would reach a more definite, albeit different, conclusion: A spoke to the physical person at the other end of the telephone line and therefore an exchange of offer and acceptance occurred between those persons. The known intention of A would have no bearing on this issue.

[8]Where the law is unclear a definitive conclusion may not be possible, but detailed analysis will gain the marks.

Clearly, the arguments as to whether the contract was concluded face-to-face or *inter absentes*, and whether an 'intent' or 'dealing' test should be employed, are finely balanced.[8] However, whatever the outcome, one should note that in the light of *Shogun* the failure of A to take reasonable steps to verify B's identity no longer appears fatal to his claim that the contract is void (a condition that was previously considered to be important, eg *Phillips v Brooks* [1919] 2 KB 243).

[9]Conclude with a brief summary of advice.

In conclusion,[9] there is probably a sufficient mutual mistake regarding the age of the car to render the contract void. There also remains the possibility that A could successfully assert that he was mistaken as to B's true identity, rendering the contract void, or, alternatively, that B misrepresented his identity in pre-contractual negotiations, rendering the contract voidable.

LOOKING FOR EXTRA MARKS?

- You might briefly discuss whether B is guilty of a misrepresentation and what effect this might have on the contract. For example, if B's statement that he is 'Mr Jones' is false, this may be a false statement of fact capable of representing an actionable misrepresentation. A may also argue that he was induced into the contract by the fraud-induced assumption that he was not dealing with a car dealer. If none of the normal bars to rescission apply, the contract is voidable at A's option.

QUESTION | 3

The single thread of principle running through the law of mistake is that, no matter how serious, the courts will not relieve mistakes of quality.

Discuss.

CAUTION!

- This essay requires a critical analysis of common, mutual and unilateral mistakes, and an investigation of whether, for example, operative mistakes relate to substance or quality. It also raises the issue of whether a meaningful distinction can be made between substance and quality in reality.
- A close knowledge of the cases is required, as well as comparing and contrasting the decisions and evaluating the rationale(s) of doctrines of mistake.

DIAGRAM ANSWER PLAN

> Introduction: identify the legal issues raised by the question.

> Point: the question requires analysis of common, mutual, and unilateral mistakes and whether operative mistakes relate to substance or quality.

> Evidence: why does the law confine the notion of mistake narrowly?

> Evidence: outline the principal theories underlying the decisions concerning mistake: formation and construction of the contract; and the independent doctrine based on the distinction between a mistake of substance and a mistake of quality.

Analysis: how can a distinction be made between substance and quality in the three recognized categories of mistake?

▼

Analysis: should a mistake as to quality be sufficient to render a contract void?

▼

Conclusion.

 SUGGESTED ANSWER

At common law, the notion of mistake is confined within narrow limits but if it is operative its effect is to render a contract void *ab initio*. By placing mistake in a straitjacket, both freedom of contract and certainty of contract are arguably preserved.[1] A may make a bad bargain due to his/her own error and receive something of inferior quality in comparison with his/her expectations but the courts will not grant relief on that ground alone, in order to preserve the essence of bargain and *caveat emptor* (although compare, for example, the **Consumer Rights Act 2015**). The general rule[2] is that, if the parties agree in the same terms on the same subject matter, they are bound and should look to the contract for 'protection from the effects of facts unknown to them' (*Bell v Lever Bros Ltd* [1932] AC 161, per Lord Atkin).

Arguably the so-called mistake cases really turn on questions of formation, contract interpretation and risk allocation, rather than representing an independent theory of mistake.[3] If so, cases of common mistake may be resolved by asking whether the contract terms put the risk on one or other of the parties, or whether a term can be implied regarding the presence or absence of the fact at issue (see, eg, *McRae v Commonwealth Disposals Commission* (1951) 84 CLR 377). Similarly, the cases on mutual mistake, where the parties are at cross-purposes, and unilateral mistake, where only one party is mistaken, arguably involve nothing more than contract formation in terms of offer and acceptance. Nevertheless, in *Bell v Lever Bros* the House of Lords appeared to acknowledge an independent doctrine of mistake based upon the distinction between *substance* and *quality/attributes*.[4] Subsequently, in *Associated Japanese Bank (International) Ltd v Credit du Nord SA* [1989] 1 WLR 255 and *Great Peace Shipping Ltd v Tsavliris Salvage (International) Ltd* [2002] EWCA Civ 1407, [2003] QB 679, it was held that the question of whether the contract allocated the risks to either party should be considered first and separately from mistake, thereby acknowledging the existence of independent rules of mistake.

[1] Explains why the law considers that the notion of mistake must be confined narrowly.

[2] State the general rule.

[3] Outline the principal theories underlying the decisions concerning mistake.

[4] Your answer must analyse this important case, and compare and contrast this and later decisions on mistake.

In *Bell v Lever Bros* Bell had been compensated by Lever Bros for the premature termination of his contract of service, both parties assuming the contract to be valid when, in fact, Bell could have been dismissed summarily without compensation because of previous breaches of duty. Lever Bros sought recovery of the money. In terms of quality, both parties thought that Bell was 'worth' £30,000 whereas he was worth nothing. The House of Lords held the contract to be valid and binding as the substance of the contract was a compensation agreement which remained unchanged by the mistake. Lord Atkin appeared to accept the possibility of a contract being declared void for mistake of quality if the contract was 'essentially different' from that which the parties agreed upon. However, as the mistake in *Bell* could not have been much worse (ie payment for no reason), some commentators argue that a contract will only be void for common mistake when the contract has no subject matter, supporting the contention in the question that quality will never be a ground of relief.[5] This may be an overly narrow interpretation of Lord Atkin's approach, but it raises the question of how the test of 'essentially different' applies to mistakes of quality. Indeed, in *Swynson Ltd v Lowick Rose LLP (In Liquidation) (formerly Hurst Morrison Thomson LLP)* [2017] **UKSC 32** Lord Sumption refused to be drawn into this 'controversy'.

It seems difficult to prove a thing could be so deficient in quality that it becomes a different thing. In *Solle v Butcher* [1950] **1 KB 671**, a mistake as to whether a lease agreement was subject to the **Rent Restriction Acts** was not insufficient to invalidate the contract at common law. The same result was reached in *Leaf v International Galleries* [1950] **2 KB 86** where the parties contracted to sell a painting which both erroneously believed to be painted by Constable. It follows that *defects* in the subject matter of the contract, no matter how serious, are rarely a ground of relief and that the threshold of operative common mistake for quality can rarely be reached (compare *Pitt v Holt* [2013] **UKSC 26**).[6]

The decision in *Great Peace* also sanctions a restricted view of common mistake. The *Great Peace* (GP) was chartered for five days to offer assistance to a stricken vessel, the *Cape Providence* (CP). The exact location of the GP was never discussed but cancellation of the contract required payment of the minimum hire charge. When the defendant was informed that the GP would take 39 hours to reach the CP, they chartered another closer vessel and cancelled the contract with the claimants, refusing to pay the cancellation charge. The defendant argued that the contract had been entered into on the basis of a common, fundamental, mistaken belief that the GP was 'in close proximity' to the CP and that the contract was either void at common law or voidable in equity. The Court of Appeal found for the claimant. First, the GP could still perform its standby function for part of the

[5] Remember to retain the focus of your argument. It is clear that it is not necessarily enough that the contract would not have been entered into if the true facts had been known: see *Triple Seven MSN 27251 Ltd v Azman Air Services Ltd* [2018] EWHC 1348 (Comm).

[6] Here your case analysis contributes to your overall argument.

five-day charter period (ie this was not a total failure of consideration). Secondly, no term could be implied that the GP should be closer to the CP as this would contradict the pre-contract negotiations where the precise location of the GP had not been mentioned—the defendants must bear the risk of their fault. Finally, the requirements of the common law doctrine of common mistake had not been met. The Court of Appeal made several observations to clarify the law relating to common mistake. If no express or implied risk allocation is evident in the contract, the test was whether the mistake was of sufficient magnitude to render performance of the contract *impossible*, and therefore void.[7] This strict test follows the narrow view of mistake from ***Bell v Lever Bros*** and appears to almost rule out a mistake of quality. A court could not draw on its equitable jurisdiction to declare the contract voidable (eg for a fundamental mistake of quality—see ***Solle v Butcher***) as this would be inconsistent with ***Bell v Lever Bros***.

[7] Address the question: should a mistake as to quality be sufficient to render a contract void?

The restrictive approach to mistake is also present in mutual mistake[8] where the parties must be at such fundamental cross-purposes that it is impossible to construe an agreement between them. If they are crossed on the question of quality alone this will not render the contract void, allowing one party to profit at the expense of the other, as in ***Scott v Littledale*** (1858) 8 E & B 815. Similarly, in unilateral mistake where only one party is mistaken as to quality and the other party knows it, the contract is still binding on the basis of *caveat emptor*.[9] In unilateral mistakes of identity, the House of Lords in ***Shogun Finance Ltd v Hudson*** [2003] UKHL 62, reinterpreted the issue as being a matter of offer and acceptance, relieving courts from attempting to distinguish identity and attributes.

[8] Address mutual mistake.

[9] Address unilateral mistake.

In conclusion, one might argue that a mistake as to quality which goes to the root of the undertaking should render a contract void. If, for example, where parties agree to buy and sell a painting which they both mistakenly believe to be painted by Picasso,[10] the identity of the artist arguably lies at the root of the contract; it would be unreasonable to argue that the subject matter of the contract is 'a painting' with the artist's identity merely an attribute relating to the painting's value rather than its substance. However, one might equally argue that, without express or implied terms of the contract indicating that the painting is by Picasso, the parties have agreed merely to buy and sell 'a painting'. While the ***Great Peace*** decision recognized an independent doctrine of mistake, this was not based on the distinction between substance and quality but, instead, upon whether performance became 'impossible'. If both parties mistakenly believe a painting to be painted by Picasso, performance of the contract is not impossible as the painting exists and it is the correct subject matter of the contract: the impossibility test in ***Great Peace*** would result in the contract being binding.

[10] The use of analogy here illustrates and reinforces your argument.

The distinction between substance and quality is criticizable as being elusive but provides a basis for distinguishing acceptable from unacceptable contractual risks. While the *Great Peace* approach avoids the terminology of substance and quality, arguably it introduces debates concerned with 'impossibility'. Regrettably, the difficulty which the terminology attempts to resolve remains as intractable as ever.

LOOKING FOR EXTRA MARKS?

■ Examples could illustrate the substance/quality divide in unilateral mistake: if S sells a painting to B knowing that it is not a Constable yet knowing that B thinks it is a Constable, the contract is valid where S has not misled B. B's mistake relates to quality or his motive for entering into the contract. If B is mistaken as to the *promise itself* and S knows it, S cannot take advantage of B, the contract being void. If S intends to sell a painting but B thinks S intends to sell a Constable and S knows of B's mistake, the contract is void, B being in error on the nature of S's promise (see also *Hartog v Colin and Shields* **[1939] 3 All ER 566**).

QUESTION | 4

Pike buys and sells paintings and antiques. He sees that Shark, an art dealer, has a Renoir for sale but he knows that Shark would never sell the painting to him as Pike still owes a debt to Shark from a previous contract. Pike therefore emails Shark, stating: 'Hello, I am Lord Chub. I am staying at the Grand Hotel. I should like to acquire the Renoir that you have advertised for sale as it fits into my personal collection perfectly.' Shark has to bribe the porter at the Grand Hotel in order to discover whether Lord Chub is staying there but when he discovers that Lord Chub is registered at the hotel he feels pleased to have attracted a prestigious customer. In fact, Pike is staying at the Grand Hotel in the name of Lord Chub, having stolen the latter's driving licence and chequebook.

The next day, Pike faxes Shark a copy of his driving licence as proof of identity and tells Shark that he will arrange for a courier to visit his premises with a cheque for the correct amount. Shark is agreeable to this proposal and when the courier arrives with the cheque Shark allows him to take the Renoir away. Pike displays the painting in his shop and sells it almost immediately to Rudd, a private collector, who pays in cash. Shark has now discovered that the cheque has been dishonoured and that Rudd is in possession of the Renoir.

Advise Shark, paying special attention to how the decision of the House of Lords in *Shogun Finance Ltd v Hudson* [2003] UKHL 62, [2004] 1 All ER 215 might have affected his rights.

Would your advice differ in any way if Pike had visited Shark's premises, heavily disguised, and had been allowed to take away the Renoir on handing over his cheque?

CAUTION!

■ Think: did Shark accept an 'offer' from Pike or from Lord Chub? The problem concerns unilateral mistake of identity. The contract may also be voidable if Pike made a misrepresentation; if so, consider the effect of the third party, Rudd.

■ Clearly, your answer must address **Shogun**.

■ You should also address rescission and how rescission can be communicated.

DIAGRAM ANSWER PLAN

Identify the issues
■ Identify the legal issues: unilateral mistake of identity; possible claim for fraudulent misrepresentation?
■ Two possible remedies for Shark.

Relevant law
■ Outline the relevant law in relation to establishing an operative unilateral mistake of identity;
■ Outline the requirements for a possible claim for fraudulent misrepresentation.

Apply the law
■ Is the contract between P and S void for mistake?
■ Is the contract between P and S voidable for misrepresentation?
■ Remember to address the impact of the decision in **Shogun**.

Conclude
■ Possible remedies for Shark? If S establishes unilateral mistake of identity, contract void. If S establishes fraudulent misrepresentation, possibility to rescind contract;
■ Conclusion.

SUGGESTED ANSWER

[1] Clearly identifies the approach of your answer.

Shark (S) can explore two possible remedies.[1] First, he can try to establish an operative unilateral mistake of identity which would render the contract with Pike (P) void. If successful, no title in the painting would transfer to P and, consequently, *prima facie* no title would pass to Rudd (R), who would potentially be liable in conversion to S. Secondly, P is almost certainly guilty of fraudulent misrepresentation which would render his contract with S voidable at the latter's option.

S could rescind the contract with P and, if communicated in time, the rescission would mean that no title could transfer to R. There are obvious difficulties here as to which of two innocent parties—the owner or the bona fide third party—should suffer for the act of a swindler who probably cannot be traced.

² Briefly state the old law and analyse to see how it would have applied to the facts of the problem.

Traditionally, to establish an operative mistake of identity, S had to show that: (a) he intended to deal with Lord Chub; (b) P was aware of this intention; (c) P's identity was crucial in the circumstances; and (d) S took reasonable steps to verify P's identity.² On one view the first requirement is easy to prove here, and (b) is self-evident as the facts demonstrate P's fraudulent mind, while requirement (d) might be established by proof of the porter's bribe (an analogy could be drawn with *Ingram v Little* [1961] 1 QB 31, where the plaintiffs' quick check of the telephone directory was treated as a reasonable method for verifying the fact that the reputable third party lived at the address provided by the swindler). However, establishing (c) (and the relationship with (a)) under the old law was difficult.

Under the old law, S had to establish that he intended to contract with Lord Chub and P's identity was crucial in the circumstances. Objective appearances were crucial. For example, in *Phillips v Brooks Ltd* [1919] 2 KB 243, a swindler named North entered the plaintiff's shop and wrote a cheque saying that he was Sir George Bullough with an address in St James's Square which the plaintiff verified by consulting a directory. North took away a ring which he pledged with the bona fide defendant. The contract was held not void for mistake as the plaintiff intended to deal with the person in front of him; however, the contract was voidable for misrepresentation but had not been avoided, so the defendant acquired a good title. The decision was seemingly ignored in *Ingram v Little*, but reaffirmed in *Lewis v Averay* [1972] 1 QB 198, where a swindler posed as the actor Richard Greene and showed an admission pass to Pinewood Studios bearing a photograph of the swindler. It was held that the plaintiff intended to contract with the person in front of him, especially as the negotiations had been conducted face-to-face. The plaintiff's mistake was only one of attributes rather than identity, so the defendant acquired a good title as the initial contract was voidable for fraud but had not been avoided by the plaintiff. These facts appear very similar to those in the problem except that here Shark (S) never meets Pike (P) in person. Older case law seemed inclined to declare a contract void for mistake where the parties dealt with each other at a distance (eg *Cundy v Lindsay* (1878) 3 App Cas 459 and *Boulton v Jones* (1857) 2 H & N 564) but S would still have to prove a fundamental difference between the person he dealt with and the person he intended to deal with: his mistake had to be of *substance* rather than *attributes*. So, under the old law, S could argue that if he had known P was an unpaid debtor he would not have dealt with him (ie the contract is void) but a court might conclude that this was simply a mistake of P's creditworthiness (ie the contract might be voidable for fraud but not void for mistake).

How does the House of Lords' decision in *Shogun* affect this analysis?[3] Here the parties never dealt with each other face-to-face, or signed a written contract. On this basis Lord Hobhouse's approach in *Shogun*, which relied on the application of the parol evidence rule to a written contract, is arguably irrelevant. The remaining Law Lords divided

[4] Makes clear that the law is uncertain.

equally on the correct approach.[4] Lords Millett and Nicholls (dissenting) advocated a *dealing test* which, in essence, sets up an irrebuttable presumption that the seller (S) intends to deal with the person with whom he physically corresponds (P), or who physically signs the contract. So, for contracts involving face-to-face dealings, that you intend to deal with the person standing in front of you. If correct, the contract between S and P would not be declared void, allowing P to pass good title to R provided S had not rescinded in the meantime. Conversely, Lords Phillips and Walker employed an *intent test*, which presupposed that A intended to direct his offer (or acceptance) to the named individual as stated in the contract or as stated in the written correspondence (ie Lord Chub). On this basis, as P pretended to be Lord Chub when emailing S with his offer (and faxed a copy of Lord Chub's driving licence), it is clearly arguable that no exchange of offer and acceptance took place between S and P: P then cannot pass good title to R.

[5] Conclusions such as this may be more appropriate to an essay, but are helpful here to indicate how the law might apply on these facts.

That there was no clear majority in *Shogun* regarding the issue of contracts being concluded *inter absentes* without any formal written instrument, makes a definitive conclusion difficult here. A future court, faced with the obvious tension between the 'dealing' and 'intent' tests, may look to the respective conduct of the two innocent parties, S and R: while R appears to have acted in good faith and would have legitimately assumed that P was the owner of the painting, S, in his dealings with P, seems to have taken too much on trust and should therefore suffer the consequences.[5]

[6] The problem is clearly one of mistake, but the facts also raise this possibility: keep mistake as the focus of your answer, and deal briefly with misrepresentation.

Assuming that the contract between P and S is not void for mistake, it will be voidable for misrepresentation.[6] P has misrepresented his identity, which constitutes a false statement of fact, and this seems to have been a key factor in inducing S to sell the painting to P. However, this does not mean S can rescind his contract with P and recover the painting from R: here, R has acquired a valid title and S has made no attempt to rescind. When addressing misrepresentation, if S had discovered the fraud before the sale to R, the possibility of rescission must be considered. The general rule is that rescission must be communicated to the other party who has the voidable title but in *Car & Universal Finance Co. Ltd v Caldwell* [1965] 1 QB 525 it was recognized that a public act (there informing the police and Automobile Association) could suffice if the swindler was deliberately evading the plaintiff. Here, S appears not to know that P perpetrated the fraud. This rule is very protective of ownership but it is of limited application. P is clearly a buyer in possession of the goods under **s. 9 of the Factors Act 1889** and **s. 25(1) of the Sale of Goods Act 1979** and the decision in *Newtons of Wembley Ltd v Williams* [1965] 1 QB 560 establishes that these statutory provisions override an attempted rescission as in *Caldwell* meaning that the third party will normally acquire title. As P sells the painting to R in his (P's) shop and R appears to be bona fide, the other requirements of the statutes would seem to be satisfied, meaning that R should acquire a valid title in the painting.

Finally, what if Pike had visited Shark's premises? Prior to the *Shogun* decision there was a strong presumption of a binding contract when formed face-to-face and it was difficult to establish a *valid reason* for contracting with some other party (ie Lord Chub) other than that he had the attributes of good reputation and creditworthiness. This would lead to the conclusion that S intended to deal with P (as in *Lewis v Averay*). The difficulty here is that P is said to be 'heavily disguised'. If this means that *his* identity is hidden, it adds nothing to this conclusion; if it means disguised so as to resemble Lord Chub, S may have a greater chance of proving that he wanted to deal only with Lord Chub.[7] It appears *Shogun* has not affected this aspect of mistake, as all of the Law Lords clearly supported the operation of the face-to-face presumption. Here, it would seem reasonable to conclude that the contract between S and P is voidable for fraudulent misrepresentation but not void for mistake of identity.

[7] Your answer addresses both possibilities.

LOOKING FOR EXTRA MARKS?

■ You could refer to the recommendations of the 1966 Law Reform Committee (Cmnd 2958) that in cases of mistaken identity the contract should be voidable so far as the acquisition of title by third parties is concerned, thereby clarifying the state of the, then, confused body of decisions.

TAKING THINGS FURTHER

■ Chandler, A. and Devenney, J., 'Mistake of Identity: Threads of Objectivity' [2004] 3(1) *Journal of Obligations and Remedies* 7.

Assesses the significance of mistaken identity in contract negotiations and considers the House of Lords ruling in **Shogun Finance Ltd v Hudson [2003] UKHL 62, [2004] 1 All ER 215**.

■ Chandler, A., Devenney, J., and Poole, J., 'Common Mistake: Theoretical Justification and Remedial Inflexibility' [2004] JBL 34.

Considers the decision in **Great Peace Shipping Ltd v Tsavliris Salvage (International) Ltd [2002] EWCA Civ 1407, [2003] QB 679**.

■ Treitel, G., 'Mistake in Contract' (1988) 104 LQR 501.

Detailed analysis of **Associated Japanese Bank (International) Ltd v Credit du Nord SA [1989] 1 WLR 255**.

Illegality and Restraint of Trade

9

ARE YOU READY?

In order to attempt the questions in this chapter you must have covered the following areas in your revision:

- The meaning and classification of illegality in contract law, including contracts contrary to law and contracts contrary to public policy;
- Illegality in the formation of contract and illegality in the performance of contract;
- The effects of illegality, including on the recovery of property and money;
- The doctrine of restraint of trade, the meaning of a protectable interest, and the reasonableness of a restraint clause in the interests of the parties and the public interest;
- Severance.

KEY DEBATES

Debate: when faced with illegality to what extent should the courts grant relief to ensure justice?

Should the approach be based upon a strict approach to the principle, expressed in the words of Lord Mansfield, that 'No court will lend its aid to a man who founds his cause of action upon an immoral or an illegal act', even if the effect leads to unfair consequences? Or should the courts adopt a more discretionary approach to the effect of illegality? This was recently considered by the Supreme Court in *Patel v Mirza* [2016] UKSC 42.

Debate: many contracts will, to some extent, restrain future activity but, it seems, not all such restraints will be subject to the restraint of trade doctrine.

When will the doctrine of restraint of trade apply?

In the Law of England and Wales only the innocent have rights under an illegal contract.
Discuss.

CAUTION!

- Avoid simply summarizing the law. Marks will be earned for a coherent structure, evaluation, and analysis of existing precedent and, in particular, an ability to concentrate on those aspects of illegality relevant to the question.

- Your answer should focus on three issues. First, in dealing with a contract illegal at its inception, when will the innocence of either party be relevant to the determination of their rights under that contract? Secondly, is there a difference if the contract is only illegal as performed? Thirdly, in which circumstances, if any, will a guilty party possess rights under an illegal contract? Remember that this area has undergone a landmark change in *Patel v Mirza* **[2016] UKSC 42**.

DIAGRAM ANSWER PLAN

Outline the courts' traditional approach to illegal contracts. Has this been affected by *Patel v Mirza* [2016] UKSC 42?

⬇

What is the difference between a contract *ex facie* unlawful and one that is only illegal as performed?

⬇

When can a party reclaim property transferred under an illegal contract?

⬇

In what circumstances will innocence entitle one party to enforce the contract (or reclaim money or property transferred under the contract)?

⬇

In what circumstances will a 'guilty' party retain the right to enforce the contract (or reclaim money or property transferred under the contract)?

⬇

Uncertainty in case law.

⬇

Remedies available to innocent parties but also to parties where some guilt attaches but the law has been unclear when remedies are available.

[1] The traditional approach of the courts to illegality is succinctly explained.

[2] There were exceptions to the traditional approach and the answer will explore these traditional exceptions. See also *Henderson v Dorset Healthcare University NHS Foundation Trust* [2020] UKSC 43.

The traditional approach of the courts to illegal contracts could be broadly summarized by the maxim *ex turpi causa non oritur actio* (no right of action arises from a disgusting cause).[1] Thus neither party would acquire enforceable rights under an illegal contract; nor, generally, would they be entitled to sue for the return of any money or property transferred. Various justifications were advanced for such an approach (indeed in *Patel v Mirza* [2016] **UKSC 42** Lord Toulson identified at least six justifications), including the deterrence of wrongdoing and protecting the integrity of the civil justice system. Yet sometimes such an approach might be viewed as disproportionate. Moreover these, and other, policy considerations sometimes pointed in different directions and so the *ex turpi* rule is subject to exceptions.[2] Unfortunately the application of the rules which developed in this area was not always straightforward or predictable due, in large part, to the unarticulated judicial balancing of competing policy aims. Indeed, the transparent balancing of competing policy aims was something which was encouraged by the Law Commission (see, for example, the Law Commission, *The Illegality Defence* ((2010) Law Com No. 320) at 1.11). Subsequently, in four Supreme Court cases—*Allen v Hounga* [2014] **UKSC 47**, *Les Laboratoires Servier v Apotex Inc* [2014] **UKSC 55**, *Bilta (UK) Ltd (in Liquidation) v Nazir* [2015] **UKSC 23**, and *Patel v Mirza* [2016] **UKSC 42**—there was disagreement between the Justices as to the future approach to the illegality defence. Some essentially argued for a retention of a rule-based approach to the illegality defence whereas others argued for a more flexible, underlying policy approach where all relevant policy aims and considerations are balanced. Ultimately in *Patel v Mirza* [2016] **UKSC 42** the latter, more flexible approach was selected. Some will argue that this brings more uncertainty to the law. Yet, arguably, it more accurately and transparently reflects the reality of what the courts were already doing (and, as such, may not radically alter the outcome of cases—compare *Gujra v Roath* [2018] **EWHC 854**). Thus, in *Okedina v Chilake* [2019] **IRLR 905** at [62], Underhill LJ stated that not all previous case law will need to be re-examined in the light of *Patel v Mirza*.

Contracts Illegal at Inception

[3] Such a rule sometimes conflicts with a competing policy aim, the desire to avoid unjust enrichment.

In keeping with the traditional approach just outlined, traditionally an agreement to do something which was expressly or impliedly prohibited by the law was unenforceable and property or money transferred under the contract could not be recovered:[3] *in pari delicto potior est conditio defendentis* (where both parties are equally at fault the position of the possessor is better). In such circumstances, generally neither party could assert that they had no intention of breaking the law, nor would any allowance be made for either party's ignorance of the law.

⁴Restitution may have been allowed in certain circumstances; it is important to explain the circumstances clearly.

Nevertheless, the courts would sometimes, for example, permit the recovery of property or money transferred under the contract where the *comparative innocence* of one party was established.⁴ Thus, if the parties were not *in pari delicto*, a court may have allowed the less blameworthy to recover money or property transferred under the contract. Precedent suggested that this might have been the case where there was some evidence of oppression or misrepresentation by the defendant, or the statute which prohibits the contract was aimed at protecting one of the parties. For example, in **Hughes v Liverpool Victoria Legal Friendly Society [1916] 2 KB 482** the plaintiff was allowed to recover premiums paid under an illegal life insurance policy as he was induced to enter into the contract by the defendant's fraudulent misrepresentation that the policy was valid. However, a claimant's innocence may have been insufficient without evidence that the defendant acted in some unconscionable manner. Thus, in **Edler v Auerbach [1950] 1 KB 359** the plaintiff lessee could not recover premiums, paid under an illegal lease, from the defendant lessor as there was no evidence that the latter had been fraudulent. Regarding class-protecting statutes, in **Kiriri Cotton Co. Ltd v Dewani [1960] AC 192** the landlord charged the tenant an illegal premium which the tenant then sought to recover. It was held that as the relevant statute placed the obligation firmly on the landlord, the tenant could recover the rent on the grounds that he was not *in pari delicto*.

⁵The paragraph uses PEA, by identifying a point, explaining relevant case law, and undertaking some analysis.

One further example of 'comparative innocence' was provided by the principle of repentance.⁵ Specifically, the recovery of property and money would be permitted if the claimant repents by discontinuing his illegal activities before the contract has been substantially performed (see **Kearley v Thomson (1890) 24 QBD 742**). Some cases suggested that the repentance must have been voluntary, the defendant thereby demonstrating that he has seen 'the error of his ways' (although compare *Patel v Mirza* [2014] EWCA Civ 1947). For example, in **Bigos v**

⁶If you decide to explain the facts of a case, you must do so concisely.

Bousted [1951] 1 All ER 92⁶ the plaintiff agreed to purchase Italian lire from the defendant, paying in sterling, which contravened existing exchange-control regulations. When the lire were not delivered, the plaintiff claimed back his money, arguing that he had repented. The claim failed as there was no evidence that the claimant would have withdrawn from the contract if the defendant had supplied the lire.

As noted earlier, in **Patel v Mirza [2016] UKSC 42** the Supreme Court adopted a more flexible, underlying policy approach to the illegality doctrine. Moreover, in that case the Supreme Court reversed the traditional general rule that money paid or property transferred under a legal contract could not be recovered with Lord Toulson stating that a claimant 'who satisfies the ordinary requirements of a claim for unjust enrichment, should not be debarred from enforcing his claim by reason *only* of the fact that the money which he seeks to recover was paid for an unlawful purpose' ([**121**] emphasis added). Presumably issues of comparative innocence and the like are not irrelevant to the underlying policy approach to the illegality doctrine.

Contracts Illegal as Performed

In this area, traditionally, an innocent party *might* have been able to exercise all of the normal contractual/restitutionary remedies available, for example recovery of property and/or damages for breach of contract (see *Marles v Philip Trant & Sons Ltd* [**1954**] **1 QB 29**). By contrast the plaintiff's claim in *Ashmore, Benson, Pease & Co. Ltd v AV Dawson Ltd* [**1973**] **1 WLR 828** failed. In that case the contract involved the transportation of a load in excess of the legal limit for the lorries used and the court held that the plaintiff had participated in the illegal performance of the contract. The argument by the *plaintiff*'s transport manager, who had actually supervised the loading of the lorries, that he had not noticed the error, was rejected by the court. Thus if the claimant's 'innocence' was compromised then he/she may have forfeited his/her rights, for example perhaps the innocent party ought to have recognized that the contract could only be performed in an illegal manner, though this seems less important if the statute is there to protect him/her in the first place (see *Shaw v Groom* [**1970**] **2 QB 504**). A similar approach was also applied, in a different context, to a collateral contract which stipulated that the defendant would obtain the required statutory licence before commencing work. The defendant failed to do so. Nevertheless, the 'innocence' of the plaintiff persuaded the court to afford him an independent cause of action based on the collateral contract (see *Strongman (1945) Ltd v Sincock* [**1955**] **2 QB 525**).[7]

[7] While the main contract was illegal, ie to do building work without a licence, the claimant's remedy was based on an alternative ground, a collateral contract.

Some of the fine distinctions previously drawn in this area was one of the drivers for the Supreme Court to move to a more flexible, underlying policy approach in *Patel v Mirza* [**2016**] **UKSC 42** and this, arguably, is a more honest approach to the case law in this area (see also *Robinson v HRH Al Qasimi* [**2021**] **EWCA Civ 862**).

So, we have seen that innocent parties may possess remedies under an illegal contract but what about a non-innocent or 'guilty' party?

Rights of a Guilty Party

The general traditional rule that no rights emerge from a contract illegal at inception has often been successfully utilized by the defendant as a defence against a claimant who seeks enforcement, damages, or recovery of property (see *Re Mahmoud and Ispahani* [**1921**] **2 KB 716**). For example, in *Pearce v Brooks* (**1866**) **LR 1 Ex 213**, although the prostitute used the carriage, she could successfully rely on the illegality of the contract when the plaintiff sued for the hire charge.

On the other hand, under traditional principles a guilty party could seek recovery of property under an illegal contract provided disclosure of the illegality is not essential to his/her cause of action. For example, in *Amar Singh v Kulubya* **[1964] AC 142** the plaintiff was the owner of land leased unlawfully to the defendant. It was held that he could recover his land on the basis of his untainted, independent title of freehold ownership. However, if the illegality was apparent from the evidence brought before the court, it was questionable whether the guilty party would be entitled to recover his property (see *Snell v Unity Finance Co. Ltd* **[1964] 2 QB 203**), although in *Tinsley v Milligan*, the House of Lords allowed the defendant's counterclaim on the ground that evidence of illegality only emerged in cross-examination rather than in her original pleadings (and a presumption of a resulting trust arose).

However, as evidenced by these four recent Supreme Court decisions in this area, there followed a period of uncertainty on the overall approach that a court would adopt in this context. There had been a growing body of case law suggesting, for example, that where a party is only guilty of a minor breach of law in performing the contract, a court may look more sympathetically on any attempt to enforce an existing contract. Initially, this approach was founded on whether enforcement of a contract would be an affront to public conscience but this was decisively rejected by the House of Lords in *Tinsley v Milligan* on the grounds that it would introduce a form of unbridled judicial discretion contrary to 200 years of precedent.[8] However, the absence of any discretion simply begs the question: why should a minor technical offence deprive one party of any contractual rights whilst preserving those rights for the other party? Surely the resultant windfall for the innocent party borders on a form of unjust enrichment?[9] Consequently, in *Les Laboratoires Servier v Apotex Inc.* **[2012] EWCA Civ 593** and **[2014] UKSC 55**, Etherton LJ called for a 'just and proportionate response to the illegality' by which a trivial or inadvertent breach of the law might not deprive the 'guilty' party of all of the normal rights under an existing contract. However, the majority in the Supreme Court, led by Lord Sumption, rejected this approach, favouring the approach in *Tinsley*. In an earlier Supreme Court case, *Hounga v Allen* **[2014] UKSC 47,** Lord Wilson said that the approach to adopt was to ask, 'What is the aspect of public policy which founds the defence?' and, then, to ask 'But is there another aspect of public policy to which application of the defence would run counter?' Lord Hughes, while not going as far as this, explained that the approach to illegality had to be case-sensitive and to consider the gravity of the illegality of which the claimant is guilty, the claimant's knowledge or intention in relation to the illegality, the purpose of the law infringed, and the extent to which to allow a civil claim nevertheless to proceed would be inconsistent with that purpose and other factors which may arise in individual cases. In *Jetivia SA v Bilta (UK) Ltd* **[2015] UKSC 23**, there was disagreement once more with Lord Sumption maintaining his previously stated

[8] The need for certainty and the view of some that this is achieved by a rules-based approach to illegality is discussed.

[9] The counter-policy to certainty is the need for justice.

[10] Should there be divergent judicial views, explanations of such views are essential to a comprehensive answer.

position, but with Lords Toulson and Hodge approving of the approach of Etherton LJ in *Les Laboratoires* and relying on the judgment of Lord Wilson in *Hounga v Allen*.[10]

Ultimately in *Patel v Mirza* [2016] UKSC 42 the law was settled in favour of the more flexible, underlying policy approach. In so doing *Tinsley v Milligan* was overruled. Moreover, in that case the Supreme Court reversed the traditional general rule that money paid or property transferred under a legal contract could not be recovered with Lord Toulson stating that a claimant 'who satisfies the ordinary requirements of a claim for unjust enrichment, should not be debarred from enforcing his claim by reason *only* of the fact that the money which he seeks to recover was paid for an unlawful purpose' ([121] emphasis added). Subsequently in *Stoffel & Co v Grondona* **[2020] UKSC 42 at [43]** Lord Lloyd-Jones (with whom Lord Reed, Lord Hodge, Lady Black and Lady Arden agreed) stated that the issue of reliance is not totally irrelevant and may have an impact on the centrality of the illegality.

As has been seen, where illegality is involved, the law provides some remedies to innocent parties but also to parties where some guilt attaches. The difficulty has been that the law was unclear as to the circumstances in which the law will give a remedy. This reflected a conflict in underlying policies—the need for certainty as against the desire to do justice between the parties. *Patel v Mirza* **[2016] UKSC 42** arguably paves the way for a much more transparent balancing of competing policy aims.

LOOKING FOR EXTRA MARKS?

- While a clear statement of the rules in this area is needed, looking at the policies underpinning the rules will demonstrate a deeper understanding of this area of law.

- Pointing to inconsistencies in the case law and disagreements amongst the judges will impress an examiner. See, particularly, the differing views expressed in four recent Supreme Court cases: *Hounga v Allen* [2014] UKSC 47; *Les Laboratoires Servier v Apotex Inc*. [2014] UKSC 55; *Jetivia SA v Bilta (UK) Ltd* [2015] UKSC 23; and *Patel v Mirza* [2016] UKSC 42. How will the approach in *Patel v Mirza* [2016] UKSC 42 develop over time?

QUESTION | 2

Sam is employed as Deputy Accountant by Albright Ltd, a firm of financial analysts located in Cardiff, Wales. Most of Sam's work involves sitting in front of a computer predicting the future profit expectations of Albright's clients located in Wales. His work has always greatly impressed these clients. Recently, Sam resigned from his job and joined a similar firm located in Swansea.

A number of Albright's clients heard about this move and transferred their allegiance to the Swansea firm. Albright Ltd has now written to Sam pointing out that there was a clause in his original contract which stated that on termination of employment he must not 'for a period of two years solicit custom from, or deal with, any Albright client with whom the employee has had contact in the year prior to termination of the contract, or join any firm of financial analysts located in Wales'.

Discuss.

CAUTION!

- The basic issue in this question will be resolved by posing the following questions: Does Albright Ltd have a legitimate protectable interest? Is the clause unduly wide in protecting that interest? Can any offending portions be severed whilst allowing the remainder to remain enforceable? The law has a clear structure in this area, follow it closely.

DIAGRAM ANSWER PLAN

Identify the issues	■ Outline doctrine of restraint of trade. ■ Doctrine applies in contracts between employers and employees.
Relevant law	■ Restraint clauses void unless shown to be reasonable. 'Reasonableness' depends upon whether an employer establishes that it has a legitimate interest to protect and that the clause is reasonable in protection of those interests. ■ Severance of clause.
Apply the law	■ What interests is Albright Ltd attempting to protect? ■ Is the clause used by Albright Ltd unreasonably wide, in terms of Sam's existing duties and his degree of influence over Albright Ltd's clients? ■ Is the clause used by Albright Ltd unreasonably wide, in terms of Albright Ltd's geographical area of influence and the commercial duration of any 'trade secrets'? ■ What scope is there to sever the offending parts of the clauses?
Conclude	■ Restraint clause may be void, even though Albright Ltd may have a legitimate interest to protect, as the clause appears to go beyond mere protection of the interest.

SUGGESTED ANSWER

The question concerns the doctrine of restraint of trade. For present purposes a contract or contract term in restraint of trade is one which seeks to restrict a person's future freedom to carry on their trade, business, or profession as that person may choose. The doctrine states that such a clause is prima facie void and will be unenforceable unless reasonable as between the parties and reasonable in the public interest: ***Nordenfelt v Maxim Nordenfelt Guns and Ammunition Co.* [1894] AC 535.**[1] The doctrine of restraint of trade may not apply to all contracts that seek to restrain in this manner (see ***Peninsula Securities Ltd v Dunnes Stores (Bangor) Ltd* [2020] UKSC 36** and ***Quantum Actuarial LLP v Quantum Advisory Ltd* [2021] EWCA Civ 227**) but it has been established that the doctrine does apply to covenants in restraint of trade in contracts of employment: ***Herbert Morris v Saxelby* [1916] 1 AC 688**.

As Sam had a contract of employment with Albright Ltd the doctrine of restraint of trade applies and the simple issue is whether the restraint clause in that contract is enforceable by Albright Ltd. The presumption with all such restraint clauses is that they are void unless shown to be reasonable. 'Reasonableness' depends, in the first instance, upon whether Albright Ltd can establish that it has a legitimate interest to protect and that the clause is not drafted in unreasonably wide terms for the protection of those interests.[2]

An employer may not merely protect against competition from a former employee. The employer may only restrain an employee in circumstances where there is a legitimate interest to protect. The law recognizes trade secrets and trade connection (ie customers) as legitimate interests: ***Herbert Morris v Saxelby*.**[3] In order to establish a trade connection the employee must have influence over the customers (***Fitch v Dewes* [1921] 2 AC 158**); merely having dealings with customers is insufficient. Does Albright Ltd possess such legitimate interests?[4] This is debatable as regards the protection of trade connections because Sam seems to have little personal contact with Albright's clients. In ***Strange (SW) Ltd v Mann* [1965] 1 WLR 629** where an employee had no face-to-face dealings with customers, merely speaking on a telephone, it was held that this did not amount to a protectable interest. However, if Sam does have the opportunity to exert personal influence over the clients, or possibly if his reputation is such that clients might move their accounts when he leaves Albright Ltd, such an interest might exist. After all, Albright Ltd is attempting to prevent departing employees from poaching their existing clients: an important asset within any firm (see ***Plowman (GW) and Son Ltd v Ash* [1964] 1 WLR 568**). Moreover, Sam may have had access to a

[1] It is important to set out the basic doctrine and the key case of ***Nordenfelt*** at the outset of your answer. In ***Harcus Sinclair LLP v Your Lawyers Ltd* [2021] UKSC 32** the Supreme Court were of the opinion that the it was not necessary to import the ***Patel v Mirza*** into this related area of law.

[2] Reasonableness is introduced and then may be used to structure the next section of the answer. Note ***Harcus Sinclair LLP v Your Lawyers Ltd* [2021] UKSC 32** where the Supreme Court held that a 'legitimate interest' was not limited to contractual obligations.

[3] It is essential to identify a legitimate interest of the employer that needs to be protected; without such an interest a restraint clause will be void.

[4] The remainder of the paragraph is an example of IRAC, with a statement of the law and its application to the facts of the problem.

considerable amount of confidential information which could be used unfairly in this context and may, therefore, constitute a relevant interest (see *Roger Bullivant Ltd v Ellis* **[1987] ICR 464**). However, it is worth remembering that Albright Ltd will need to *prove* that Sam had actively solicited ex-clients to transfer their business to his new employer. In *Towry EJ Ltd v Bennett* **[2012] EWHC 224 (QB), [2012] All ER (D) 148**, clients decided to transfer their business in this way but the court refused to accept that the claimant had proven that these clients had been 'persuaded' to do so by the relevant employee. However, an anti-*dealing* clause is wider and may prevent Sam from dealing with customers who approach him.

Should a protectable interest be established, is the clause unreasonably wide in terms of the *type* of activities which it restricts? This requires consideration of what is reasonably necessary to protect the interest.[5] As Albright Ltd will want to enforce the clause it will be for it to establish the reasonableness of the restraint clause as between the parties; should the clause be reasonable then it is for Sam to show the clause to be against the public interest: *Herbert Morris v Saxelby*. Insofar as the clause prevents the solicitation of clients, this is likely to be reasonable if, for example, the two-year period accurately reflects how long it would take the employer to reinstate *influence* over the clients; and should receive a more sympathetic hearing from a court because it is limited in the scope and range of clients affected (see *Plowman (GW) & Son Ltd v Ash*). However, the clause also prevents Sam from joining a competing firm. This is much more difficult to defend. Reasonableness here will depend upon: (a) Sam's duties and his degree of influence over Albright Ltd's clients; and (b) the area and time limits imposed within the clause.

First, it may be that Sam was employed as a backroom expert with little personal contact with clients. This would suggest that the clause is unreasonable (see *Strange (SW) Ltd v Mann*) because the clause does not reflect the employee's job. However, it seems that Sam did occupy a senior position within the firm and his work impressed the clients for whom he worked. This may represent an effective substitute for personal contact as clients are often more interested in ability and results, rather than general personality traits. As these positive factors induce reliance and some degree of attachment, a properly drawn restraint might be considered reasonable (see *Marley Tile Co. Ltd v Johnson* **[1982] IRLR 75**). The actual wording of the clause imposes a blanket prohibition on working for another firm of 'financial analysts'. There is no mention in what capacity Sam would seek employment, for example as a clerk, an auditor, or an accountant. As such, the clause may appear too widely drawn insofar as it prevents Sam from diversifying into other types of employment.[6] The question notes that the clients have moved their business. It is irrelevant

[5] Having established a protectable interest, the reasonableness of the restraint clause must be tested in terms, for example, of area of operation and duration.

[6] This point relates to the scope of the clause in terms of employment area. The clause must be relevant to the interest to be protected.

here whether they would or would not wish to continue dealing with Albright Ltd in any event.

On the second point, there must be a functional correspondence between the area circumscribed by the clause (ie not to work in Wales) and the area particularly associated with the employee's place of work[7] (see *Spencer v Marchington* **[1988] IRLR 392**). The guiding principle is that the wider the geographical area of restraint, the more likely that it is unreasonable, although density of population should be taken into account. In *Mason v Provident Clothing and Supply Co. Ltd* **[1913] AC 724** an employee worked as a canvasser in Islington in London. A restraint clause prevented the employee from seeking similar employment within 25 miles of London. The clause was said to be unreasonable as it covered an area much greater than was needed to protect the interest. In Sam's position we do not know whether his clients are located throughout Wales or within a narrower area. If the clients are widely dispersed, the clause seems more reasonable, whereas if they are all situated within a few miles of Cardiff, a court might reach a different conclusion.

Regarding the time constraint,[8] this period must not be longer than the projected useful life of any trade secrets which Albright Ltd is attempting to protect (see *Faccenda Chicken v Fowler* **[1986] ICR 297**). Nor must any restraint regarding trade connections usually be longer than it would take Albright to recruit a replacement and for that employee to gain the same status and contacts as Sam possessed. Both these points are questions of fact, although current precedent suggests that one year is often a generally accepted norm for protecting trade connections.

If the clause is reasonable in the interests of the parties, it still could be held to be unreasonable in the public interest: *Wyatt v Kreglinger and Fernau* **[1933] 1 KB 793**. However, if a clause is reasonable in the interests of the parties, it is unlikely to be held to be unreasonable in the public interest.[9]

Finally, should the clause be unreasonable as between the parties could any reasonable portions of the clause be enforced? The principle of severance does not countenance the rewriting of contracts by the courts.[10] The 'blue pencil' test, as far as employee-focused restraint of trade clauses are concerned, ensures that an objectionable part of a clause can only be severed if it leaves the remainder in a grammatically correct and understandable form and does not '…generate any major change in the overall effect of all the post-employment restraints in the contract' (*Tillman v Egon Zehnder Ltd* **[2019] UKSC 32** at **[87]**). On our facts, it would be possible to delete the words 'or join any firm of financial analysts located in Wales', leaving the non-solicitation clause intact. However, it would not be possible to substitute a different length of time for the restraint, so if the existing period was unreasonable the clause would fail in its entirety. It should also be noted that at one time if a court decided that the clause was not a combination of two undertakings but, rather, an indivisible covenant, the clause would again fail completely (see **Attwood v Lamont** [1920] **3 KB 571**) but that no longer represents the law (see **Tillman v Egon Zehnder Ltd** [2019] **UKSC 32** at [83]).

In conclusion, it may be argued that the restraint of trade clause in Sam's contract is void. The key issues are whether Albright Ltd has a protectable interest and whether the clause protects that interest or goes much further than is needed. Sam's ability to influence Albright Ltd's customers seems limited although it may be argued that Sam has access to confidential information in the nature of a trade secret. The clause does appear to go further than is needed in seeking to prevent Sam from working for 'any firm of financial analysts located in Wales' in any capacity. The length of the restraint is also problematic. Severance may be possible, but if the length of time is excessive the clause will be void as severance does not allow the clause to be rewritten.

 ## LOOKING FOR EXTRA MARKS?

- A restraint of trade clause is an express term in a contract. You could mention that implied terms in employment contracts also offer protection of particular interests, for example an employee cannot use or reveal an employer's trade secrets before or after terminating employment: **Printers and Finishers v Holloway** [1965] **1 WLR 1**.
- Consider further the way in which the restraint clause is drafted, contrasting the operation of an area clause with that of a solicitation clause.

 ## TAKING THINGS FURTHER

- Buckley, R.A., 'Illegality in the Supreme Court' (2015) 131 LQR 341.
  *Reviews (before **Patel v Mirza** [2016] **UKSC 42**) **Hounga v Allen** [2014] **UKSC 47** and highlights the judicial differences of opinion as to how to resolve illegality cases; that is, is resolution based upon application of rules of law or upon a consideration of policy issues?*
- Davies, P., 'The Illegality Defence: Two Steps Forward, One Step Back' [2009] Conv 182.
  *Considers the Law Commission's **The Illegality Defence: A Consultative Report**. Davies concludes that more extensive legislative intervention is needed than the report suggested.*
- Lim, E., 'Ex Turpi Causa: reformation not revolution' (2017) 80 MLR 927.
  *Discusses the recent case of **Patel v Mirza** [2016] **UKSC 42**.*
- Smith, S., 'Reconstructing Restraint of Trade' (1995) 15 OJLS 565.
  Reviews four issues: (a) which contracts should be excluded from the ambit of the doctrine; (b) defining legitimate interests; (c) the significance in assessing procedural and substantive fairness in assessing restraints; and (d) the importance of the 'public interest' requirement.

Frustration

10

ARE YOU READY?

In order to attempt the questions in this chapter you must have covered the following areas in your revision:

- The concept of frustration and its relationship to breach of contract;
- The types of event that may frustrate a contract and the courts' reluctance to allow a party to escape a bad bargain;
- The limitations on the operation of the doctrine of frustration. Broadly a court will consider whether the contract expressly provides for the frustrating event; whether the event was foreseeable and the risk implicitly allocated by the contract; and/or whether the event was self-induced;
- The impact of frustration at common law;
- The effect of the **Law Reform (Frustrated Contracts) Act 1943**.

KEY DEBATES

Debate: a self-induced event will not frustrate a contract.

Case law has established that if an alleged frustrating event was brought about by the actions of a contracting party, the contract generally will not be frustrated. However, the limits of self-induced frustration are not clear.

Debate: the consequences of frustration under the Law Reform (Frustrated Contracts) Act 1943.

It is argued that the **Law Reform (Frustrated Contracts) Act 1943** concerns the prevention of unjust enrichment but should the purpose of the law be to apportion loss instead?

IMC own a piece of land in Dorset, 80 square miles in area, with planning permission to mine for tungsten ore. IMC agree to lease this land to Dig Deeper Ltd (DD Ltd) which will extract the tungsten ore. The contract provides that DD Ltd will supply all relevant plant, machinery, and technology for the extraction of the tungsten ore and that the lease rental will become payable when the first tonne of tungsten has been extracted from the land.

A year later, when the site has been developed and mining operations are due to commence, local pressure groups force a public inquiry. As a result of the inquiry, planning permission for mining operations is restricted to an area of 20 square miles. DD Ltd claims that the contract has been frustrated.

Advise the parties.

CAUTION!

Problem questions involving frustration can be answered by adopting the following structure:

- Has there been a subsequent radical change in circumstances?
- Are there any rules of law preventing the contract from being frustrated?
- If frustrated, what are the effects?
- Remember, you are presenting arguments and explaining the outcomes for the parties. Do not arrive at definite conclusions, for example, that there was never a radical change in the first place, unless this is unavoidable as this will then curtail further discussion of the issues raised by the question.

DIAGRAM ANSWER PLAN

Identify the issues	■ Is the restriction on mining a potentially radical change in circumstances (eg was the common object to lease the land or extract the ore)? ■ What rules might prevent the frustration of the contract? ■ The effects of frustration.
Relevant law	■ Object of contract: see *Krell v Henry, Herne Bay Steamboat Co. v Hutton* and *Canary Wharf (BP4) T1 Ltd v European Medicines Agency*; ■ Allocation of risk—event foreseeable? *Amalgamated Investment and Property Co. Ltd v John Walker & Sons Ltd, Ocean Tramp Tankers Corp. v VO Sovfracht, The Eugenia* and *Canary Wharf (BP4) T1 Ltd v European Medicines Agency*; ■ Lease capable of frustration: *National Carriers Ltd v Panalpina (Northern) Ltd*.
Apply the law	■ Object to mine for tungsten ore, possible radical change in circumstances—possible frustration; ■ No clear allocation of risk and arguably no inference to be drawn from foreseeability; ■ Discharge from future obligations. **Law Reform (Frustrated Contracts) Act 1943, s. 1(2)** no application, possible valuable benefit under **s. 1(3)**.
Conclude	■ Possible frustration. Parties' future obligations end but any benefit conferred to be recompensed under **Law Reform (Frustrated Contracts) Act 1943, s. 1(3)** unless 'benefit' of no value.

SUGGESTED ANSWER

[1] The opening sentence identifies the general area of law to be discussed.

This question concerns the possible discharge of contract, and particularly the operation of the doctrine of frustration.[1]

Is the Event Capable of Frustrating the Contract?

[2] A statement of what constitutes frustration with authority is given in the first paragraph.

The doctrine of frustration potentially applies when, after conclusion but before complete performance of a contract, a change of circumstances renders a contract physically or legally impossible to perform or the changed circumstances transform the expected contract performance into something which is radically different from that which the parties intended when they entered into the contract;[2]

see *Davis Contractors Ltd v Fareham Urban District Council* **[1956] AC 696**. On the present facts the mining of tungsten ore is still physically possible, albeit restricted to only 20 square miles. The same considerations apply to legal possibility. Two questions arise in this context: first, what was the object of the contract and, secondly, in the light of this object, has the contract become commercially sterile?[3]

How clear is the object of the contract?[4] For example, it might be: (a) to lease land; or (b) to lease land for the purpose of mining tungsten ore; or (c) to mine the land for tungsten ore. This is particularly important, for if object (a) is correct, frustration would be difficult to argue as the actual lease would remain unaffected by the changed circumstances. Although some further problems concerning leases will be considered later, it would seem appropriate to state that claim (a) is the least likely to succeed as the object of the contract. First, IMC are not just leasing land and washing their hands of it; rather, IMC's future profits are linked inextricably with DD Ltd's effective use of the land. Secondly, the pre-contractual negotiations between IMC and DD Ltd must have focused on DD Ltd's intended use of the land. One can hardly imagine IMC advertising the availability of a lease without a clear and specific reference to the presence of tungsten deposits. Clear parallels could be drawn with *Krell v Henry* **[1903] 2 KB 740** where the initial advertisement stated the intended use to which the room and balcony would be put, that use eventually constituting the object of the contract. As Marcus Smith J stated in *Canary Wharf (BP4) T1 Ltd v European Medicines Agency* **[2019] EWHC 335 (Ch) at [37]**: 'What the parties were buying and selling [in *Krell*] was, quite literally, a room with a view.'

If claim (b) or (c) is correct, the next question is whether the planning limitations constitute a sufficiently radical change in circumstances to warrant a finding of frustration.

On a purely mathematical basis, the 75 per cent restriction in the mining area appears fundamental.[5] But what if the tungsten ore is primarily located in the specified area? If so, the public inquiry has made little difference to the expectations of the parties. Note that an event that reduces profitability (or makes a contract loss-making), increases logistical hardship, or simply causes inconvenience, is not per se sufficient to frustrate the contract (see *Tsakiroglou & Co. Ltd v Noblee Thorl GmbH* **[1962] AC 93**, involving a carriage of goods by sea contract that was rendered unprofitable by the closure of the Suez Canal). Conversely, if the tungsten ore is distributed evenly across the whole 80 square miles and the initial site development costs remain the same, it is more arguable that there has been a radical change in circumstances. *Herne Bay Steamboat Co. v Hutton* **[1903] 2 KB 683** might be relevant. There a plea of frustration failed, as the

[3] The first issue, of whether the contract is frustrated, is identified.

[4] Once the object of the contract is established, this allows consideration of whether the event makes the performance of the contract something radically different.

[5] The paragraph illustrates the use of IRAC, containing an explanation of the law, application of the law, and an appropriate conclusion.

defendant could attain one of the two primary objectives from performance of the contract. However, on the present facts, a 75 per cent reduction appears rather more drastic.

Will Any Rule of Law Render Frustration Inoperative?

6 This part of the answer considers whether the operation of the doctrine of frustration is limited by (a) the event potentially being foreseeable and (b) the contract being one for a mining lease.

There are two important questions here:[6] (a) was the decision of the public inquiry foreseen by either party and/or did either party take the risk of such an event occurring; and (b) can a mining lease be frustrated?

Generally, where land is intended to be redeveloped it is the buyer who is assumed to take the risk that planning permission will be refused unless the contract states otherwise. For example, in *Amalgamated Investment and Property Co. Ltd v John Walker & Sons Ltd* **[1956] 3 All ER 509**, the buyer purchased a warehouse for business redevelopment purposes. The building was worth over £1.7 million with planning permission, without which it was worth only £200,000. Subsequent to the sale, the warehouse was legally designated as a building of historic importance, making the intended redevelopment all but impossible. The court concluded that in such circumstances the buyer was taken to have accepted the risk of such an event. But the present facts are slightly different. When IMC and DD Ltd entered into the contract, planning permission had already been successfully obtained. In these circumstances it might be difficult to place the risk on DD Ltd unless, for example, it was clear at the time of contracting that local pressure was mounting for a public inquiry. Equally, in a more environmentally friendly society it might indeed be reasonably foreseeable that large-scale projects might attract unfavourable media comment but unless the contract specifically allocates this risk to one or other of the parties, there is arguably nothing to prevent a court from discharging them. For example, in *Ocean Tramp Tankers Corp. v VO Sovfracht, The Eugenia* **[1964] 2 QB 226**, involving carriage of goods via the Suez Canal, Lord Denning MR recognized that *both* parties had foreseen the possible closure of the canal. However, as they had been unable to reach agreement on any provision to meet this contingency, Lord Denning was quite prepared to make a finding of frustration when the relevant vessel became trapped in the canal. A useful summary on the relevant law was given by Marcus Smith J in *Canary Wharf (BP4) T1 Ltd v European Medicines Agency* **[2019] EWHC 335 (Ch) at [211]** who stated that the foreseeability of the event is relevant to determining whether one or both of the parties accepted the relevant risk.

In the present case, there is nothing to suggest that the parties turned their minds to the possibility of a planning limitation so frustration seems possible (see also *Edwinton Commercial Corp.*

v Tsavliris Russ (Worldwide Salvage & Towage) Ltd (The Sea Angel) **[2007] EWCA Civ 547)**.

The second point concerns leases of land. Traditionally it had been argued that a lease could not be frustrated as it creates not only a contract but also an estate in land. If land is requisitioned by the government, for instance, the lessee would still be expected to pay the rent as the act of requisition has not affected the ownership of the estate (eg *Whitehall Court Ltd v Ettlinger* **[1920] 1 KB 680**). But there are two cases which have doubted that, *as a matter of law*, leases are incapable of being frustrated. First, in *Cricklewood Property and Investment Trust Ltd v Leighton's Investment Trust Ltd* **[1945] AC 221**, the Law Lords were divided equally on the matter (Lord Porter expressing no view).[7] Lords Simon and Wright argued persuasively that a special purpose lease (eg a building lease), in which that purpose could not be performed, might be capable of being frustrated. Secondly, in *National Carriers Ltd v Panalpina (Northern) Ltd* **[1981] 1 All ER 161**, the House of Lords expressed the opinion that frustration should 'hardly ever' apply to leases rather than discounting the possibility entirely (see also *London Trocadero (2015) LLP v Picturehouse Cinemas Limited, Gallery Cinemas Limited, Cineworld Cinemas Limited* **[2021] EWHC 2591 (Ch)**). As DD Ltd have taken a lease exclusively for the mining of tungsten ore (ie a special purpose lease), which may now be commercially redundant, it is arguable that the lease has been frustrated (see also *BP Exploration Co. (Libya) Ltd v Hunt (No. 2)* **[1979] 1 WLR 783**, affirmed **[1983] 2 AC 352**, where an oil concession, similar in many ways to a mining lease, was held capable of being frustrated).

Effects

If a contract is frustrated it is discharged from the date of the frustrating event and thereafter both parties are excused further performance; see *Hirji Mulji v Cheong Yue Steamship Co. Ltd* **[1926] AC 497**. However, the position at common law has been qualified, to some extent, by the **Law Reform (Frustrated Contracts) Act 1943**.[8]

Under the 1943 Act, the general rule is that any money paid or payable before the frustrating event ceases to be payable or is recoverable.[9] There is no evidence of such a payment so the general rule is inapplicable. Moreover, as the lease rental was only payable when mining had actually commenced, this liability is extinguished under the normal common law rules (eg *Fibrosa Spolka Akcyjna v Fairbairn Lawson Combe Barbour Ltd* **[1943] AC 32**). Finally, insofar as **s. 1(2)** offers the possibility of wasted expenses being recovered, this again has no application in the absence of any obligation to make payments before the frustrating event.

[7] Here there is an appreciation shown of controversy in the case law.

[8] The common law effect of discharging future obligations, ie after the frustrating event, is noted and the effect of the 1943 Act on performance of obligations prior to the frustrating event is considered.

[9] **Section 1(2)** and the proviso to **s. 1(2)** are considered and correctly determined to be inapplicable.

[10] Part-performance of a contract and the effect of **s. 1(3)** are discussed. What constitutes a valuable benefit and the award of a just sum are considered.

However, under **s. 1(3)** of the 1943 Act, the court may award a 'just sum' where one party has obtained a 'valuable benefit' *before* discharge of the contract.[10] Can DD Ltd claim that IMC has retained the benefit of land which has been suitably adapted to mineral extraction? Recourse should be made to the judgment of Robert Goff J in *BP Exploration Co. (Libya) Ltd v Hunt (No. 2)* on this point. The learned judge stressed that the value of any benefit must be equated with the end product of services not their cost of provision. This causes DD Ltd some difficulty as much of the site development may be worthless to IMC in the light of planning restrictions. In particular, Robert Goff J commented that the effect of the frustrating event might be to reduce, or even extinguish, the value of the benefit received. If DD Ltd has built roads on IMC land which are now unusable, there appears to be little benefit to IMC.

LOOKING FOR EXTRA MARKS?

The following issues could be explored further:

■ Whether the mining of 20 square miles is radically different from the mining of 80 square miles or whether it merely causes additional hardship and a consequential reduction in profitability;

■ Whether the object of the contract was to lease land or extract tungsten ore;

■ If the contract is frustrated, whether a 'valuable benefit' has been conferred on either party, noting alternative interpretations of **s. 1(3)**.

QUESTION | 2

Victor, as secretary of his local tennis club, hires a bus from the Rambler Bus Co. (RBC) to take 45 members of the club to see the final of the Men's Singles Championships, held at Wimbledon. A term of the contract provides: 'This contract may be cancelled provided that notice of three working days is given to the company, otherwise the full hire charge is payable'.

The contractual price is £1,500 and Victor pays a deposit of £250 in advance. As RBC guarantees the roadworthiness of all of its buses, the designated bus is properly serviced the day before its intended use. However, on the morning of the trip it is announced that none of the tennis matches will be played as political demonstrators have dug holes in the tennis courts. Victor immediately claims that the contract has been frustrated and demands the return of the £250 deposit.

Advise the parties.

CAUTION!

- It is useful to consider the 'object of the contract'. Is it to hire a bus or to facilitate the viewing of the sporting event? If the former, a plea of frustration will almost certainly fail.

- The following questions may be considered: is there a radical change in circumstances, what is the effect of the cancellation clause, was the event foreseen or foreseeable, can RBC recover its servicing costs, and has any valuable benefit been conferred?

- Be aware of the ambit of the **Law Reform (Frustrated Contracts) Act 1943**. The Act does not deal with all elements of the doctrine of frustration; it only deals with aspects of the effect of frustration.

DIAGRAM ANSWER PLAN

Identify the issues	■ Is the common object of the contract to hire out a bus or to facilitate the viewing of the tennis event? Has there been a radical change in circumstances? ■ Was the event foreseen or foreseeable? Does the clause in the contract cover the event?
Relevant law	■ Frustration: *Davis Contractors Ltd v Fareham Urban District Council* and *Krell v Henry*. ■ Foresight and the contractual clause: *Walton Harvey Ltd v Walker & Homfrays Ltd*, *The Eugenia* and *Metropolitan Water Board v Dick, Kerr & Co*. ■ Effect of frustration common law and **Law Reform (Frustrated Contracts) Act 1943**.
Apply the law	■ Object of contract depends upon circumstances and intentions of parties. ■ Who takes risk of an event occurring depends upon, for example, foresight and whether the contract makes provision for the event. ■ If frustration, future obligations discharged. Under 1943 Act money paid is recoverable, subject to court's discretion to award expenses to payee. If a valuable benefit is conferred by performance, a court may award a just sum.
Conclude	■ Arguable frustration. ■ Possible that event should have been foreseen but the contract clause arguably does not provide for the event. ■ If frustration, future obligations under contract discharged. Under 1943 Act money paid by Victor recoverable, but RBC may seek expenses under **s. 1(2)** proviso. Appears no valuable benefit.

[1] This paragraph introduces and contextualizes the issues raised by the question.

In advising the parties the law relating to the discharge of contracts, particularly the doctrine of frustration, requires discussion.[1] Generally a contract is to be performed and failure to do so may amount to a breach of contract. However, the law excuses non-performance of a contract where the contract is said to have been frustrated. In the question, the cancellation of the tennis matches raises the issue of whether, on the facts, there is an event sufficient to frustrate the contract and, if so, with what effect?

Is the Event Capable of Frustrating the Contract?

In broad terms a contract will be discharged by frustration where (often unforeseen) events render performance of the contract radically different from that which was originally intended by the parties: 'it was not this that I promised to do' (*Davis Contractors Ltd v Fareham Urban District Council* **[1956] AC 696** at 729 per Lord Radcliffe).

The contract to hire the bus can still be performed, as RBC would readily argue. However, from Victor's viewpoint, performance would be pointless as the motive for hiring the bus has disappeared. To decide this issue, one must identify the *object* of the contract. Have the changed circumstances made performance of this object impossible? *Krell v Henry* **[1903] 2 KB 740** considered the hypothetical example of a contract for the hire of a cab to go to Epsom on Derby Day. The races were subsequently cancelled. The court felt that the contract would not be frustrated as it would be viewed as one in which the passenger was transported to Epsom, his motive of seeing the Derby being irrelevant to the cabby.

[2] Having explained the relevant rule, an argument in favour of RBC's position is presented.

This argument would be used by RBC, contending that the contract was merely to transport Victor and his passengers rather than to facilitate the viewing of Wimbledon tennis matches.[2]

[3] A counter-argument in favour of Victor is then raised, offering an alternative analysis of the facts.

Conversely, Victor could rely on the actual decision in *Krell v Henry* where the contract was frustrated as the court considered that the basis of the contract was to afford a private view of the coronation procession rather than the simple hire of a room.[3] As Marcus Smith J stated in *Canary Wharf (BP4) T1 Ltd v European Medicines Agency* **[2019] EWHC 335 (Ch)** at [37] the parties in *Krell* were negotiating for a room with a view.

[4] This paragraph shows an ability to assess the arguments and acknowledges that the facts of the question may be incomplete and require further investigation.

Which argument is stronger? Although both are possible, it is submitted that the court's decision will be determined by the manner in which RBC advertised its services and the general intentions of the parties.[4] In *Krell*, for example, the plaintiff advertised the room specifically for the purpose of viewing the coronation—the room hire and its intended use became inseparable. If the facts show that RBC advertised their services in this way (eg 'hire our bus and see Wimbledon tennis') Victor may be successful on this point. If not, RBC will be entitled to claim that the contract remains in force and that, consequently, the cancellation fee is payable.[5]

[5] This sentence gives a qualified conclusion on the possible factual scenarios.

If Victor's arguments prevail it is clear that the cancellation of Wimbledon will be of sufficient magnitude to frustrate the contract. It is proposed to proceed on the basis that Victor succeeds on this first point.[6]

[6] The answer states that the analysis is to continue on the basis that the argument in favour of frustration may be successful.

Will Any Rule of Law Render Frustration Inoperative?

A party may be unable to rely on an event which he/she has foreseen in order to claim frustration[7] (eg *Walton Harvey Ltd v Walker & Homfrays Ltd* [1931] 1 Ch 274). The rationale is that if an event has been foreseen, then in the absence of an express provision covering that event, one or other of the parties will often be taken to have accepted the risk of its occurring (see also *Canary Wharf (BP4) T1 Ltd v European Medicines Agency* [2019] EWHC 335 (Ch)).[8]

[7] Consideration is given to the limits to the operation of the doctrine of frustration.

[8] The element of foreseeability may determine the allocation of risk. Whether foresight of the event will prevent frustration from operating is considered using the IRAC analysis.

In considering this issue courts have, on occasion, distinguished between events that were foreseen by the parties (or one of them) and events which were foreseeable at the time of the contract. In the first situation, if the event and its magnitude have been foreseen, then a plea of frustration will usually fail except, perhaps, where there is evidence that the parties intended 'to leave the lawyers to sort it out' (see *The Eugenia* [1964] 2 QB 226, per Lord Denning MR). On the present facts, there is nothing to intimate that the parties foresaw that a political demonstration would lead to the event's cancellation.

If the event was foreseeable at the time of the contract, it becomes a question of construction as to whether the contract allocates the risk of the event (eg *Larrinaga & Co. v Societe Franco-Americaine des Phosphates de Medulla* (1923) 92 LJKB 455). It is arguable that in the modern age of violent political demonstration, the possibility that people will resort to such activity in order to enhance the publicity of a particular campaign cannot be discounted. If so, the disruption of a major event is foreseeable (compare also *Edwinton Commercial Corp. v Tsavliris Russ (Worldwide Salvage & Towage) Ltd (The Sea Angel)* [2007] EWCA Civ 547). The question then becomes: have the parties made provision for this eventuality by incorporating a clause which restricts the effects of the potentially frustrating event? In particular, what is the effect of the cancellation clause?

Victor appears to have accepted responsibility for any cancellation which takes place *within* three days of the anticipated performance.

[9] Another possible limitation, an express provision in the contract, is identified in this paragraph and linked to the issue of risk.

However, in this area courts traditionally apply a very strict test: as the frustrating event, by definition, is usually unforeseen (though not necessarily unforeseeable), clear evidence is required that the parties intended the clause to cover the said event (eg *Metropolitan Water Board v Dick, Kerr & Co.* **[1918] AC 119**).[9]

On the present facts, it is arguable that the parties merely intended the clause to cover a situation where, for example, Victor was unable to find enough passengers to make the trip cost-effective. Moreover, if the object of the contract is to arrange transport to a sporting event, it is arguable that Victor does not so much 'cancel' the contract as that the political demonstrators 'frustrate' it; that is to say, Victor does not notify a desire to cancel as the events have already brought the contract to an end. On this basis it might be justifiably concluded that as the cancellation clause does not cover political demonstration, there is no other evidence from which one could deduce that the parties had allocated that particular risk in a certain way. Hence, although the event might be foreseeable, arguably the contract is still capable of being frustrated.

Effects

[10] Separate the common law effect of frustration from the effect of the **Law Reform (Frustrated Contracts) Act 1943**.

[11] Once the common law position has been considered, attention may then be turned to the **Law Reform (Frustrated Contracts) Act 1943**.

[12] Note the order in which the issues are addressed: **s. 1(2)** sums paid or payable; the proviso to **s. 1(2)**, expenses incurred by the payee; and **s. 1(3)** valuable benefit.

At common law the effect of frustration is that future obligations are automatically discharged; see *Hirji Mulji v Cheong Yue Steamship Co. Ltd* **[1926] AC 497**. So here RBC would no longer have to provide the bus and Victor would no longer be under an obligation to pay the remaining £1,250.[10] Under the Law Reform (Frustrated Contracts) Act 1943[11] the general rule is that any money paid or payable before the frustrating event ceases to be payable or is recoverable by the payer: s. 1(2) of the Law Reform (Frustrated Contracts) Act 1943.[12] However, if the payee, RBC, incurred expenses in performance of the contract, a court has discretion to allow that party to retain some or all of the specified prepayment under the proviso to **s. 1(2) of the Law Reform (Frustrated Contracts) Act 1943**. On the present facts, Victor will be reclaiming his £250 deposit whereas RBC will argue that it should retain some part of the deposit as compensation for its servicing costs. Under the proviso to **s. 1(2)**, the court has a discretion to award a sum not exceeding the amount of the prepayment in respect of such expenses. It is unlikely that RBC's claim will succeed as RBC presumably services its buses at periodic intervals anyway, making it unfair to saddle Victor with the ensuing costs. Support for this can be found in *Gamerco SA v ICM/Fair Warning Ltd* **[1995] 1 WLR 1226** where the court refused to deduct an amount from the prepaid sum to cover the defendants' expenses as the plaintiff's loss had been so much greater. However, an alternative argument might be that servicing only takes place because the buses are actually hired for future use; that is, without use, the need to service disappears.

[13] The possibility of a valuable benefit is considered, but discounted. Note that the answer, in consequence, deals with this issue more briefly.

Has any valuable benefit been conferred on either party by anything done in, or for the purpose of, the performance of the contract?[13] Technically speaking, RBC is now in possession of a 'recently serviced' bus but a court would probably ignore this: under **s. 1(3)** the valuable benefit must be conferred by the other party, whereas here RBC does its own servicing. It would seem that **s. 1(3)** is inapplicable.

In conclusion, it is arguable that the contract between Victor and RBC is frustrated should the common object of the contract be seeing Wimbledon tennis. While the event may be foreseeable, this would not necessarily prevent the doctrine of frustration from applying, nor would the express provision in the contract necessarily cover the event. The consequence of the contract being frustrated is that at common law future obligations are discharged. Under the **Law Reform (Frustrated Contracts) Act 1943** the sum of £250 is recoverable by Victor but may be subject to RBC setting off a sum in respect of expenses incurred in servicing the bus. This, however, seems unlikely. Finally, as there does not appear to be a valuable benefit conferred on either party, no just sum is payable under **s. 1(3)**.

LOOKING FOR EXTRA MARKS?

- What is important, especially in frustration, is that you try to look at the potential arguments of *both* sides. An answer needs to be balanced in identifying the issues raised by the question but also shows depth of analysis rather than a superficial treatment of such issues.

- The treatment of 'effects' will normally separate the average/good script from the excellent script. Always consider the payer's, payee's, and valuable benefit rules.

- In explaining and applying the **Law Reform (Frustrated Contracts) Act 1943** it is advisable to deal with **s. 1(2)**, the proviso to **s. 1(2)**, and then **s. 1(3)** in that order. This will allow you to arrange your answer logically and spot cross-issues between the proviso to **s. 1(2)** and **s. 1(3)**.

QUESTION 3

When comparing the common law with the **Law Reform (Frustrated Contracts) Act 1943**, it becomes clear that the latter is more clearly directed towards equitably apportioning the loss between the parties.

Discuss.

CAUTION!

- Before starting to write, read the question carefully and seek to unpack the sentence—what is the subject matter of the essay?—this determines relevance; what tasks am I expected to consider?—(a) compare common law and statute and (b) assess whether the Act is designed to apportion loss fairly.

- This is not a general question about frustration, but is targeted at the impact of the **Law Reform (Frustrated Contracts) Act 1943**.

DIAGRAM ANSWER PLAN

Contextualize the question by briefly explaining the concept of frustration.

▼

What was the approach of the common law prior to the passing of the **Law Reform (Frustrated Contracts) Act 1943**?

▼

What inadequacies remained after the House of Lords' decision in *Fibrosa*?

▼

How did the 1943 Act change the law?

▼

What discretion does a court have under the 1943 Act to compensate either party for wasted expenditure, or even to apportion losses?

▼

How have the courts interpreted and applied the 'valuable benefit' rule?

▼

What weaknesses remain under the present system?

SUGGESTED ANSWER

[1] This paragraph introduces and contextualizes the issues raised by the question.

The question requires a consideration of the effect of the **Law Reform (Frustrated Contracts) Act 1943** on a contract which has been frustrated.[1] When a contract is frustrated the parties are excused from the performance of any future obligations, as at the date of discharge further performance has become impossible in circumstances which involve no liability in damages for the failure of either party (see *Fibrosa Spolka Akcyjna v Fairbairn Lawson Combe Barbour Ltd* **[1943] AC 32**).

[2] The common law is explained prior to the *Fibrosa* case.

At common law the logical corollary was that any obligation that had accrued before the frustrating event still had to be performed.[2] This could cause considerable injustice as illustrated in *Chandler v Webster* **[1904] 1 KB 493** where the plaintiff hired a room for the purpose of overlooking the coronation procession but the coronation was subsequently cancelled. The price exceeded £140 and was payable in advance. Although the plaintiff actually paid £100 he was still held liable for the balance. The Court of Appeal rejected counsel's submission that there had been a total failure of consideration. As the doctrine of frustration only released the parties from *future* performance, as opposed to past and future obligations, the court held that there could be no total failure of consideration.

[3] Note the facts of the *Fibrosa* case are explained for the purpose of highlighting the difficulties inherent in the law.

In *Fibrosa*, the House of Lords took a different approach and mitigated the harshness of the common law by ruling that in such cases there could be a total failure of consideration, in terms of non-performance, releasing the other party from the performance of an accrued obligation and allowing him/her to recover payments already made.[3] The facts of *Fibrosa* are instructive. The respondents agreed to make and deliver machinery according to the appellant's specifications. The contract price was £4,800, £1,600 payable in advance of which only £1,000 had been paid at the time of the frustrating event. As no machinery had been delivered, the House of Lords held, overruling *Chandler v Webster*

[4] Using PEA, the Point, harshness of the common law, and the Evidence, how the law was developed through case law, is evident in the paragraph.

[1904] 1 KB 493, that there was a total failure of consideration and that the appellants need not pay the outstanding £600 and were entitled to recover their £1,000.[4]

[5] The difficulties within the common law are explained, emphasizing where loss falls. This paragraph provides the Analysis to the Point and Evidence of the previous paragraph.

At first glance the *Fibrosa* decision appears perfectly logical: the appellants did not receive any benefit so they were not expected to pay any money. However, closer examination reveals certain flaws.[5] First, the respondents were merely performing their contractual obligations by manufacturing machinery in accordance with the appellant's specifications. Why should the respondents bear the whole loss for performance stipulated by the appellants? Secondly, the machinery was almost complete when the contract was frustrated; on the facts, it seems that it could have been sold without loss. But what if the machinery had been 'custom-built' and was only saleable at a loss? Would it be just and equitable for the respondents to receive no recompense for work done? On these hypothetical facts, the respondents' prudence in stipulating for a prepayment would be side-stepped, which is especially worrying in view of their blameless conduct. Yet the common law would still place the whole loss on their shoulders.

Thirdly, consider a variation on these facts in which the appellants received a very small part of the anticipated delivery of machinery. Insofar as this represented only a partial failure of consideration, the appellants would forfeit their £1,000 and be liable for the balance of £600, even if the delivery had been unusable without the remainder of the consignment.

These points demonstrate the inadequacies of the common law even after *Fibrosa*. Moreover, that decision was limited to the recovery of money payments and did not offer any general restitutionary relief for the conferment of non-monetary benefits.[6]

[6] A running conclusion is given on the previous discussion.

The **Law Reform (Frustrated Contracts) Act 1943** addressed some of these issues. It introduced a general principle that all money paid or payable before the frustrating event was recoverable or ceased to be payable, irrespective of whether there had been a total failure of consideration. However, this rule was subject to two exceptions.

First, under **s. 1(2)** a court could allow the payee to retain the whole or part of any advance payment (paid or payable before the frustrating event) in order to compensate for expenses incurred in performance of the contract. Applied to the facts of *Fibrosa*, this might have allowed the respondents, subject to the court's discretion, to retain and/or claim a part of the £1,600 advance payment as recompense for their manufacturing expenses. However, this exception only applies if the contract provides for an advance payment prior to the frustrating event (or an actual payment *is* made), otherwise compensation for expenses is unavailable. Equally, if expenses exceed the advance payment, a court is powerless to award the excess under this provision, emphasizing another deficiency in the 1943 Act. The moral is to negotiate for payment of the entire contract price in advance.[7] These two points, taken together, suggest that the 1943 Act was never intended to apportion losses equitably as, otherwise, the expenses rule would operate without the need for an advance payment. Additionally, it is unclear on what basis the discretion is to be exercised under the proviso to **s. 1(2)**. In *Gamerco SA v ICM/ Fair Warning Ltd* **[1995] 1 WLR 1226** Garland J said that the words of **s. 1(2)** conferred a broad discretion on a court. There is no clear guidance given, either in the statute or in the case law, as to how the discretion is to be exercised.

[7] This is a good point showing how the law can be used to the advantage of a payee. An examiner would be impressed by this insightful comment.

Secondly, under **s. 1(3)** of the 1943 Act the court may award a 'just sum' where one party has obtained a 'valuable benefit' before discharge of the contract. Robert Goff J in *BP Exploration Co. (Libya) Ltd v Hunt (No. 2)* **[1979] 1 WLR 783** (affirmed [1983] 2 AC 352) made a number of useful observations. Most importantly, the value of any benefit was to be equated with the end product of services,

8 This statement goes to the heart of the question—the 1943 Act is concerned with the prevention of unjust enrichment rather than the apportionment of loss.

not the cost of their provision. Perhaps for this reason Robert Goff J emphasized that the 1943 Act was more concerned with preventing unjust enrichment rather than providing for an equitable apportionment of loss.[8] For example, if the benefit conferred was destroyed by the frustrating event, no sum would be payable except, possibly, where one party had benefited from insurance cover. This confirms that a valuable benefit must be conferred, rather than payment made for *work done*. Thus, if the facts of *Fibrosa* were to be repeated, there would be no valuable benefit as no machinery had been delivered.

9 The judgment of Robert Goff J in *BP v Hunt* has been the subject of academic criticism, eg Treitel argues for an alternative interpretation of **s. 1(3)**.

Robert Goff J's interpretation has been criticized.[9] It is true that under **s. 1(3)(b)** the court must take account of the effect of the frustrating event upon the said benefit, thereby suggesting that destruction of the benefit will render it valueless. However, **s. 1(3)** expects a court to value the benefit *before* the time of discharge and then have 'regard to all the circumstances', including the effect of the frustrating event. This implies that a court could value a benefit before discharge and only *partially* reduce its value in the event of its subsequent destruction. The decision in *BP v Hunt* ignores this potential flexibility, thereby emphasizing the role of unjust enrichment at the expense of an equitable apportionment of loss. As the law stands, the effect of Robert Goff J's judgment would be that, on the facts of *Appleby v Myers* (1867) LR 2 CP 651, the claimants would still bear the whole loss as the frustrating event destroyed the machinery.[10]

10 Here the answer draws another comparison with the common law position in relation to part-performance of a contract before the time of discharge.

Robert Goff J's judgment also considered that, although the Act was silent on the matter, the best guide to valuing a benefit was the contract price. These points, taken together, establish clear limits on a court's flexibility to apportion losses fairly. Nevertheless, there are exceptions.

First, **s. 1(3)** requires a court to take into account any advance payment made which the court has allowed the payee to retain under **s. 1(2)**, thereby preventing a double payment for the same benefit. In the same context, any expenses incurred by the benefited party have to be deducted from the benefit received rather than the 'just sum' which is eventually awarded by the court. Secondly, the Act can apportion benefits; that is, if both parties confer benefits on each other, a court would be entitled to award the balance to the less favoured party. Thirdly, **s. 1(3)** can include 'benefits' of a more intangible nature, such as the knowledge and experience gained from pre-frustration contractual performance (eg *BP v Hunt*). This might allow the provider of specialist advice to be paid a reasonable sum of money for its potential post-frustration use by the recipient.

11 The previous discussion is summarized and related to the requirements of the question.

In summary, the 1943 Act offers considerable advantages over the common law by allowing courts greater flexibility in the awards that can be made.[11] However, the scheme is not perfect (compare also the

European Law Institute's *Principles for the COVID-19 Crisis*, Principle 13(3)). Expenses cannot be recovered in the absence of a provision for prepayment or actual payment and compensation for benefits conferred is dependent upon those benefits surviving the frustrating event. Indeed the 1943 Act, as Robert Goff J indicated, concerns the prevention of unjust enrichment and not, it would seem, apportionment of loss. This clearly falls short of any scheme aimed at apportioning losses equitably between the parties.

LOOKING FOR EXTRA MARKS?

- The answer divides broadly into two parts. First, a brief description of the common law and an assessment of its advantages and disadvantages, setting this in the context of the House of Lords' decision in *Fibrosa*. Secondly, the changes brought about by the 1943 Act and whether they improved the situation, focusing especially upon the analysis adopted in *BP* and *Gamerco*.

- Better students will try to answer the question by including their own evaluation of whether the 1943 Act ensures a more equitable distribution of loss. Consideration should be given to the interpretation of **s. 1(3)**.

TAKING THINGS FURTHER

- Baker, J.H., 'Frustration and Unjust Enrichment' (1979) 38 CLJ 266.
  Raises issues concerning the meaning of valuable benefit under **s. 1(3) of the Law Reform (Frustrated Contracts) Act 1943**.

- Chandler, P.A., 'Self-Induced Frustration: Foreseeability and Risk' (1990) 41 NILQ 362.
  Looks at the issues arising out of **Lauritzen AS (J) v Wijsmuller BV, The Super Servant Two [1990] 1 Lloyd's Rep 1**.

- Clark, P., 'Frustration, Restitution and the Law Reform (Frustrated Contracts) Act 1943' [1996] LMCLQ 170.
  Provides an analysis of **Gamerco SA v ICM/Fair Warning (Agency) Ltd [1995] 1 WLR 1226***, exploring the application of the discretion under the proviso to* **s. 1(2) of the Law Reform (Frustrated Contracts) Act 1943**.

- Hall, C.G., 'Frustration and the Question of Foresight' (1984) 4 LS 300.
  Explores the views of Professor Treitel in relation to the issue of foresight.

- Haycroft, A.M. and Waksman, D.M., 'Frustration and Restitution' [1984] JBL 207.
  The article considers the **Law Reform (Frustrated Contracts) Act 1943** *and argues that the basis of the Act is apportionment of loss.*

11 Damages

ARE YOU READY?

In order to attempt the questions in this chapter you must have covered the following areas in your revision:

- The generally compensatory nature of damages;
- The nature of loss;
- The appropriate measure of damages—for example, the difference between expectation and reliance losses;
- The availability of damages for non-pecuniary losses;
- Remoteness of damage;
- Mitigation of loss;
- The difference between an agreed or liquidated damages clause and a penalty clause.

 KEY DEBATES

Debate: the meaning of loss.

What is the difference between expectation and reliance losses? To what extent is there flexibility in identifying loss (as in a case such as *Wrotham Park Estate Co. Ltd v Parkside Homes Ltd* which was more recently discussed in *Morris-Garner v One Step (Support) Ltd* [2018] UKSC 20)? To what extent does the law allow damages to be recovered for inconvenience, distress, injury to feelings, or other non-pecuniary losses?

Debate: the rule of remoteness.

There are uncertainties surrounding the operation of the rule of remoteness in *Hadley v Baxendale* and further uncertainty has been created by *Transfield Shipping Inc. v Mercator Shipping,* which may require an assumption of responsibility for loss to be recoverable. Interestingly, more recently in *Attorney General of the Virgin Islands v Global Water Associates Ltd* [2020] **UKPC 18 at [26]** the Privy Council was keen to stress that the case before it was not concerned with 'unusual volatility in the market or questions of market understanding' as in *Transfield Shipping Inc v Mercator Shipping Inc (The Achilleas)*.

Debate: penalty clauses.

In *Makdessi v Cavendish Square Holdings BV* the Supreme Court considered the operation of the penalty rule, the first time the Supreme Court (or House of Lords) had done so in a century. In that case the Supreme Court restated the principles used to distinguish penalty clauses from liquidated damages clauses. To what extent did this restatement alter traditional principles?

Q **QUESTION** **1**

Jack is a manufacturer and seller of frozen food. Botchit & Co. agree to lay the floor in Jack's newly constructed factory, the work to be completed on 1 April at a cost of £25,000. Clause 12 of the contract provides: 'If Botchit & Co. fail to complete the contract within the stipulated time, we undertake to pay, by way of penalty, a sum of £10,000 in full satisfaction of our liability.'

Jack also enters into a contract with Marko & Co. to install machinery in his factory (5–14 April), for the purposes of converting fresh food into frozen, at a cost of £750,000. Botchit & Co. is informed of Jack's contract with Marko & Co.

Jack intends to commence production of frozen food on 15 April and, in consequence, he enters into a contract with Fatts Ltd for fresh food to the value of £200,000 to be delivered to the factory on 14 April.

Botchit & Co. only complete the floor on 8 April. As a result, Jack decides to pay Marko & Co. an extra £50,000. This sum of money is intended to cover overtime payments for Marko's employees caused by the shortened time for completion, thus enabling the machinery to be installed by 14 April. Whether Marko & Co. was contractually entitled to any compensation remains unclear. Jack finally commences frozen food production on 18 April. Unfortunately, the fresh food that had been delivered by Fatts Ltd on 14 April had to be sold off by Jack for £10,000 to local pig farmers.

Advise the parties.

 CAUTION!

■ Nearly all problem questions involving damages require you to adopt the same structure: was there a breach of contract? If there was a breach of contract, is there a valid damages clause? If there is not a valid damages clause, how are damages measured? What losses were caused by the breach? Are any losses too remote? Can damages for any non-pecuniary losses be awarded? What steps were taken to mitigate losses?

■ This represents the archetypal damages question. It contains the main ingredients of the law relating to damages: causation, remoteness, mitigation, and agreed damages clauses. Note that if an agreed damages clause is valid, then a claimant cannot claim unliquidated damages at common law.

 ## DIAGRAM ANSWER PLAN

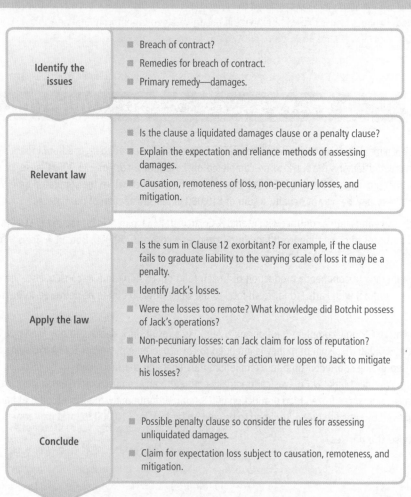

Identify the issues
- ■ Breach of contract?
- ■ Remedies for breach of contract.
- ■ Primary remedy—damages.

Relevant law
- ■ Is the clause a liquidated damages clause or a penalty clause?
- ■ Explain the expectation and reliance methods of assessing damages.
- ■ Causation, remoteness of loss, non-pecuniary losses, and mitigation.

Apply the law
- ■ Is the sum in Clause 12 exorbitant? For example, if the clause fails to graduate liability to the varying scale of loss it may be a penalty.
- ■ Identify Jack's losses.
- ■ Were the losses too remote? What knowledge did Botchit possess of Jack's operations?
- ■ Non-pecuniary losses: can Jack claim for loss of reputation?
- ■ What reasonable courses of action were open to Jack to mitigate his losses?

Conclude
- ■ Possible penalty clause so consider the rules for assessing unliquidated damages.
- ■ Claim for expectation loss subject to causation, remoteness, and mitigation.

[1] This outlines the subject of the question and raises the two main issues to be addressed.

This question concerns breach of contract and remedies for breach of contract, particularly damages. Damages may be assessed by the courts or may be agreed in advance by the parties in the form of an agreed damages clause.[1] The difficulty in predicting the damages recoverable for a breach of contract often encourages the parties to insert an agreed damages clause into the contract, thereby obviating the need to go to court. Should a clause, rather than leaving damages to be assessed at common law by the courts, provide a contractual remedy (this is a secondary obligation) on breach of a contract obligation (the primary obligation), then it will be subject to control by the courts through the penalty rules: *Makdessi v Cavendish Square Holdings BV* **[2015] UKSC 67**.[2] If, as seems to be the case, Botchit & Co are in breach of contract, is the clause 12 a penalty clause?

[2] This sentence indicates the 'policing' of agreed damages clauses through the penalty rules and provides a link to the restatement of the law in this area by the Supreme Court.

Agreed Damages Clause

[3] The test for establishing the existence of a penalty clause is explained although note in *CFL Finance Limited v Jonathan Bass* **[2019] EWHC 1839 at [48]** Judge Briggs stated: 'There is little guidance on what may constitute a legitimate interest, save that there can be no legitimate interest in punishing the defaulting party.'

Following the *Makdessi v Cavendish Square Holdings BV* case, the test is whether the clause (as a secondary obligation) 'imposes a detriment on the contract-breaker out of all proportion to any legitimate interest of the innocent party in the enforcement of the primary obligation' (Lord Neuberger).[3] An assessment must be made of what is a legitimate interest and whether the contractual remedy is out of all proportion to that interest. Punishment of a contract-breaker is not a legitimate interest but compensation for a breach will amount to a legitimate interest. Is the clause in the contract a penalty and unenforceable, essentially allowing the court to award damages in accordance with the normal rules of contract damages; or is it a liquidated damages clause, which means the common law rules (eg remoteness) are disregarded and the parties can rely on their agreed remedy in the event of the specified breach?

[4] This paragraph explains how to distinguish a penalty clause from an agreed damages clause.

In *Dunlop Pneumatic Tyre Co. v New Garage and Motor Co. Ltd* **[1915] AC 79** the following guidelines were formulated by the House of Lords (guidelines which, in many cases, continue to be helpful after *Cavendish Square Holings BV v Makdessi*).[4] First, the clause will be considered penal if the sum stipulated is extravagant or unconscionable in comparison with the greatest conceivable loss which could arise. Consequently, as recognized in *Murray v Leisureplay plc* **[2005] EWCA Civ 963, [2005] IRLR 946**, the recovery of a sum greater than the actual loss suffered does not inevitably lead to the clause being deemed penal in nature. On the facts, Botchit is expected to pay Jack £10,000 for the delay. It is arguable that this is not an exorbitant sum, bearing in mind the expected loss of production and the dislocation of other arrangements caused by significant delays.

Secondly, the clause is normally a liquidated damages clause if the consequences of the breach are such as to make precise pre-estimate impossible and the actual amount specified bears a reasonable relation to the probable consequences of the breach (see the facts of **Dunlop v New Garage**). Superficially, it appears difficult to estimate the real loss resulting from delay. On the other hand, the specified sum is not graduated in accordance with the severity of the breach. For example, the loss sustained by Jack might be minimal if Botchit & Co. delayed by only one day but it might be considerable if the delay exceeded two months. Thus, the clause is arguably not linked to any legitimate interest of Jack and so could be considered a penalty clause.[5]

On the basis that the damages clause is penal, the court will have to assess Jack's actual losses under the normal common law rules of recovery. At common law the purpose of damages is usually to compensate the victim for the loss caused by the defendant's breach of contract, rather than to punish the defendant, in this case Botchit & Co.[6]

Measure

Presumably Jack will want to claim 'expectation' damages equivalent to being put in the position he should have occupied if the contracts had been properly performed (see **Robinson v Harman** (1848) **1 Ex 850**). More specifically, Jack will want to claim any lost profits resulting from the delay in commencing production, the loss incurred in selling off the fresh food consignment as pig food, and the additional payment of £50,000 to Marko & Co.[7] The first question, therefore, is whether these losses were caused by Botchit and Co.'s breach (we are not, for example, informed why, after the additional payment to Marko & Co., production did not commence until 18 April). The second question is whether these losses are too remote.

Remoteness

The basic principle in **Hadley v Baxendale** (1854) **9 Exch 341** states that losses are too remote if, at the time of the contract, they were not in the reasonable contemplation of the parties as liable to result from the particular breach.[8] The courts will have to consider a number of questions in deciding the issue of remoteness. For example, as Botchit & Co. knew about the anticipated installation of machinery by 14 April, a court might conclude that Botchit & Co. had implicitly accepted liability for any production delays suffered by Jack as a consequence of the late completion of the factory floor, although whether knowledge of the facts should *always* be equated with acceptance of loss where the contract is broken remains a moot point

---

[5] As it is concluded that the clause *may be* a penalty this allows consideration of how the courts would assess damages for Botchit's delay.

[6] An explanation of the nature of damages at common law is provided.

[7] The good student *might* also consider the loss to Jack's reputation—see later section on 'Non-Pecuniary Losses'.

[8] This paragraph illustrates IRAC. The issue is that of remoteness, the concept is explained, applied, and arguable conclusions reached. In **Attorney General of the Virgin Islands v Global Water Associates Ltd** [2020] UKPC 18 the Privy Council were of the view (at **[32]**) that '[t]o be recoverable, the type of loss must have been reasonably contemplated as a serious possibility…'.

(compare *Transfield Shipping Inc. v Mercator Shipping Inc., The Achilleas* [2008] UKHL 48, [2008] 4 All ER 159, *Sylvia Shipping Co. Ltd v Progress Bulk Carriers Ltd (The Sylvia)* [2010] EWHC 542 (Comm), [2010] 2 Lloyd's Rep 81 and *Attorney General of the Virgin Islands v Global Water Associates Ltd* [2020] UKPC 18). Conversely, if Botchit & Co. was not aware that Jack was intending to start production from 15 April, would any loss of profits resulting from the delay have been reasonably contemplated? Support may be found in *Hadley v Baxendale* where the carrier was not expected to foresee the consequences of his delay as the mill owner failed to inform him of the absence of any spare shaft.

Moreover, the ability of the defendant to foresee possible losses may arise from the capacity in which he contracted. For example, in *The Heron II* [1969] 1 AC 350 the shipowners were expected to know of the fluctuating prices on the commodity markets. It was, therefore, within their reasonable contemplation that a delay might cause loss to their clients if the market price moved against them. Equally, if Botchit & Co. are experienced builders they might be expected to predict more accurately the consequences of their actions. As a factory floor is often laid as a precursor to the installation of machinery, any delay in completion might foreseeably cause a consequential delay to that installation.

As all these issues raise questions of fact, it is difficult to come to a specific conclusion. However, in practice, it is arguably likely that the loss caused by a delay in commencing production seems the most foreseeable as Botchit & Co. must realize that Jack is a frozen food manufacturer who wishes to utilize his assets (factory) as quickly as possible. The claim for overtime payments is potentially dependent upon the success of the first claim: if the delay in frozen food production was too remote, surely an additional payment to a third party to ensure timely installation of the production machinery would be equally remote? However, Jack's counsel will refer to *John Hunt Demolition Ltd v ASME Engineering Ltd* [2007] EWHC 1507 (TCC), [2008] 1 All ER 180 which suggests that the payment to Marko & Co. will be recoverable from Botchit & Co. provided it is viewed as a 'reasonable settlement' by the court—such reasonableness potentially being established even though the legal enforceability of that payment was questionable. As Botchit & Co. was aware of the tight deadline for installation of the machinery by Marko, a court may conclude that the overtime payments that were made were reasonably foreseeable under the second branch of the *Hadley v Baxendale* remoteness principle. Finally, the sale of the fresh food seems the most remote as it requires Botchit & Co. to foresee the possibility of Jack organizing a consignment of food before the works had definitely been completed and the potential consequences of food storage facilities being unavailable.

Non-Pecuniary Losses

[9] The claim relating to non-pecuniary loss is difficult to argue so the answer raises the possibility but deals with the issue briefly.

In relation to non-pecuniary losses,[9] one might consider the possible impact of delay on Jack's reputation. Generally, damages for injured reputation are difficult to recover in the law of contract, especially as the law of tort offers remedies in defamation and malicious falsehood. But there are exceptions. In particular, it may be possible to claim damages for injury to commercial reputation, for example see *Anglo-Continental Holidays Ltd v Typaldos Lines (London) Ltd* **[1967] 2 Lloyd's Rep 61**. Jack's reputation might also suffer if he has entered into contracts to supply frozen food to certain customers by a particular date. However, it is submitted that Jack would fail in such a claim as these losses would be considered too remote.

Mitigation

[10] Mitigation is another key issue in relation to damages. IRAC again may be used in relation to this issue.

Jack has a 'duty' to mitigate[10] any loss. A court will not expect him to take the *most* reasonable course of action or explore every avenue in order to minimize his losses. Rather, he must adopt a reasonable course of action. Presumably, Jack must have known by 2 April that Botchit & Co. would not be completing on time. Should (and could) he have contacted Fatts Ltd and delayed delivery until he was confident that his processing plant would be operational by a specific date? Ought he to have considered temporary storage of the fresh food, assuming that such facilities were available? Could he have obtained a better price for the food? If an affirmative answer to *any* of these questions is forthcoming, it will raise serious doubts as to whether Jack's course of action could be regarded as 'reasonable'. Alternatively, if the court decided that such actions involved too much practical inconvenience for Jack, then such possible courses of action would be ignored (see, generally, *Pilkington v Wood* **[1953] Ch 770**).

 LOOKING FOR EXTRA MARKS?

■ Explain the nature of damages, especially the purpose of damages for breach of contract. An explanation of the relationship between unliquidated damages and liquidated damages; that is the relationship between the common law rules on damages and the parties determining damages for themselves in an agreed damages clause.

■ The penalty clause jurisdiction of the courts following the decision of the Supreme Court in *Cavendish* could be explained further.

Deco Ltd purchased an eighteenth-century property to be used as its new business premises from 19 April. The property needed to be completely repainted and have a central heating system installed. Deco Ltd hired Jerry for the sum of £1,000 to do the painting, all work to be completed by 18 April otherwise a deduction of 5 per cent in the contract price would be made for each day that completion was delayed. Deco Ltd also purchased a new heating system from Warmwall & Sons. The contract stipulated that the system needed to be installed by 18 April, with Warmwall & Sons being required 'to pay £1000 by way of penalty to Deco Ltd for any late completion of the work'.

Jerry did not complete the work until 28 April (ten days late). This meant that Deco Ltd was unable to operate normally from its new premises until 29 April, causing an approximate loss of profits in the region of £500 per day (from 18 April).

Coincidentally, the heating system was not fully installed until 28 April, so Deco Ltd was required to hire six portable electric heaters as the house was cold and damp—total hire charge and electricity was approximately £150 per day, for ten days. Moreover, two days later, owing to a gas leak, the heating system exploded, causing severe structural damage to the property and ruining an antique tapestry which had recently been acquired by Deco Ltd for hanging within its client reception area.

Advise Deco Ltd.

CAUTION!

- As mentioned earlier, consider adopting a simple structure to your answer: breach, impact of agreed damages clause, causation, remoteness, special types of damages, and mitigation.
- When considering agreed damages clauses, be careful about concluding that the clause is *definitely* valid as this may leave very little left to write about.

DIAGRAM ANSWER PLAN

Identify the issues
- ■ Breach of contract?
- ■ Remedies for breach of contract causing financial loss and damage to property.
- ■ The validity of the agreed damages clauses.

Relevant law
- ■ Is the clause a liquidated damages clause or a penalty clause?
- ■ Types of loss.
- ■ Remoteness: *Hadley v Baxendale*.
- ■ Non-pecuniary losses: *Farley v Skinner*.
- ■ Mitigation.

Apply the law
- ■ Are the agreed damages clauses valid or are they invalid penalties?
- ■ Remoteness—what knowledge did Jerry and Warmwall possess of Deco's operations? How will this affect Deco's damages?
- ■ Have Deco suffered any non-pecuniary losses? Apply *Farley v Skinner* to the facts.
- ■ Did Deco adopt a reasonable course of action in order to minimize losses?

Conclude
- ■ Damages assessed by the courts will only be recoverable if agreed damages clauses are penalties and therefore invalid;
- ■ Damages recoverable if not too remote and Deco has taken reasonable steps to mitigate; unlikely that non-pecuniary losses are recoverable.

SUGGESTED ANSWER

The question concerns damages for breach of contract. The facts disclose that the contracts between Deco and Jerry and between Deco Ltd and Warmwall & Sons have been broken. Both Jerry and Warmwall had promised to finish the work by 18 April and by failing to complete on time are in breach, being strictly liable. Moreover, in the contract between Deco and Warmwall, in the absence of express provision, there will be an implied term that Warmwall will take reasonable care and skill in providing the service. If the gas leak is Warmwall's fault, then there will be a breach of this term. Deco, as the victim of these breaches of contract, has suffered a loss of profits as well as damage to its property. A victim's first decision is to choose whether to claim damages for expectation loss ('loss of bargain'),[1] putting it in the position it should have occupied if the contract had been performed correctly (see **Robinson v Harman (1848) 1 Ex 850**), or 'reliance losses', representing compensation for any out-of-pocket expenses and costs associated with performance,[2] as well as placing it back in the position it occupied before the contracts had been concluded (see **McRae v Commonwealth Disposals Commission [1951] 84 CLR 377**). Presumably Deco Ltd will wish to claim his expectation loss from Jerry so as, for example, to recover lost profits. Deco may also wish to claim expectation loss from Warmwall & Sons in respect of the loss which should have been avoided.

[1] The answer identifies damages as a key subject for discussion and explains the nature of loss of bargain damages.

[2] Shows an understanding of an alternative measure of loss, ie reliance interest.

Agreed Damages Clauses

[3] This sentence indicates to the examiner that you are aware of the relationship between an agreed damages clause and damages assessed by the courts at common law.

However, Deco may not be able to claim damages for its actual loss, if the agreed damages clauses in its contracts with Jerry and Warmwall are valid and not penalty clauses.[3] In **Makdessi v Cavendish Square Holdings BV [2015] UKSC 67** Lord Neuberger said the test for a penalty clause is whether the clause (as a secondary obligation) 'imposes a detriment on the contract-breaker out of all proportion to any legitimate interest of the innocent party in the enforcement of the primary obligation'. In applying this test to a straightforward damages clause where the interest is merely compensation for breach, reference may be made to **Dunlop v New Garage and Motor Co. Ltd [1915] AC 79**. In this case Lord Dunedin established a number of guidelines[4] including: if the sum stipulated is extravagant or unconscionable in comparison with the greatest conceivable loss, it is a penalty clause; and where a single fixed sum is payable on the occurrence of varying events, necessarily causing different amounts of loss, the presumption is that it is a penalty clause. At first glance the sums of money mentioned in either clause do not appear to be unduly extravagant. However, Jerry might be deprived of any payment if he is more than 20 days late. Is this out of proportion to Deco's legitimate interest; that is, compensation? If yes, then it is a penalty clause and unenforceable—requiring the court to apply the normal common law rules regarding the recovery of damages.

[4] The relevant guidelines are stated and then applied to the facts of the question.

Secondly, although both sums of money are payable for one particular type of breach, the clause in Warmwall's contract does not appear to graduate its liability. Whether Warmwall completes one hour late or one year late seems to make no difference: the same amount of money is payable. Thus, under the guidelines in **Dunlop**, it might be difficult to argue that the sum of £1000 bears a reasonable relation to the probable consequences of the breach. As already noted, this would make the clause penal in nature, again requiring the court to resort to the normal common law rules on recovery.

Remoteness

[5] This sentence identifies an issue.

On the basis that these clauses are arguably penal in nature, we will need to consider the normal common law rules on damages. In particular, Deco Ltd will need to identify each loss suffered, establish that it was caused by the breaches, and that it was not too remote[5] from Jerry or Warmwall's breaches of contract; that is, that there is a sufficiently strong causal connection between the breach of contract and the claimed loss. Adopting the principle first stated by Alderson B in *Hadley v Baxendale* **(1854) 9 Exch 341**, damages are only recoverable if: (a) they are fairly and reasonably considered to arise naturally from the breach; or (b) they were in the contemplation of the parties at that time of contract formation as liable to result from the breach.[6] This offers a single test for awarding damages for breach of contract based on the 'reasonable contemplation' of the parties, the level of liability depending upon the degree of knowledge possessed by the contract-breaker.

[6] Here there is a clear statement of the rule relevant to the issue. Note that in *Attorney General of the Virgin Islands v Global Water Associates Ltd* [2020] UKPC 18 the Privy Council were of the view (at [32]) that '[t]o be recoverable, the type of loss must have been reasonably contemplated as a serious possibility...'.

Clearly Jerry and Warmwall & Sons have been asked to complete their respective contractual duties by 18 April. As traders they must encounter many situations where time limits are imposed and, consequently, late completions will inevitably cause their customers some inconvenience. However, Deco's losses generally result from the need to occupy and operate from their premises from 18/19 April. Was this known to Jerry and Warmwall & Sons and also that delays in completion might prevent Deco from opening for business? Perhaps Deco can rely on the first branch of the remoteness principle set out in *Hadley v Baxendale*;[7] namely, that the losses were fairly and reasonably considered to arise naturally from the breach (ie delayed completion prevented occupation of the premises for business purposes). However, in *Hadley v Baxendale* the court decided that the mill owner's failure to inform the carrier of the absence of a spare shaft prevented him from claiming any loss of profits resulting from the delayed return of the repaired shaft. Surely any failure by Deco to inform either party of its intention to use the offices from 19 April would be treated similarly? Moreover, has either set of contractors assumed responsibility for such loss[8] (see *Transfield Shipping Inc. v Mercator Shipping Inc., The Achilleas* [2008] UKHL 48, [2008] 4 All ER 159 and *Siemens Building Technologies FE Ltd v Supershield Ltd* [2010] EWCA Civ 7, 129 Con LR 52; cf *Sylvia Shipping Co. Ltd v Progress Bulk Carriers Ltd (The Sylvia)* [2010] EWHC 542

[7] The answer considers the application of the first branch of the rule in *Hadley v Baxendale*.

[8] The answer acknowledges the uncertainty in the law following the decision in *The Achilleas*.

(Comm), [2010] 2 Lloyd's Rep 81 and *Attorney General of the Virgin Islands v Global Water Associates Ltd* [2020] **UKPC 18**)? Alternatively, what if Jerry and/or Warmwall had been notified of the consequences of late completion?[9] Applying the second branch of the rule in *Hadley v Baxendale*, this would prove that the consequences of late completion were reasonably contemplated. Whilst this would not necessarily prove that either of the builders had accepted liability for such losses, following *John Grimes Partnership Ltd v Gubbins* **[2013] EWCA Civ 37, [2013] BLR 126**, a court might imply a term to such effect, provided circumstances did not suggest otherwise.

[9] Here there is an application of the second branch of the rule in *Hadley v Baxendale*; which completes IRAC in this paragraph.

The damage caused by the gas leak offers interesting possibilities. Assuming that Warmwall & Sons caused the leak, and that Deco Ltd was not expected to have been checking for such problems (compare this with *Beoco Ltd v Alfa Laval Co. Ltd* **[1994] 4 All ER 464**), it would seem that the two rules in *Hadley v Baxendale* would cover the situation. The only issue would be whether the purchase of the antique tapestry, *after* the contract with Warmwall had been entered into was a relevant consideration. Is it likely that gas leaks will cause damage to any artefacts stored on premises and that Deco, as a company, might well have expensive ornaments in order to impress its clients? Arguing that Warmwall should have been told the value of the precise items on the premises as a pre-condition of liability would appear needlessly burdensome for Deco.

Non-Pecuniary Losses

Apart from the normal pecuniary loss, it seems unlikely that Deco Ltd could recover any other special damages. The main objects of the contract are all business-related.[10] It may well be that the owners of Deco Ltd will be 'disappointed' by the delays but that is insufficient. In *Bliss v SE Thames Regional Health Authority* **[1987] ICR 700** it was clearly stated that such damages were irrecoverable in an arm's-length commercial contract, although certain *obiter* comments in *Farley v Skinner* **[2001] UKHL 49** would suggest that the distinction between 'business' and 'non-business' contracts should not be the critical determinant in such circumstances. Similar reasoning could be used as regards any physical inconvenience suffered by Deco employees. Presumably, the purpose of the contract is primarily to enhance the earnings potential of Deco Ltd, not to improve the working environment of its employees.

[10] The loss suffered depends upon what has been promised under the contract and also what the law allows to be claimed.

Mitigation

To what extent would Deco Ltd be expected to mitigate its losses? It will only be expected to act reasonably, rather than taking the most reasonable course of action. In relation to the breach of contract by

Jerry, could Deco have stayed at its old premises for another few days, or was the move irreversible? Was alternative accommodation available or would the inconvenience and disruption caused to Deco make that option unreasonable? In relation to the breach of contract by Warmwall & Sons, the hire of portable heaters at that cost seems extravagant. What other options did Deco Ltd consider and with which other suppliers did it communicate?[11]

[11] The purpose of posing such questions is that it demonstrates to the examiner an understanding of how the rules of mitigation would be theoretically applied by a court.

LOOKING FOR EXTRA MARKS?

■ Clearly you cannot always predict the decision of the court on any issue involving a question of fact. What is important is that you state the law accurately, identify any specific problems, and make several remarks on how the law might sensibly be applied to the facts.

■ Indicate where there are uncertainties in the law and how this may impact upon your answer. For example, consider the differences in relation to remoteness apparent in the cases of *Parsons Ltd v Uttley Ingham Ltd* [1978] QB 791 and *Victoria Laundry (Windsor) Ltd v Newman Industries Ltd* [1949] 2 KB 528.

QUESTION | 3

The overriding principle in the award of damages for breach of contract is that the victim should be fully compensated for all the losses which flow from that breach.

Discuss.

CAUTION!

■ The mere regurgitation of lecture notes must be avoided and an attempt made to answer the question (for example, you might identify particular situations where the claimant's actual losses are not fully recoverable).

■ The answer adopts one of many possible structures. You might also consider other aspects, such as the basis upon which damages are awarded (eg compare reliance and expectation losses), or problems over the meaning of loss as seen in *Ruxley Electronics and Construction Ltd v Forsyth* [1996] AC 344, or the quantification of loss (eg non-delivery of goods which thwarts a profitable sub-sale by the buyer), or the enforceability of agreed damages clauses which may not fully compensate the victim of a breach.

DIAGRAM ANSWER PLAN

Damages for breach of contract generally compensate for losses caused by a breach but the law places limits on recoverable losses. Give examples throughout your answer that illustrate how the victim's damages do not always fully compensate him/her for all the losses resulting from the breach.

▼

What is the meaning of causation?

▼

How will the contract-breaker's knowledge at the time of contracting affect the application of the remoteness test?

▼

What is meant by reasonably contemplated losses?

▼

What limitations are imposed on the recovery of non-pecuniary losses?

▼

What steps should the victim take in order to minimize his/her losses?

▼

Conclusion.

SUGGESTED ANSWER

[1] As the question concerns damages, an explanation of the nature and purpose of damages should be given.

The purpose of awarding damages for breach of contract is generally to compensate the claimant rather than punish the defendant, thereby excluding the award of exemplary damages.[1] Thus, although damages can be claimed as of right by the victim of a breach, such damages may only be nominal, substantial damages requiring proof that actual losses were sustained as a result of the breach. Where the claimant has suffered no loss, he/she will not normally be awarded substantial damages even if there is proof that the defendant's breach was committed deliberately and with a view to profit, unless the court is prepared to disguise such an award under the general heading of injury to the claimant's feelings (eg *Cox v Phillips Industries Ltd* [1976] 1 WLR 638 but compare *Bliss v SE Thames Regional Health Authority* [1987] ICR 700). The general aim of damages is to compensate the claimant for a loss suffered.

However, three questions emerge from the quotation.[2] How does one assess whether the loss suffered is actually *caused* by the breach? Is the recovery of damages based upon an assessment of the direct consequences of the breach or is it limited by a test of foreseeability? Finally, will the victim be fully compensated for *all* the losses suffered?

Causation

[3] This paragraph employs PEA. The first sentence explains the *point*, the next lines explain the law (providing *evidence*), and the final sentence offers *analysis* in applying it to the question.

There must be a sufficiently strong causal connection between the loss suffered and the actual breach.[3] In this context, causation is not exclusively subsumed within the remoteness principle. For example, if the breach of contract is one of two causes for the loss suffered, both causes acting concurrently, then a court may still award normal damages (see *Heskell v Continental Express Ltd* [1950] **1 All ER 1033**). Thus, in *Smith, Hogg & Co. v Black Sea Insurance Co. Ltd* **[1940] AC 997**, the cargo was lost because of bad weather and also because, in breach of contract, the ship did not fulfil the seaworthiness criterion. It was held that the breach was sufficient to support a claim for damages. However, if the bad weather had been so extreme that no ship would have survived, then damages might not have been recoverable. In this way, the principle of causation ensures that the claimant does not recover for losses under the notional pretext that a breach has occurred.

Remoteness

The principle of remoteness limits the recovery of losses directly caused by the breach. The courts have traditionally adopted a test which limits recoverable loss to that which was in the reasonable contemplation of the parties as liable to result from the particular breach (see *Hadley v Baxendale* **(1854) 9 Exch 341** and *The Heron II* **[1969] 1 AC 350**). In *Attorney General of the Virgin Islands v Global Water Associates Ltd* **[2020] UKPC 18** the Privy Council were of the view (at **[32]**) that '[t]o be recoverable, the type of loss must have been reasonably contemplated as a serious possibility…'.

The knowledge of the parties is the determining factor and can be illustrated by a comparison of the following cases. In *Diamond v Campbell-Jones* **[1961] Ch 22** the defendant, in breach of contract, refused to sell a house to the plaintiff. The defendant knew that the plaintiff was a dealer in real property but not that he intended to convert the premises into offices and flats. It was held that, as the defendant did not possess any knowledge of the plaintiff's specific intentions, he was not liable for the loss of redevelopment profits. Conversely, in *Cottrill v Steyning & Littlehampton Building Society* **[1966] 1 WLR 753**, the vendor of a hotel knew that the purchaser intended to convert the premises into flats, and erect a further six houses on the land. It was held that in refusing to sell the hotel, in breach of contract, the vendor was liable to pay damages assessed upon the lost redevelopment potential. It can be seen that in both cases[4] the defendant *caused* the plaintiff's losses but that the defendants' state of knowledge was crucial in determining whether the court would award their full recovery. The test of remoteness, following *Transfield Shipping Inc. v Mercator Shipping Inc., The Achilleas* [2008] UKHL 48, [2008] 4 All ER 159 (see also *Siemens Building Technologies FE Ltd v Supershield Ltd* [2010] EWCA Civ 7, 129 Con LR 52), may require consideration of whether a defendant has assumed responsibility for a particular loss and this may require a consideration of the commercial background to the contract.[5]

[4] A comparison of alternative cases would suffice, eg *Horne v Midland Railway* (1873) LR 8 CP 131 versus *Simpson v L & NW Ry* (1876) 1 QBD 274.

[5] The potential impact of the *Achilleas* on recovery of damages is briefly considered. Compare *Attorney General of the Virgin Islands v Global Water Associates Ltd* [2020] UKPC 18.

Recovery of Losses

There are four general issues which arise here: the recovery of nonpecuniary loss, the general duty imposed on the claimant to mitigate his/her losses, developments in the way loss may be calculated, and exceptional cases where damages for breach of contract may have a punitive flavour.

With regard to the first aspect, there are clear limitations on the recovery of such losses. In *Addis v Gramophone Co. Ltd* [1909] AC 488, the House of Lords stated that damages for injured feelings were generally not recoverable in a pure contract action. This prohibition was eventually questioned, with the current position being that nonpecuniary losses (eg disappointment) are recoverable provided only that *one* of the main objects of the contract is the provision of enjoyment, peace of mind, or freedom of distress, such as occurs with a standard holiday contract (eg *Jarvis v Swan Tours Ltd* [1973] 1 QB 233, *Farley v Skinner* [2001] UKHL 49). Nevertheless, these types of damages are exceptional, as illustrated by the position in most commercial contracts where even the clearest indication that the claimant will experience anguish and vexation as a consequence of the breach will not be compensated (see *Hayes v James and Charles Dodd* [1990] 2 All ER 815). The limitations that are being imposed are not fully explicable by recourse to the principle of remoteness (ie the defendant could easily have been expected to contemplate such losses) but are referable to wider policy considerations. However, the more relaxed approach of the House of Lords in *Farley v Skinner* and the recovery of damages for mental distress in *Hamilton Jones v David & Snape* [2003] EWHC 3147 (Ch), [2004] 1 All ER 657 have recognized further losses for which damages are recoverable.

[6] A point is made about the duty to mitigate loss, potentially reducing the amount of damages to be awarded.

Secondly, even if the loss which the claimant has suffered is recoverable in principle, damages will be reduced on evidence that the victim failed to mitigate his loss properly.[6] This requires the claimant to act reasonably in trying to minimize his/her loss and not to act unreasonably in increasing his loss. Precedent suggests that the claimant need only adopt a reasonable course of action rather than the *most* reasonable course of action. Thus, an employee who is wrongfully dismissed must take reasonable steps to find another, hopefully comparable, position. But he/she would not be expected to accept an offer of re-engagement from the original employer where his/her original dismissal occurred in particularly humiliating circumstances (compare *Payzu v Saunders* **[1919] 2 KB 581** with *Brace v Calder* **[1895] 2 QB 253**). One can justify this rule of mitigation[7] on the following grounds: either that a claimant's inaction causes the loss to occur rather than the defendant's breach, or that the defendant reasonably contemplated that the claimant would wish to minimize his/her loss rather than seek redress through the courts (but see *White & Carter (Councils) Ltd v McGregor* **[1962] AC 413**). Either way, the effect seems generally to be that the defendant should not be liable for losses which are not of his/her own making.

Finally, case law demonstrates that the courts are sometimes willing to devise novel mechanisms for quantifying damages or to award non-compensatory awards where the traditional methods of calculating damages might lead to injustice. For example, in *Attorney General v Blake* **[2001] 1 AC 268**[8] an account of profits was awarded against the defendant equivalent to the profits which the defendant had secured in publishing his memoirs as an ex-employee of the UK Secret Intelligence Service, in breach of his undertaking of confidentiality, even though the information no longer remained confidential. The normal rules for the award of damages suggested that the claimant had not suffered a pecuniary loss but the House of Lords held that the claimant possessed a *legitimate interest* in preventing publication of the said memoirs for reasons of staff morale and the need to discourage revelations from other employees, the account of profits securing those twin aims. Comparable innovations can be observed in the line of cases[9] stemming from *Wrotham Park Estate Co. Ltd v Parkside Homes Ltd* **[1974] 2 All ER 321** where courts have been prepared to award damages based on the release of a hypothetical order for specific performance, or a hypothetically negotiated payment for the relaxation of an existing covenant within a contract (although note the curtailing of this line of authority in *Morris-Garner v One Step (Support) Ltd* **[2018] UKSC 20**—discussed in **Chapter** 12).

Conclusion

In conclusion,[10] the foregoing analysis demonstrates the limits on the recovery of loss caused by the defendant's breach; that is causation,

[7] Having identified and explained relevant case law, the paragraph is concluded by analysing the reasons for the duty to mitigate.

[8] Here there is a discussion of a difficult case, which does not fit neatly into the law of damages relating to compensation of loss.

[9] Other developments in this area are identified and supported by case authority.

[10] A conclusion draws together the points made and their relationship to the question asked.

remoteness, non-pecuniary losses, and mitigation. In a commercial sense it seems fair that the defendant should not be liable for losses which he could never have contemplated. Both parties take risks when entering into a contract and part of the allocation of those risks is that non-recoverable loss might be suffered by the victim of a breach. Conversely, case law, such as *Blake*, has demonstrated that courts are prepared, in exceptional circumstances, to bend those rules where a purposeful breach of contract leaves the claimant without any damages under traditional principles. In so doing, the law continues to reflect the ever-present tension between the layman's assumption that all losses flowing from a breach of contract should be compensated and the economist's view that a contract represents a man-made instrument of risk allocation, in which the precise reimbursement of loss for breach is often of secondary importance to the strategic commercial imperatives governing the original process of contract formation.

LOOKING FOR EXTRA MARKS?

■ In relation to non-pecuniary loss, the good student might also consider the difficulties of recovering damages for injured reputation. A summary of the general principle linked to a couple of exceptions might demonstrate to the examiner a useful breadth of knowledge, for example, damage to reputation and *Anglo-Continental Holidays Ltd v Typaldos Lines (London) Ltd* **[1967] 2 Lloyd's Rep 61**; or even damage to personal reputation and *McLeish v Amoo-Gottfried* **(1993) 10 PN 102.**

■ The time available for your answer will not permit you to deal with all the issues raised in great depth. Ensure that you raise all the issues relevant to the question, and that these are clearly linked to the argument in your answer.

TAKING THINGS FURTHER

■ Capper, D., 'Damages for Distress and Disappointment—Problem Solved' (2002) 118 LQR 193.
Considers the decision of the House of Lords in **Farley v Skinner [2001] UKHL 49, 2002 2 AC 732** *and its relationship with* **Ruxley v Forsyth [1996] AC 344**.

■ Chandler, A. and Devenney, J., 'Breach of Contract and the Expectation Deficit: Inconvenience and Disappointment' [2007] 27 LS 126.
Argues that development of the law justifies the award of damages for inconvenience and disappointment as compensation for lost expectation.

■ Coote, B., 'Contract Damages, *Ruxley* and the Performance Interest' (1997) 56 CLJ 537.

Explores the impact of the case of **Ruxley Electronics and Construction Ltd v Forsyth [1996] AC 344** *and protection of the performance interest.*

■ Hunter, H., 'Has *The Achilleas* Sunk?' (2014) 31 JCL 120.

An exploration of the rule of remoteness as stated in **Transfield Shipping Inc. v Mercator Shipping Inc., The Achilleas [2008] UKHL 48, [2008] 4 All ER 159** *in the light of subsequent case law and offers a comparison with the law in Singapore.*

■ Kramer, A., 'The New Test of Remoteness in Contract' (2009) 125 LQR 408.

Gives an analysis of the rule of remoteness as stated by the House of Lords in **The Achilleas***.*

■ McKendrick, E., 'Breach of Contract and the Meaning of Loss' [1999] 52(1) CLP 53.

Looks at the meaning of loss and argues that damages should be available for non-financial losses caused by breach of contract.

■ Summers, A., 'Unresolved issues in the law on penalties' [2017] LMCLQ 95.

Discusses **Makdessi v Cavendish Square Holdings BV [2015] UKSC 67***.*

Additional Remedies

ARE YOU READY?

In order to attempt the questions in this chapter you must have covered the following areas in your revision:

- When the standard common law remedy of compensatory damages might not prove adequate for the victim of a breach of contract, and when additional discretionary equity remedies may be relevant;

- The nature of the remedy of specific performance;

- The nature of mandatory and prohibitive injunctions;

- When injunctions will be ordered;

- When a claim to specific performance (or injunction) can be combined with claims for damages (see **ss. 49–50 of the Senior Courts Act 1981**);

- When courts have been prepared to consider the award of 'restitutionary damages', based on the recovery of gains secured by the defendant (as opposed to an award based on the loss suffered by the claimant).

 ## KEY DEBATES

Debate: the nature of the remedy in *Attorney General v Blake* [2001] 1 AC 268.
Is the aim of this remedy to punish the party in breach of contract? When will it be available?

Debate: the nature of the award in the line of authority emanating from *Wrotham Park Estate Co. Ltd v Parkside Homes Ltd* [1974] 1 WLR 798 (although compare *Morris-Garner v One Step (Support) Ltd* [2018] UKSC 20).

There has been a lot of debate about whether the defendant is being asked to: *restore* unjustly acquired profits to the victim; account for profits; or pay a sum of money equivalent to that which the non-breaching party would have charged the defendant for release from an existing legal/contractual duty.

The circumstances in which a court may be prepared to order specific performance or grant an injunction in respect of a breach of contract are so limited as to make such remedies almost superfluous nowadays.

Discuss.

CAUTION!

- It is very unlikely, although not impossible, that an examination question would be set exclusively on equitable remedies. It is more likely that some aspect of equitable remedies will arise in a damages question or form part of a mixed question (see **Chapter** 14 on mixed questions).

- Questions in this area are most likely to comprise essays, so you can use the PEA structure.

DIAGRAM ANSWER PLAN

Introduction

Point: the question requires a discussion of the factors that might influence a court when ordering specific performance or injunction.

Evidence: what factors might influence a court when ordering specific performance. Why might a court refuse to make such an order?

Evidence: factors that might influence a court when ordering an injunction.

Analysis: has there been any recent change in attitude towards when a court might make an order for specific performance?

Why is injunctive relief more likely where the breach refers to a negative stipulation within the contract?

Analysis: what other options are available to a court?

Conclusion.

SUGGESTED ANSWER

This essay requires a discussion of the equitable remedies of specific performance and injunction in relation to breach of contract.

Specific Performance

The remedy of specific performance (where a court orders performance) is a discretionary remedy sometimes granted by the courts in connection with a breach of contract: 'The court gives specific performance instead of damages, only when it can by that means do more perfect and complete justice' (***Wilson v Northampton and Banbury Junction Ry Co.* (1874) 9 Ch App 279** at 284 per Lord Selborne). In particular, a court will consider certain questions.[1]

The first question to be addressed is whether damages are an adequate remedy; if so, a court would be very unlikely to grant an order of specific performance. Consequently, specific performance of contracts of sale of goods are rarely ordered where the contract involves goods which are readily available in the market. Thus, in cases of non-delivery of such goods, purchasers would be expected to purchase the required goods elsewhere; if that came at a higher price, or the purchaser is put to costly inconvenience, the court can award damages to cover this. In such circumstances, damages would be considered an adequate remedy. However, if the purchaser finds that he/she cannot obtain a satisfactory substitute elsewhere, damages may be viewed as inadequate (see ***Phillips v Lamdin* [1949] 2 KB 33**, at 41, involving the wrongful removal of an Adam door, and ***Gregor Fisken Ltd v Carl* [2020] EWHC 1385 (Comm)** where the court awarded specific performance in respect of a unique and original gearbox to a Ferrari purchased for \$US44 (approved on appeal: **[2021] EWCA Civ 792**)). Other examples of inadequacy potentially include the speculative nature of the claimed damages, the difficulty of proving loss (see also ***AB v University of XYZ* [2020] EWHC 2980 (QB)** where specific performance of a contract between a student and a university was ordered on the ground that there was, in that case, no realistic way to assess damages for the student not being able to have legal representation at a disciplinary hearing.) or the irrecoverability of the claimed loss in law (see, generally, ***Decro-Wall International SA v Practitioners in Marketing Ltd SA* [1971] 1 WLR 361**).

However, more recent case authority suggests some relaxation in this overall approach, possibly making orders for specific performance a little more likely.[2] In ***Laemthong Lines Co. Ltd v Artis (The Laemthong Glory) (No. 2)* [2005] EWCA Civ 519, [2005] 1 Lloyd's Rep 632**, specific performance was ordered as the assessment of damages in similar circumstances had not been 'an entirely

---

[1] There are some key questions—address each in turn.

[2] Examine the case law that helps to build an argument.

straightforward matter'. More importantly, in *Thames Valley Power Tool Ltd v Total Gas and Power Ltd* [2005] EWHC 2208 (Comm), [2006] 1 Lloyd's Rep 441 the defendant sought to be released from an obligation to supply gas to the claimant for 15 years, at a rate that was subject to a complicated formula, on grounds of *force majeure*. This argument was rejected and, seemingly, the obligation to supply the gas was specifically enforceable as the original contract had been based on the claimant's need to receive gas from a first-rate supplier for a minimum period of time; in effect, as the claimant would not have been able to secure supply from an equivalent, substitute source, damages were an inadequate remedy. A separate justification revolved around the difficulty of calculating future losses and the delay that might be encountered in obtaining payment of any damages.

In deciding whether to award an order for specific performance, a court '. . . will only grant specific performance if, under all the circumstances, it is just and equitable to do so' (see *Stickney v Keeble* [1915] AC 386 at 419 and see also *NaviG8 Chemicals Pool Inc v Aeturnum Energy International Pte Ltd* [2021] EWHC 3132 (Comm) on the relevance of the defendant's conduct). An order will usually only be made if:[3] (a) the contract could also be enforced by the defendant, at the time of the hearing (see *Sutton v Sutton* [1984] 1 All ER 168); (b) the defendant can comply with the order (see *Watts v Spence* [1976] Ch 165; *The Sea Hawk* [1986] 1 WLR 657); (c) the claimant has not taken unfair advantage of the defendant (eg negotiating with a drunkard) or has acted dishonestly or in some other unconscionable way (compare *Watkin v Watson-Smith* [1986] CLY 424 with *Shell UK Ltd v Lostock Garages Ltd* [1976] 1 WLR 1187); and (d) it will not cause the defendant severe hardship (see *Patel v Ali* [1984] Ch 283 and compare **UTB LLC v Sheffield United Ltd** [2019] EWHC 2322 (Ch)), or the costs of performance are not wholly disproportionate to the benefit conferred on the claimant (see *Tito v Waddell (No. 2)* [1977] Ch 106 at 326). These cases demonstrate the overarching 'fairness' considerations of the existing judicial approach to specific performance of a contract. The possibilities of enforcement are wide-ranging, but their use is significantly influenced by the individual circumstances of both parties. Recent cases have not undermined that approach.

Finally, when deciding whether or not to award an order for specific performance, there are certain types of contract that courts generally do not enforce. This would include, for example, a contract of personal service; so, employees cannot be forced to work for their employer and an employer who is found to have unfairly dismissed an employee ultimately cannot be compelled to reinstate or re-engage him/her (this is an area supplemented by statute). The courts are also wary of

[3] Note: some examiners might dislike use of (a), (b), etc. within essays.

enforcing contractual performance where constant supervision would be required. For example, in *Ryan v Mutual Tontine Association* **[1893] 1 Ch 116** the lease of a flat gave the tenant a right to have a porter 'constantly in attendance' but the court's reluctance to supervise such activities on a daily basis led to a refusal to grant an enforcement order. Yet the courts have shown some flexibility: in *Co-operative Insurance Society Ltd v Argyll Stores (Holdings) Ltd* **[1998] AC 1** the House of Lords stated its disquiet with any refusal of an enforcement order based *solely* on the need for constant supervision, helpfully highlighting the difference between supervision of an ongoing 'activity' and a 'result', the latter being far easier to execute. Since then, courts have been prepared to enforce building/repair obligations where the required work could be described with greater certainty (eg *Rainbow Estates Ltd v Tokenhold Ltd* **[1999] Ch 64**), whilst in *Thames Valley Power (see earlier)* the potential problems of supervising the maintenance of a gas supply contract that still had five years to run were seemingly ignored by the court.

These comments potentially suggest, at the very least, that orders of specific performance remain an important remedy for dealing with contract breaches.[4] Can the same be said for the use of injunctions?[5]

Injunctions

Traditionally, an injunction would be refused if it would compel the defendant to perform acts which could not form the basis of a decree of specific performance (eg a contract of personal service—see *Chappell v Times Newspapers Ltd* **[1975] 1 WLR 482**). There are some important exceptions to the general rule.[6]

First, if the contract contains a negative stipulation it may be possible for the injunction to be framed in such a way as to enforce this negative aspect without compelling positive performance of the whole contract. For example,[7] when an employee resigns in order to take up employment with another firm, the (now) ex-employer may wish to enforce a restraint clause in the relevant employment contract which prevents ex-employees from working for competing firms within a specified area: a properly framed injunction could enforce this negative obligation (if not an invalid restraint of trade) without forcing the employee to work for his old employer; for example, he could find work outside the specified area or join a non-competing firm (see *Fitch v Dewes* **[1921] 2 AC 158**; *Littlewoods Organisation Ltd v Harris* **[1977] 1 WLR 1472**). However, the employee must possess a reasonable, alternative way of earning his/her living, otherwise an injunction serves as a disguised form of specific performance (see, generally, *Page One Records v Britton* **[1968] 1 WLR 157**).

[4] Reach some form of conclusion here before moving to the next part of the question.

[5] Make sure to address both remedies indicated in the question.

[6] Answers often require consideration of a legal rule and its exceptions. Here, address the three exceptions.

[7] This is quite a complicated point, so using an example can help the explanation.

Secondly, except in contracts of personal service, the courts have sometimes been prepared to *imply* negative stipulations into the contract even though the contract, as a whole, may not be specifically enforceable. In *Associated Portland Cement Manufacturers Ltd v Teigland Shipping A/S* **[1975] 1 Lloyd's Rep 581**, an injunction was granted to prevent a shipowner from employing a ship under charter in ways that were inconsistent with the charterparty.

Thirdly, a negative stipulation which is too wide can be severed and enforced in part. For example, in *Warner Bros Pictures Inc. v Nelson* **[1937] 1 KB 209**, the defendant undertook neither to act for third parties without the plaintiff's consent nor to 'engage in any other occupation' without requisite permission. An injunction was awarded to enforce the former obligation, but the latter was considered unenforceable as it would force the defendant, an actress, to work for her existing employer.

[8]This shows awareness of how the remedies can interact.

The courts are not compelled to adopt an 'either/or' approach to the award of damages or specific performance/injunction.[8] Although **s. 50 of the Senior Courts Act 1981 (SCA 1981)** allows courts to award damages in lieu of, or in substitution for, specific performance and injunction, **s. 49 of the SCA 1981** permits courts to entertain a *combined* claim to damages and specific performance or injunction. Consequently, a court can prevent future breaches via the grant of an injunction whilst compensating a claimant for past breaches via the award of damages (see *Experience Hendrix LLC v PPX Enterprises Inc. and Edward Chaplin* **[2003] EWCA Civ 323, [2003] EMLR 25**).

[9]A brief conclusion should suffice as the argument has been clearly developed throughout.

In conclusion,[9] it would appear that specific performance and injunctions continue to perform important roles, even if at common law damages remains the primary remedy for dealing with breaches of contract.

LOOKING FOR EXTRA MARKS?

■ Be wary of questions that seemingly encourage you to adopt a particular stance. Essay questions give you an opportunity to reveal the extent of your knowledge, but their primary purpose is to see how you can use that knowledge to produce a well-thought-out argument that is directed towards defending or attacking a particular proposition. To ensure higher marks, your answer must achieve this.

QUESTION | 2

The concept of 'restitutionary damages', as exemplified in *Attorney General v Blake* **[2001] 1 AC 268**, can displace the standard rules for assessing recoverable loss in a breach of contract action in favour of measuring the claimant's loss by the value of the defendant's unjust enrichment.

Discuss.

CAUTION!

- This is a difficult question, requiring analysis of a number of complex cases relating to an area of law with many uncertainties.
- Don't be afraid to acknowledge that this may be an area where 'there is never one answer'.

DIAGRAM ANSWER PLAN

Introduction.

Point: the question requires a consideration of what is meant by 'standard rules for assessing recoverable loss in a breach of contract action'.

Evidence: outline the facts of *Attorney General v Blake* and the decision reached in the House of Lords.

Evidence: outline the interpretation of *Blake* in subsequent decisions.

Analysis: did *Blake* represent a fundamental departure from existing precedent in that the damages were restitutionary rather than compensatory?

Analysis: consider the future for 'restitutionary damages'.

Conclusion.

SUGGESTED ANSWER

In the landmark case of *Attorney General v Blake* [2001] 1 AC 268 the House of Lords considered the traditional focus of the courts on *compensating* a claimant for actual losses suffered as result of a breach of contract and also whether a different measure might be adopted where, for example, a defendant purposely breaches a contract in order to secure an additional benefit or profit but the claimant suffers no financial loss.

[1] First address what is meant by the phrase 'standard rules for assessing recoverable loss in a breach of contract action'.

[2] Review the case law on this point.

The traditional purpose of an award of damages for breach of contract[1] is to ensure that the victim is compensated for his/her losses, provided those losses would have been reasonably contemplated as liable to result from that breach (at the time of contract formation). This focus is evident in a number of cases, including recently in *Morris-Garner v One Step (Support) Ltd* **[2018] UKSC 20**.[2] The court will seek to place the victim, so far as money can do this, in the position he/she should have occupied if the contract had been properly performed (*Robinson v Harman* **(1848) 1 Ex 850**). Such damages usually compensate the victim for lost expectations although where, for example, such expectations are difficult to value, the courts have been prepared to award reliance damages as a substitute (eg *McRae v Commonwealth Disposals Commission* **(1951) 84 CLR 377**). As damages are traditionally intended to offset the victim's loss, rather than punish the defendant for his/her breach, damages would usually be nominal if the claimant suffered no loss. Awarding damages predicated on the claimant's lost consumer 'surplus' simply represents the value that a court would have attributed to the claimant's known, subjective expectation (eg in *Jarvis v Swan Tours Ltd* **[1973] 1 QB 233**, the level of enjoyment anticipated from going on holiday). This is also illustrated by *Ruxley Electronics and Construction Ltd v Forsyth* **[1996] AC 344 (HL)** where the plaintiff was awarded damages for loss of an 'enjoyable amenity' arising from the installation of a swimming pool that failed to conform to the original contract specification in terms of its required depth, consequently potentially limiting the plaintiff's level of enjoyment from its use (see also *Morris-Garner v One Step (Support) Ltd* **[2018] UKSC 20** at **[40]**).

[3] Outline the facts of ***Blake*** and what decision the House of Lords reached.

However, in ***Blake***[3] the House of Lords addressed a case where the defendant purposely breached a contract to secure an additional benefit or profit but the claimant apparently suffered no financial loss. In that case the defendant, a former member of MI5, defected to the Soviet Union and wrote his autobiography. Publication of this book breached the defendant's former employment contract. It was held that, in *exceptional* circumstances, where the normal basis for damages provided inadequate compensation, and particularly where the discretionary remedies of specific performance and injunctions were unavailable (the autobiography had already been published), the defendant could be compelled to account to the victim for any benefits secured from the breach. Such damages would protect the claimant's 'interest in performance'. In *Morris-Garner v One Step (Support) Ltd* **[2018] UKSC 20** Lord Reed stressed at **[82]** that the correctness of the ***Blake*** decision was not in question in that appeal.

Whilst some argued that the approach adopted in ***Blake*** seemed to follow the earlier decision in ***Wrotham Park Estate Co. Ltd v***

Parkside Homes Ltd **[1974] 1 WLR 798** where a form of 'gains-based' damages had arguably been awarded for the breach of contract (although such a view of *Wrotham Park* was subsequently rejected in *Morris-Garner v One Step (Support) Ltd* **[2018] UKSC 20**, where the Supreme Court regarded *Wrotham Park* as compensatory in nature), *Blake* appeared to go much further: the Crown successfully recovered *all* of the defendant's profits. How could this be justified?[4] Lord Nicholls, representing the majority view, appeared to emphasize the quasi-fiduciary nature of the parties' employment relationship: arguably the defendant's breach of confidentiality fundamentally undermined the morale and trust of existing MI5 personnel and their informers and, more importantly, the general operational effectiveness of the intelligence services. Beyond that, Lord Nicholls's speech offers some general indications. First, this type of award could only be justified in *exceptional* circumstances. Secondly, a claimant would need to establish the existence of a *legitimate interest* in preventing the defendant's profit-making activity. Finally, evidence of 'skimped performance', or proof that the defendant had profited by doing the very thing he had contracted not to do, were insufficient per se to be considered 'exceptional'.

Although *Blake* was initially viewed as a 'one-off' decision, it was soon followed by *Esso Petroleum Co. Ltd v Niad Ltd* **[2001] EWHC 6 (Ch), [2001] All ER (D) 324**.[5] In that case the parties had entered into a petrol solus agreement, with the claimant also providing a monetary inducement to each of its tied customers, including the defendants, to charge specified (and lower) petrol prices to its forecourt customers. On proof that the defendants had failed to discount the forecourt price, the court held that 'restitutionary damages', following *Blake*, were potentially available. No attempt was made to justify this award on grounds that it represented the price for which the defendants would have paid for being released from an existing contractual commitment (as on a compensatory view of *Wrotham Park*). *Niad* raised a number of questions, including whether the circumstances were sufficiently 'exceptional' (as per *Blake*) for an award of restitutionary damages.[6] However, it is clear that the court was prepared to award damages on the basis of the defendant's gain rather than the claimant's financial loss.

The crucial problem lies in identifying the basis upon which damages were awarded in *Blake*.[7] The damages were not clearly punitive; although the defendant had to give up all profits received or expected, no *additional* financial penalty was imposed. Two possible interpretations subsequently emerged. First, that the decision was a logical extension of a compensatory view of *Wrotham Park* and, therefore, represented a new method of compensating the claimant

[4] Don't be afraid to pose questions, and then provide an answer.

[5] The point here is whether subsequent decisions interpreted *Blake* expansively or sought to limit its application.

[6] Acknowledge where the law is uncertain.

[7] Analyse whether *Blake* represented a fundamental departure from existing precedent in that the damages were restitutionary (not compensatory) in nature.

for a breach of contract whilst complying with the overriding 'compensatory' approach in *Robinson v Harman*. Alternatively, the decision represented a form of restitutionary relief whereby the level of damages was determined by the size of the defendant's gains rather than the hypothetical amount the claimant might have charged for releasing the defendant from an existing contractual commitment.

[8] Refer to subsequent case law.

The current weight of authority clearly favours the view that compensatory damages were awarded in *Wrotham Park* (see *Morris-Garner v One Step (Support) Ltd* [2018] UKSC 20);[8] that is, reflecting the plaintiff's loss rather than the defendant's gain— an important conclusion because much of the analysis in *Blake* relies upon this case. Indeed, in *Jaggard v Sawyer* [1994] EWCA Civ 1, [1995] 1 WLR 269, Sir Thomas Bingham pointed out that the court in *Wrotham Park* had been influenced by the level of the defendants' profits *not* for the purposes of stripping them of those profits, but because it provided a suitable context within which to identify the amount they would have been willing to pay to secure a release from the relevant contractual commitment (see also *Gafford v Graham* [1998] EWCA Civ 666, (1998) 77 P & CR 73). However, the more important question is whether one can extrapolate from *Jaggard* that the damages awarded in *Blake* were also compensatory. Clearly the result achieved in *Niad* suggested otherwise, whilst the court in *Harris v Wynne* [2005] EWHC 151 (Ch), [2006] 2 P & CR 595 again adopted the label of 'restitutionary damages' in referring to *Blake* (at [34]) and treated the defendant's 'underhand dealings' as essential when making such an award.

This ongoing debate was revisited in *WWF-World Wide Fund for Nature (formerly World Wildlife Fund) v World Wrestling Federation Entertainment Inc.* [2007] EWCA Civ 286, [2007] 1 All ER 74. Chadwick LJ (delivering the main judgment) found 'puzzling' any suggestion that restitutionary damages had been awarded in *Wrotham Park*. He considered the remedy adopted in *Wrotham Park*, and the account of profits in *Blake*, as being 'juridically highly similar', especially as their common underlying feature was the need to compensate in circumstances where the claimant could not establish an identifiable loss. This suggested that the dividing line between hypothetical release damages and an account of profits was becoming blurred.[9] However in *Morris-Garner v One Step (Support) Ltd* [2018] UKSC 20 Lord Reed (with whom Lady Hale, Lord Wilson, and Lord Carnwath agreed) was of the opinion that the award in *Blake* *was not* compensatory in nature. By contrast Lord Reed felt that the award in *Wrotham Park* *was* compensatory in nature. That award was made in lieu of an injunction (as permitted under Lord Cairns' Act) and, as such, one 'possible method of quantifying damages under

[9] Acknowledges that the law is unclear.

this head is on the basis of the economic value of the right which the court has declined to enforce, and which it has consequently rendered worthless'; in valuing such a right 'the amount which the claimant might reasonably have demanded as a quid pro quo for the relaxation of the obligation in question' (so-called 'negotiating damages'). Moreover, Lord Reed recognized that negotiating damages might also be awarded at common law in appropriate circumstances. In particular, such damages might be awarded where the breach of contract results in the 'loss of a valuable asset created or protected by the right which was infringed'. Examples might include the breach of a restrictive covenant over land, the breach of an intellectual property agreement, or the breach of a confidentiality agreement ([**92**]). In such cases, the imaginary negotiation is merely a tool for determining the value of the relevant asset ([**91**]). Crucially Lord Reed was of the opinion that not all contract rights were to be considered as an asset in this sense ([**93**]) although it is, perhaps, not clear how the distinction will be made. More recently in *Priyanka Shipping Limited v Glory Bulk Carriers Pte Limited* **[2019] EWHC 2804 (Comm)** David Edwards QC (sitting as a Judge of the High Court) held that 'negotiating damages' were not available where the purchaser of a ship used the ship in breach of a provision as to the permitted use of the ship.

Moreover, in *Morris-Garner v One Step (Support) Ltd,* Lord Reed disagreed with some of the statements in *Experience Hendrix LLC v PPX Enterprises Inc* **[2003] EWCA Civ 232** that negotiating damages could be used more widely to achieve 'practical justice'. Nevertheless, Lord Reed agreed with the decision in the case on the basis, as discussed earlier, that it involved the breach of an intellectual property agreement.

It would, therefore, seem that *Blake* represents a judicial preparedness to award gains-based damages in *exceptional* circumstances. Whilst *Niad* appears to go further, it is arguably unlikely to be followed,[10] with the *Blake* principle primarily operating where the parties have an existing fiduciary or quasi-fiduciary relationship, which will magnify the responsibilities of the defendant not to abuse a dominant position.

Therefore, the original question is only partly correct.[11] A court can compensate the victim of a breach of contract in the most effective way possible, including either the award of damages predicated on the claimant's lost expectation (*Robinson v Harman*), or the costs of his reliance (*McRae v Commonwealth Disposals Commission*), or the deprivation of a valuable asset, which may be best informed by the gains secured by the defendant (*Wrotham Park* and *Morris-Garner v One Step (Support) Ltd* **[2018] UKSC 20**). It is true that

[10] This appears quite a confident statement, but it is offered as an opinion.

[11] Here is the conclusion, based on the preceding analysis.

the damages awarded in **Blake** were measured by the defendant's gain but this approach can also, to some extent, be adopted in calculating compensatory damages (**Wrotham Park** and **Morris-Garner v One Step (Support) Ltd** [2018] UKSC 20). Case law demonstrates that the use of the term 'restitutionary damages' can be misleading as compensatory damages measured by the defendant's gain (**Wrotham Park**) are not the same as damages specifically intended to strip the defendant of his/her profits (**Blake**). This analysis is reinforced by posing one simple question: how can damages in **Blake** be viewed as compensatory when the parties never concluded a bargain and in no circumstances would have done so (ie compensation for loss of bargain was never possible)?

LOOKING FOR EXTRA MARKS?

- Additional marks may be awarded for noting that in **Jaggard v Sawyer** Sir Thomas Bingham's approach to **Wrotham Park** conflicted with the view of **Wrotham Park** as an example of an award of 'restitutionary damages reversing the defendants' unjust enrichment' in the Law Commission Report (*Aggravated, Exemplary and Restitutionary Damages*, Law Com Report No. 247, 1997, at para. 1.36). See now **Morris-Garner v One Step (Support) Ltd** [2018] UKSC 20.

TAKING THINGS FURTHER

- Bartlett, E. and Humphreys, E., 'One Step Could Not Side-Step Usual Contract Breach Principles' (2018) 191 Emp. LJ 22.
  Considers **Morris-Garner v One Step (Support) Ltd** [2018] UKSC 20.

- Cunnington, R., 'The Assessment of Gains-Based Damages for Breach of Contract' (2008) 71 MLR 559.
  Considers the **Wrotham Park** *measure and the* **Blake** *measure as two different measures of gain-based damages for breach of contract.*

- Fox, D., 'Restitutionary Damages to Deter Breach of Contract' (2001) 60 CLJ 33.
  Suggests that, following **Attorney General v Blake** [2001] 1 AC 268, *the deterrent nature of restitutionary damages removes the financial incentive for defendants to walk away from the contract.*

- Schwartz, A., 'The Case for Specific Performance' (1979) 89 Yale LJ 271.
  Argues for routine availability of specific performance.

Privity of Contract

13

ARE YOU READY?

In order to attempt the questions in this chapter you must have covered the following areas in your revision:

● The doctrine of privity of contract which provides that, generally, only parties to a contract can have rights and liabilities under that contract;

● The interrelationship of the doctrine of privity of contract with the doctrine of consideration. Although entwined, two separate policy issues can also be identified: privity of contract relates to those *who* can enforce a contract; consideration concerns the *types* of promise that can be enforced;

● Common law and equitable mechanisms to evade the doctrine of privity of contract, including: trusts, restrictive covenants, and collateral contracts;

● The concept of agency as an exception to the doctrine of privity of contract: an agent may contract on behalf of his/her principal with a third party and form a binding contract between principal and third party;

● Statutory developments: the **Contracts (Rights of Third Parties) Act 1999**;

● That the Act gives freedom to the contracting parties to exclude the provisions of the Act or to set out procedures for post-contractual variation of arrangements that avoid the need to obtain the third party's consent.

QUESTION | **1**

It was clearly desirable to amend, by the **Contracts (Rights of Third Parties) Act 1999**, the rule that a third party may not sue on a contract, which is made for his/her benefit.

Discuss.

CAUTION!

- Questions centring entirely on the doctrine of privity often require a good knowledge of pre-1999 common law case law.

- This essay requires an understanding and evaluation of the traditional doctrine of privity of contract in the context of contracts which are made for the benefit of third parties.

- You would also be expected to critically examine whether the law needed reform in 1999; this will require knowledge of the Law Commission's recommendations regarding contracts made for the benefit of third parties (Report No. 242, 1996) and the **Contracts (Rights of Third Parties) Act 1999**.

DIAGRAM ANSWER PLAN

Introduction.

▼

Point: the question requires a critical examination of the traditional rules on privity and the reforms in 1999.

▼

Evidence: the original purpose of the doctrine of privity and how the rule interacts with the modern doctrine of consideration.

▼

Analysis: why does the rule have so many exceptions?

▼

Evidence: outline the guiding principles of the **Contracts (Rights of Third Parties) Act 1999**.

▼

Analysis: what limits are imposed by the Act on those wishing to amend existing contracts?

▼

Conclusion.

SUGGESTED ANSWER

This question concerns the doctrine of privity of contract, which provides that, generally, only parties to a contract can have rights and liabilities under that contract. Before the passing of the **Contracts (Rights of Third Parties) Act 1999** (the 'Act') it was clear that a third party generally could not sue on a contract to which he/she was not privy, even if the sole purpose of the contract was to benefit that third party. The privity rule was criticized as being unfair, yet common law attempts to circumvent it were also often criticized as artificial and often questionable. However, whilst the Act arguably gives effect to the intentions of the contracting parties and the legitimate expectations of named third parties, it also raises complex legal issues.[1]

The rule that a third party could not sue on a contract to which he/she was not privy became entrenched in the nineteenth century (see, for example, *Tweddle v Atkinson* (1861) 1 B & S 393), although since then it has been subject to much criticism.[2] The arguable injustice of the doctrine of privity was reinforced by the rules relating to damages.[3] In *Jackson v Horizon Holidays Ltd* [1975] 1 WLR 1468, the defendants contracted with the plaintiff to provide holiday accommodation for the plaintiff, his wife, and their two children. The accommodation was inadequate. The plaintiff recovered damages including £500 for 'mental distress'. Lord Denning MR considered £500 to be excessive for the plaintiff's *own* distress but adequate where the plaintiff contracted for the benefit of himself *and his family*; and Lord Denning MR allowed the plaintiff to recover in respect of the loss suffered by his family. Some of Lord Denning's wider comments in this case were strongly disapproved by the House of Lords in *Woodar Investment Development Ltd v Wimpey Construction UK Ltd* [1980] 1 WLR 277 although the promisee's general inability to recover damages in respect of loss suffered by the third party was described as 'most unsatisfactory' and in need of re-evaluation.[4] The perceived injustice of the doctrine led to common law attempts to evade privity, for example via trusts (*Affréteurs (Les) Réunis SA v Leopold Walford (London) Ltd* [1919] AC 801), but the rule remained.[5] Indeed, such attempts were on an ad hoc basis and were often both artificial and overcomplicated (eg *New Zealand Shipping Co. Ltd v AM Satterthwaite & Co. Ltd (The Eurymedon)* [1975] AC 154).

Several justifications have been advanced in support of the general denial of rights to third parties under the traditional privity rule.[6] First, contractual rights and duties are essentially the personal domain of those who create them; thus, as the third party has played no part in the technical formation of the contract, some would argue that the third party should not obtain contractual rights. On the other hand, the Law Commission emphasized that requiring consent in contracts protected personal autonomy but that allowing third parties to obtain *benefits* under a contract would not necessarily undermine such autonomy. Secondly, the third party's failure to provide any consideration is often thought to prohibit his/her having any rights under the contract. Again, the Law Commission noted that consideration was provided by the promisee meaning that the promisor's promise had

[1] These are the points that you will develop in your answer.

[2] The historical context is necessary here to explain the rule.

[3] Here you explain how the law could be regarded as 'unfair'.

[4] Demonstrates the uncertainties in the law.

[5] You do not need detailed analysis of these cases; the point is made concisely here.

[6] Explain and analyse each in turn.

been paid for, albeit not by the third party. Thirdly, it may be unjust to treat someone as a party to a contract for the purpose of suing on it when he/she could not be sued. However, the promisor's interests are protected by his/her having a claim against the promisee whereas the third party has no such security under the traditional rule of privity.

Fourthly, it is sometimes argued that giving a third party the right to enforce the contract could subject the promisor to two actions (from both the promisee and the third party). The Law Commission suggested that this could be dealt with by making it clear that there was only *one* promise giving rise to *one* cause of action; once the promise is enforced it is extinguished, the promisor then ceasing to be liable. Fifthly, whilst privity does not permit the creation of contractual rights in third parties, appropriate drafting can achieve the same result in practice. However, the Law Commission noted that laymen often fail to draft around the rule and that problems arise even where the parties have taken legal advice (eg ***Beswick v Beswick* [1968] AC 58**). Finally, the ability of third parties to sue on the contract made for their benefit may detract from the rights of the contracting parties to rescind or vary their contract and would expose the promisor to a potentially wide range of possible third-party claimants. The Law Commission acknowledged that any reform had to safeguard the rights of the parties and to define 'third parties' so as to prevent a flood of litigation.

One might, therefore, question how far the doctrine of privity was ever justifiable. The Law Commission considered that a 'detailed legislative scheme' was needed to guarantee the rights of third parties. It is not clear, however, whether the Act was the most appropriate way forward.[7]

[7] Introduces your analysis of the statutory provisions.

On the central issue of the test of an enforceable benefit, **s. 1** provides that a third party will be entitled to enforce a contractual term in his/her own right if either the contract 'expressly' so provides (**s. 1(1)(a)**), or the term '*purports* to confer a benefit' on the third party (**s. 1(1)(b)**). As regards the latter possibility, the Act, in effect, sets up a rebuttable presumption that if the parties confer a benefit on a third party, they intend that the third party is empowered to enforce the term that creates the benefit (see **s. 1(2)**). The word 'purports' may be contentious:[8] for example, the mere fact that a third party will be better off if a contract is performed does not mean that the contract had the purpose of conferring a benefit on that party (see ***Prudential Assuance Co Ltd v Ayres* [2007] EWHC 775** (reversed on other grounds **[2008] EWCA Civ 52**)). Case law suggests that courts are prepared to find the requisite intent via a process of implication or *default* reasoning: for example, in ***Nisshin Shipping Co. Ltd v Cleaves & Co. Ltd* [2003] EWHC 2602 (Comm), [2004] 1 Lloyd's Rep 38**, or ***Laemthong International Lines Co. Ltd v Artis* [2005] EWCA Civ 519, [2005] 1 Lloyd's Rep 688**.

[8] Analyse possible shortcomings in the law.

Nevertheless, the possible unintended consequences of interpreting **s. 1(1)** too widely are partly mitigated by **s. 1(3)**, which requires any third party to be expressly identified in the contract by name, or as a member of a class, or as answering a particular description (**s. 1(3)** although compare *Starlight Shipping Co v Allianz Marine and Aviation Versicherungs AG* **[2014] EWHC 3068 (Comm)**, at [88], for a broad approach to this provision). So, on the facts of *Jackson v Horizon Holidays*, as the family members were all referred to in the contract (ie satisfying **s. 1(3)**), they travelled together on a 'family trip', and the cost clearly encompassed all the family, a court would likely conclude that the contract had purported to confer the benefit of the contract terms on all the claimant's family. Moreover in *Chudley & Others v Clydesdale Bank Plc (Trading as Yorkshire Bank)* **[2019] EWCA Civ 344**, Flaux LJ stated at [80] that it is not a requirement of the Act that the third party was aware of the relevant contract at the time it was made.

[9] Indicate any remaining difficulties with the law.

However, problems arise where the contract does not specify the names of third parties but refers to categories or classes of people.[9] *Avraamides v Colwill* **[2006] EWCA Civ 1533** suggests that the word 'expressly' did not permit a 'process of implication or construction'; a clause directed towards a wide range of unidentified persons would not make individuals 'expressly' identified for the purposes of **s. 1(3)**.

Section 2 concerns the difficult issue of variation and rescission. In general, it recognizes that where a third party has a right under **s. 1** to enforce a term of the contract, the contracting parties cannot, by agreement, rescind the contract, or vary it in such a way as to alter that right without prior permission from the third party. This restriction presupposes that the third party has communicated to the promisor his assent to the term, or the promisor is aware that the third party has relied upon the term, or the promisor could reasonably foresee reliance by the third party on the term and such reliance has in fact occurred. In this, the Act seems to uphold the right to vary the subject only to express intervention by the third party. In practice, as it will often be reasonably foreseeable that the third party might rely on the term in question, the contracting parties should contact the third party before any variation to check whether such reliance had indeed taken place.

[10] The doctrine of consideration was seen by some as one of the impediments to reform.

Finally, the Act makes no mention of consideration.[10] The Law Commission seemingly reinterpreted *Tweddle* by distinguishing promises that are supported by consideration (albeit enforced by a third party) and promises that are wholly gratuitous. This interpretation of the Act will therefore focus on the right to enforce a promise supported by consideration, even though the third party conferred no benefit.

[11] A general conclusion pulls together the arguments, completing the analysis of the question.

In conclusion, the Act means that the artificial and often questionable exemptions that the common law created to circumvent the unfairness of the privity rule are less relevant today.[11] However, while the Act gives effect to the intentions of the contracting parties and the legitimate expectations of named third parties, it raises further complex legal issues.

LOOKING FOR EXTRA MARKS?

- For the House of Lords' criticism of the privity rule after *Tweddle*, compare *Dunlop Pneumatic Tyre Co. Ltd v Selfridge & Co. Ltd* [1915] AC 847 and *Midland Silicones Ltd v Scruttons Ltd* [1962] AC 446, with *Beswick* and *Woodar Investment*.

- You might also refer to Dillon J's description of the position before the Act as 'a blot on our law and most unjust' (see *Forster v Silvermere Golf and Equestrian Centre* (1981) 125 SJ 397).

- Remember: the Act allows contracting parties to exclude the provisions of the Act or to set out procedures for post-contractual variation of arrangements that avoid the need to obtain the third party's consent.

TAKING THINGS FURTHER

- Adams, J., Beyleveld, D., and Brownsword, R., 'Privity of Contract—The Benefits and the Burdens of Law Reform' (1997) 60 MLR 238.
  Considers the Law Commission Report, Privity of Contract: Contracts for the Benefit of Third Parties (Law Com. No. 242, Cm 3329, 1996).

- Andrews, N., 'Strangers to Justice No Longer—The Reversal of the Privity Rule under the Contracts (Rights of Third Parties) Act 1999' (2001) 60 CLJ 353.
  In favour of the privity reform.

- MacMillan, C., 'A Birthday Present for Lord Denning: The Contracts (Rights of Third Parties) Act 1999' (2000) 63 MLR 721.
  In favour of the privity reform.

- Smith, S., 'Contracts for the Benefit of Third Parties: In Defence of the Third Party Rule' (1997) 7 OJLS 643.
  Critical of the privity reform.

- Stevens, R., 'The Contracts (Rights of Third Parties) Act 1999' (2004) 120 LQR 292.
  Critical of the privity reform.

Mixed Topic Questions

14

Introduction

This chapter introduces you to examination questions with mixed topics. Key purposes of such questions include testing your ability to identify different topics contained within one question and your ability to manage responses to the different issues within the question. For example, a contract question might include aspects of mistake, undue influence, and misrepresentation or may contain all aspects of formation of contract; that is offer and acceptance, intention to create legal relations, and consideration. Clearly, if students identify all the relevant areas, then they will have established a firm base from which a good answer can be developed.

In answering mixed questions, it is important to identify and address the issues raised by the question. It may be that you will not have time to look at all of the issues in great depth and the explanation of relevant law may have to be brief. Where the weight of your answer should lie is for you to judge, in the light of the question asked.

Questions of this type are less common but entirely possible in first-year contract examinations. However, guidance may be gained from the seminar programme delivered and past examination papers from your university. As always, if in doubt consult your tutors.

 QUESTION | **1**

For the past five years Fastbuild Ltd, a company that specializes in the building of housing estates, has entered into one-year contracts with Bricklast Ltd for the supply of house bricks. Each of these contracts has been preceded by protracted negotiations in which new terms and conditions have been agreed between the parties. In the most recent set of negotiations, for a proposed contract in 2018, the parties had agreed on the type and quantity of bricks to be supplied, with the specified quantity easily exceeding Bricklast's expectations bearing in mind previous contracts. Fastbuild thereupon sends Bricklast a letter of intent which includes the following statement:

▶

'As per negotiations we intend to contract with you, purchasing 2.5 million bricks (type agreed) for the year 2018 at a price to be confirmed.' Bricklast purchases additional machinery in order to manufacture the increased quantity of bricks and goes into immediate production.

Consider the legal position of the parties if negotiations between them break down and Fastbuild Ltd refuses to purchase any bricks from Bricklast Ltd.

CAUTION!

■ The question raises a number of issues, and you must ensure that you deal with all of them. It is a question of judgement how long you spend on each issue.

DIAGRAM ANSWER PLAN

Identify the issues	■ Identify the legal issues—offer and acceptance, certainty of terms, intention to create legal relations, letters of intent, and consideration.
Relevant law	■ Outline the relevant law: what is an offer; is there sufficient certainty of terms; is a letter of intent consistent with an intention to contract; what is an acceptance; what is consideration?
Apply the law	■ Possible intention to be bound by a definite proposal but problem over price. ■ Letter of intent coupled with problem over price might suggest no intention to be contractually bound. ■ If an offer exists, acceptance arguably arises by conduct. ■ Consideration: is there, for example, an exchange of promises?
Conclude	■ It is arguable that no contract has been formed due to lack of an offer, problems over certainty of terms, and, should an offer exist, the difficulty of linking an acceptance to an offer. Consideration may also be lacking.

SUGGESTED ANSWER

[1] The question is generally about formation of contract and raises a number of specific issues. Each issue will be subsequently dealt with in turn.

[2] The first issue concerns the existence of an offer and the related issues of certainty and the effect of a letter of intent.

[3] The focus of the inquiry into the existence of an offer initially must be on the words used in the communication.

[4] Having considered intention, the proposed terms and the question of certainty need to be explored.

This question deals with the formation of a contract and involves a discussion of offer and acceptance, certainty of terms, letters of intent, and consideration.[1]

First, does the letter of intent constitute an offer?[2] An offer has to be certain, be specific, and demonstrate an intention to be bound. Leaving aside the particular problems associated with letters of intent, Fastbuild Ltd's communication does contain specific terms (quantity and period of delivery), but two problems remain: use of the word 'intend' and omission of an agreed price. The word 'intend' imports some degree of reticence and might be referring merely to *future* intentions.[3] For example, in *Clifton v Palumbo* **[1944] 2 All ER 497** the claimant's statement that he was 'prepared to offer' was held to constitute a mere invitation to treat (see also *Gibson v Manchester City Council* **[1979] 1 All ER 972**). Equally, omission of an agreed price would detract from the letter's certainty although use of the word 'confirmed' might suggest possibly that the parties have already reached a definite agreement elsewhere.[4] Contrast the cases of *Hillas & Co. Ltd v Arcos Ltd* **(1932) 147 LT 503** and *Scammell (G) and Nephew Ltd v Ouston* **[1941] AC 251**, the first case showing that the omission of a price might not affect contractual validity if viewed in the light of the parties' previous course of dealing. It may be that *Hillas & Co. Ltd v Arcos Ltd* may be distinguished as in the present scenario the terms are negotiated each year and, if the terms do not establish a course of dealing which may be used to resolve uncertainties in the current agreement, then this may be fatal to the enforceability of the agreement. If the words used mean that no price has been agreed and are to be interpreted as an agreement to agree on a price in the future, then the courts may consider the 'agreement' to be too uncertain to be enforced, as in *May and Butcher v R* **[1934] 2 KB 17**. Note the general policy that courts will usually seek to implement rather than defeat the reasonable expectations of the parties, particularly where the parties have acted on an agreement (see *Foley v Classique Coaches Ltd* **[1934] 2 KB 1**). However, acting on an agreement by itself may not be enough to convince a court of the existence of a contract should the parties have failed to agree or disagree or left too many issues open; see, for example, *British Steel Corp. v Cleveland Bridge and Engineering Co. Ltd* **[1984] 1 All ER 504**. It might also be relevant to consider the impact of *Blackpool and Fylde Aero Club Ltd v Blackpool Borough Council* **[1990] 1 WLR 1195** in that the clear intentions of the parties might override

[5] Many of the issues concerning the certainty of an offer would be equally applicable to the certainty of the final contract, assuming an offer and acceptance had actually taken place, eg *Foley v Classique Coaches Ltd* [1934] 2 KB 1.

the technical requirements of offer and acceptance. Finally, lack of certainty[5] might be argued with reference to *Walford v Miles* [1992] 2 AC 128—even if the letter implies an undertaking not to contract with anyone else, this does not establish an enforceable, positive contract to negotiate in good faith as it is too uncertain.

As Fastbuild have characterized their communication as a 'letter of intent', what is the impact of the use of such words? Letters of intent,[6] as do letters of comfort, raise questions of contractual intention. The decision in *Kleinwort Benson Ltd v Malaysia Mining Corp. Bhd* [1989] 1 WLR 379 shows that the courts have no preconceived notion as to the enforceability of letters of comfort. Rather, the enforceability of such letters will depend upon the precise wording used. In *Kleinwort*, the words 'it is our policy' were not considered to be promissory in nature and not contractual. On the present facts, the word 'intend' might be considered to import an unacceptable degree of uncertainty, although contrast this with the decision in *Wilson Smithett & Cape (Sugar) Ltd v Bangladesh Sugar and Food Industries Corp.* [1986] 1 Lloyd's Rep 378, where the court construed a letter of intent as an acceptance of an offer made by the claimant. The effect of a letter of intent is part a matter of construction of the document and part legal analysis. If a communication is labelled as a 'letter of intent' a court may find it to have the attributes of an offer or an acceptance or indeed of neither. In the final analysis are the words used, and any conduct, consistent with an intention to be bound or do the words negative an intention to contract? The absence of a clear intention to be bound coupled with the uncertainty over price suggest a lack of contractual intention.

[6] This paragraph deals with the impact of the words 'letter of intent'. Does the use of these words negative any intention to contract?

Secondly, if an offer has been made, has there been an acceptance? Acceptance can take many forms: written, spoken, or through conduct. Although there is no suggestion that Bricklast has responded formally to Fastbuild's letter, there is clear evidence of reliance. At first glance, *Brogden v Metropolitan Railway Co.* (1877) 2 App Cas 666 seems applicable but in that case *both* parties acted on the strength of the new agreement (see also *Wettern Electric Ltd v Welsh Development Agency* [1983] QB 796). This is important as, in general, acceptance is ineffective until it has been communicated[7] (see *Powell v Lee* (1908) 99 LT 284). Thus, no contract will have come into existence unless Bricklast can argue that starting work constitutes acceptance of an offer and thus creates a contract.[8] In *RTS Flexible Systems Ltd v Molkerei Alois Muller GmbH* [2010] UKSC 14 the Supreme Court held that even though the parties had not, as anticipated, executed a formal contract, they had agreed terms which were essential to being legally bound and, when coupled with significant performance, there was a contract. However, in *British*

[7] The problem of acceptance is explored, highlighting the absence of communication.

[8] The problems in seeking to argue that acceptance has occurred are considered.

Steel, which concerned the twin impact of an existing letter of intent and reliance by the recipient that a contract would be finalized, the court refused to find the existence of a contract as the action of commencing work could not be seen as acceptance of the claimant's offer, as the defendant had made plain that the claimant's terms were unacceptable. An alternative approach would be to consider cases where courts have been prepared to adapt, if not modify, the orthodox rules of offer and acceptance (eg *Blackpool* and *Kleinwort*, mentioned earlier; and *Evans (J) & Son (Portsmouth) Ltd v Andrea Merzario* **[1976] 1 WLR 1078**). Naturally, it would help if the parties during their negotiations had set up independent machinery (eg arbitration) to determine the meaning of uncertain terms (see *Sudbrook Trading Estate Ltd v Eggleton* **[1983] 1 AC 444**).

[9]Consideration is based on an exchange.

Finally, even if a court is prepared to find an offer that has been accepted, is there consideration for this agreement?[9] To make a promise binding, the law requires that an act, forbearance, or promise be given in exchange. Without consideration a promise will not be enforceable. Briefly, if there has been no exchange of promises, a court would find great difficulty in identifying valid consideration (see *Combe v Combe* **[1951] 2 KB 215**).

[10]The answer ends with a general conclusion on the issues raised by the question.

In conclusion,[10] it would seem that it is difficult to argue for the existence of an offer given the language used by Fastbuild. Moreover, the lack of a price creates uncertainty if interpreted as requiring further agreement by the parties. The presence of the words 'letter of intent' may not be fatal to an enforceable agreement if they do not negative an intention to contract. But, once again, an argument must be made for the existence of an offer; that is, on the facts, is there is an intention to be bound by a definite set of certain terms? Should an offer exist, then it has to be established that there has been an acceptance. Generally, communication of acceptance is required but, should the offer be one of a unilateral nature, then conduct of itself may constitute acceptance. While there is commencement of brick manufacture it is unclear whether this may be linked to an offer. Finally, has consideration been given by Bricklast for any promise of Fastbuild's? An exchange of promises may be required, as usually reliance, in itself, would not be sufficient to make a promise binding.

LOOKING FOR EXTRA MARKS?

- The interplay between the law relating to offer and acceptance, certainty of terms, and contractual intention could be emphasized, explaining the overlap in the operation of these rules. Further, the relationship between an intention to contract and an intention to create legal relations could be explored, see *Baird Textile Holdings Ltd v Marks & Spencer* **[2001] EWCA CIV 274**.

Q QUESTION | 2

Financial Systems Ltd (FSL) is experiencing intermittent interruptions to its gas supplies and therefore requests a quote from Solheat & Co. (S) for the installation of a new solar-powered heating system that will avoid reliance on outside energy suppliers. The sales representative of S delivers the quote to FSL and adds the following comments: 'This system is a world-beater. It achieves the highest "Ecology Rating", based on research by government environmental agencies. Moreover, I guarantee that you will recover the initial installation costs within five years.' FSL is impressed by these comments.

Two days later FSL signs a contract with S regarding the installation of the new heating system. The contract does not incorporate any guarantee of cost recoupment, nor any reference to the system's ecology rating.

The solar-powered heating system is installed into FSL's offices, with the parties agreeing that the system conforms to the specifications contained within the contract. Two months later FSL discovers that the new heating system had lost its government-approved 'ecology rating' because of superior products coming on to the market, while a recently published report confirms previous research that the start-up costs of solar-powered heating systems can never be recovered by purchasers. FSL demands the removal of the new heating system, a full refund of the original contract price, and the repair of all office walls and partitions caused by the original installation of the new heating system. S refuses to comply with any of these requests.

Advise FSL.

 CAUTION!

- You have to think carefully about this type of 'mixed' question and how much depth is required in answering each part.

- The problem broadly relates to contractual terms and representations, and you will see that the suggested answer refers to terms, parol evidence, classification of terms, assessment of damages, misrepresentation, and remedies for misrepresentation.

DIAGRAM ANSWER PLAN

Identify the issues	▣ Identify the legal issues. ▣ Three possible grounds of action: breach of contract, breach of a collateral contract, and/or misrepresentation.
Relevant law	▣ Outline the elements of a successful claim of breach of contract. ▣ Remedies for breach of contract. ▣ Outline the elements of an actionable misrepresentation, in particular the important concepts of inducement and reliance. ▣ **Misrepresentation Act 1967.**
Apply the law	▣ Are the statements terms of the contract? Outline and apply the parol evidence rule. ▣ Availability of remedies for breach of contract on the facts of the problem? ▣ Outline the elements of an actionable misrepresentation present in the problem facts. ▣ Explain any possible problems with a misrepresentation claim on the facts. ▣ Requirements for remedies for misrepresentation under **Misrepresentation Act 1967, s. 2(1).**
Conclude	▣ Advisability of pursuing a claim for misrepresentation and/or breach of contract. ▣ Conclusion.

 SUGGESTED ANSWER

[1]Identify the areas of law raised by the question. Here you see that it covers different areas, each of which should be addressed in your answer.

[2]The first question to consider is whether FSL has a remedy in breach of contract. Set out the relevant rule(s) in your answer.

FSL may consider pursuing an action for breach of contract and/or misrepresentation.[1]

Breach of Contract

Here FSL must prove that any relevant pre-contractual statements made by S's sales representative were terms of the contract as opposed to merely representations.[2] This requires ascertaining the parties' objective intention, helped by considering certain questions (***Heilbut, Symons & Co. v Buckleton* [1913] AC 30**). First, is there a substantial lapse of time between the oral statement and the writing?

If the period is short—two days here—the court is more likely to consider the oral statement to be a term (eg *Routledge v McKay* **[1954] 1 WLR 615** in which a period of seven days was crucial); however, other relevant factors, such as the nature of the goods sold, and the surrounding factual matrix, mean that this is not definitive. Secondly, if the sales representative possesses expert knowledge, more weight will attach to his/her statements (see *Harling v Eddy* **[1951] 2 KB 739**). This should not be too difficult to establish on these facts.[3] Thirdly, does FSL rely on the relevant statements? *Schawel v Reade* **[1913] 2 IR 81** demonstrates that a statement may have contractual effect if it was clearly of importance to the other party and was a dominating factor in the contract's formation. The facts suggest this to be the case. Finally, if there is evidence that FSL was asked to verify the statement, this would seriously undermine the statement being a term (see *Ecay v Godfrey* **(1974) 80 Ll LR 286**; *Leaf v International Galleries* **[1950] 2 KB 86**).

[3] Remember to apply the law to the specific question throughout your answer.

This analysis would suggest that statements made by S's sales representative should be treated as terms of the contract. If so, the parol evidence rule, and the type of remedy available for any breach must be addressed. The parol evidence rule states that extrinsic evidence may not be adduced to add to, vary, or contradict writing. There is a strong presumption that if the parties have committed their agreement to an all-embracing written contract, it must represent their finalized intent. Here there does not seem to be any evidence that the parties were intending to contract on terms that were partly written and partly oral (see *Allen v Pink* **(1838) 4 M & W 140**), so S might be able to rely on the parol evidence rule to avoid any oral statements being incorporated into the contract.[4]

[4] For extra marks you could suggest that FSL may then try to establish a collateral contract.

If the statements made by the sales representative were terms of the contract, FSL is potentially entitled to repudiate the contract and claim damages. However, it may be that a court would not permit FSL to repudiate the contract when the new heating system has already been installed for a period of time and the old one has been removed (and possibly disposed of). Consequently, if the award of damages was the most likely outcome, the standard common law rules of measure, remoteness, and mitigation should be applied.

Misrepresentation

FSL's alternative possible cause of action is misrepresentation. Broadly, a misrepresentation is a false statement of fact/law made by the representor, which is intended to induce and, in fact, does induce the representee to enter into the contract.[5] S's representative made several statements, each of which must be analysed.

[5] Define the elements constituting the doctrine of misrepresentation.

S could argue that the first statement (it is a 'world-beater') was too vague a statement or should be classed as an opinion (see *Dimmock v Hallett* (1866) 2 Ch App 21—the words 'fertile' and 'improvable' were considered too vague to constitute 'facts'). However, FSL could argue that any reasonable person would have assumed that the opinions of a specialist salesperson were based on some clear supporting evidence (see *Smith v Land & House Property Corp.* (1884) 28 Ch D 7 where use of the word 'desirable' to describe a tenant who was habitually late in paying rent was considered to be a false statement of fact). *Brown v Raphael* [1958] Ch 636 established that an opinion may be actionable as a misrepresentation where the representor is in a much stronger position to ascertain the facts than the representee, which is clearly relevant here.

The comment regarding the ecology rating appears to be an unequivocal, false statement of fact as the relevant government agency has withdrawn its top ecology rating for S's product. However, FSL must establish that it was a false statement of *existing* fact (ie that the ecology rating was withdrawn *before* FSL entered the contract). If the statement was correct when made, but incorrect at the time the contract was formed, S may have an obligation to inform FSL of this change of circumstances (eg *With v O'Flanagan* [1936] Ch 575), although if this information was only disclosed post-contractually no liability would arise.

The final statement (recoupment of costs) appears to be a definite misrepresentation: the language used, and intention conveyed seem obvious, a clear fact is mentioned, and S is in a superior position to know the truth (again, as in *Smith v Land & House Property*). The timing of the research report, referred to in the facts, is immaterial as the statement remains false, irrespective of when publication took place (ie before or after the contract was made), although the date of its publication might be relevant to the type of misrepresentation made (eg innocent or fraudulent).

Assuming a false statement of fact has been identified, FSL must prove that it relied on that statement and was thereby induced to enter the contract. There is no evidence that FSL was given the opportunity to check the truth of the statements before a contract came into existence (eg *Attwood v Small* (1838) 6 Cl & F 232), nor would it be sufficient for S to argue that FSL could/ought to have known about previous research on cost recoupment, particularly as *Redgrave v Hurd* (1881) 20 Ch D 1 established that the *opportunity* to discover untruths is irrelevant as constructive knowledge is insufficient to disprove reliance. So FSL only needs to prove that the comments of S's sales representative (particularly as to cost

⁶Continue to address each element of misrepresentation, applying the law to the facts in each case.

⁷This is directly relevant to the remedies which might be available.

⁸This is a clear and concise explanation and application of the law.

⁹Although see *Smith New Court Securities Ltd v Scrimgeour Vickers (Asset Management) Ltd* [1996] 4 All ER 769 and its explanation of the direct consequence test.

recoupment) were a factor in persuading FSL to enter the contract (see *Edgington v Fitzmaurice* **(1885) 29 Ch D 459)**. This seems likely on the facts, as economy and ecology issues would likely be material to the purchaser of a solar heating system, meaning that FSL could claim misrepresentation.⁶

On this basis, what type of misrepresentation has occurred?⁷ It is unlikely that FSL could establish a fraudulent misrepresentation unless there was proof that the sales representative intentionally misled FSL (see *Le Lievre v Gould* **(1893) 1 QB 491**; *Derry v Peek* **(1889) 14 App Cas 337)**. In addition, as FSL could rely on the liability imposed by **s. 2(1) of the Misrepresentation Act 1967**, it would seem unnecessary for FSL to bring an action in deceit and/ or for negligence at common law, under the principles of *Hedley Byrne & Co. Ltd v Heller and Partners Ltd* **[1964] AC 465**. In effect, **s. 2(1)** imposes liability for negligent misrepresentations and reverses the normal burden of proof: once the representee proves that there has been a misrepresentation, the burden shifts to the representor to show that he had 'reasonable grounds to believe and did believe up to the time the contract was made that the facts represented were true'. It is clear from *Howard Marine and Dredging Co. Ltd v A Ogden & Sons (Excavations) Ltd* **[1978] QB 574** that it is extremely difficult to discharge this burden: honest belief is insufficient as the representor must positively establish the reasonableness of his belief. Consequently, the question is whether S's representative *ought* to have known about the research on cost recoupment and/or the lost ecology rating, with the safest conclusion being that, if the information was publicly available before the contract was formed, it is unlikely that S will be able to discharge the burden under **s. 2(1)**.

As FSL wishes to return the system and obtain a refund of the price, it would be seeking rescission of the contract. This seems unlikely on the facts.⁸ FSL may not have affirmed the contract by continuing with its use for two months (compare *Long v Lloyd* **[1958] 1 WLR 753** with *Leeds City Council v Barclays Bank Plc* **[2021] EWHC 363 (Comm)** at [165]) but, more importantly, it seems impossible to restore the parties to their original position as it would arguably require FSL's old heating system to be reinstalled and connected, whilst the new system would have significantly depreciated in value through use.⁹

As regards damages, FSL will presumably pursue its claim under **s. 2(1)** of the 1967 Act (see earlier), so damages will be assessed in the tort of deceit. FSL will be entitled to reclaim all those damages which *directly* flow from its reliance upon the misrepresentation, such as the failure to recoup its losses within the stipulated time. Following *East v Maurer* [1991] 2 QB 297, damages may encompass lost opportunity costs, so this could cover the benefits that FSL would have obtained if it had purchased an alternative system capable of meeting the standards originally specified by FSL.

LOOKING FOR EXTRA MARKS?

- When considering whether FSL has a remedy in breach of contract, additional marks would be available for also reflecting on the prospects of FSL establishing a collateral contract.

- On assessing the likely award of damages, the lost ecology rating (assuming it occurred pre-contractually), and the inability to recoup installation costs within five years are primary 'losses' suffered by FSL. Using the standard expectation measure (*Robinson v Harman* (1848) 1 Exch 850), with the normal rules of remoteness (see *Hadley v Baxendale* (1854) 9 Exch 341), the court would need to identify the objective value attributable to the ecology rating, and the pecuniary loss sustained by failing to recoup initial installation costs within the prescribed period. Note also *Transfield Shipping Inc. v Mercator Shipping Inc., The Achilleas* [2008] UKHL 48, [2008] 4 All ER 159.

15 Skills for Success in Coursework Assessments

When preparing and writing an answer to a coursework question you need to consider the purpose of the exercise. For example, the exercise will often be designed to allow you to demonstrate to a marker that you understand an area, or areas, of law and that the process you have employed shows a sound method of collection, interpretation, and use of appropriate legal source material. Depending on the type of exercise set, it will also often allow you to demonstrate higher level skills such as analysis, synthesis, evaluation, and application. So before embarking on this process you should consider carefully what is expected of you; guidance will be found in the assessment criteria as it is against these that your answer will be judged.

Researching, Planning, and Preparing to Write

Your starting point must be a careful analysis of the question asked. Identify the subject matter of the question and then consider what you are asked to address in answering the question. Are you expected to compare the law pre- and post- a particular change or to seek to reconcile authorities or to make a judgement on the effectiveness of the operation of the law? Key words in the question must be identified and, of course, the instruction, for example, to discuss or critically evaluate must be followed. In answering a question, you will be required to make express reference to primary, and possibly secondary, legal source materials.

Having unpacked the question and identified the subject matter of the question, your next task will be to locate relevant materials. Starting points will include your lecture notes and appropriate textbooks. Consult the major textbooks such as: *Treitel*; *Anson*; *Cheshire, Fifoot, and Furmston*; and/ or *Chitty*. Read these to get an overall appreciation of the area of law and the important source materials available.

In researching an area of contract law, the sources you will be seeking to locate are primary source materials, such as cases and legislation, and secondary sources, such as textbooks, journal articles, and reports. Make a list of materials as your research progresses, ensuring that you fully note the reference for each (it is very time-consuming to hunt down a source reference when you are putting the finishing touches to your coursework). Journal articles are an important source of analysis of cases and of reviews of areas of law. An essay will benefit from the arguments or interpretation of legal authorities provided by academics. Of course, the sources must be carefully attributed in footnotes and bibliographies, so it is clear that you are using the ideas or comments of another person.

What you have learned about IRAC and PEA in answering examination questions may be used in writing your coursework. The important point to recognize is that writing skills are transferable between forms of assessment and indeed subject areas.

Critical Analysis and Evaluation

Use of IRAC and PEA will form the basis for the analysis of the question asked. By using these approaches, you should avoid producing a merely descriptive account of the area of law identified in a question.

In problem questions the first stage of your analysis is to identify the issues raised and then to explain the law relevant to each issue before applying the law to the specific issue.

Structure

A clear and logical structure to your answer is essential. An introduction should identify the elements of the question, thus demonstrating that the requirements of the question have been understood, and then indicate briefly how such issues are to be tackled in the body of the essay. The main body of the essay should then deal with the issues in turn. Having discussed the issues, an overall conclusion may be reached based upon the material already explored; new material should not be introduced in a conclusion.

Writing Your Answer

One difficulty faced by law students is determining the level of explanation to be employed in an answer. It is crucial to identify the audience at which your writing is directed. If you are writing for a lawyer, you may be able to assume that lawyers will possess basic legal knowledge which therefore need not be explained. However, if you are writing for a layperson, such an assumption may not be made, and basic concepts must be explained. At first-year undergraduate level your tutors will usually be seeking to assess, amongst other things, *your* understanding of basic legal concepts and rules so you will be expected to give explanations, for example, of what is an offer, what is meant by consideration, what is misrepresentation, and so on. Undergraduate students in later years or GDL students may face questions which are more searching or have a different emphasis. The question asked should give an indication of the audience to be addressed. As always, if in doubt ask your tutor.

The style of writing you employ will depend upon the task that has been set, for example, are you instructed to write an essay or a report or an advice note for a lawyer? Look for examples of the type of writing that is required and make notes of the features that may be used in your answer.

In producing an essay, it is more usual to write in the third person singular; rather than saying 'I think the argument is . . .', you should write 'It may be argued that . . .' or 'It may be contended . . .'. Ensure that your writing does not use colloquialisms and avoids a conversational style of writing. Adopt a more formal style of expression; examples of formal styles of writing may be found in journal articles in publications such as the *Cambridge Law Journal* and *Law Quarterly Review*. It is also advisable wherever possible to keep sentences short and not to overcomplicate writing by using long words where shorter words would suffice. Remember, you are seeking to demonstrate that you understand a particular area of law and/or that you can construct an argument. However, in legal writing precision and accuracy are paramount so the use of legal language is expected. Detailed advice on writing style is beyond the scope of this chapter but you may like to consider S.I. Strong's *How to Write Law Essays and Exams* (6th edn, Oxford University Press, expected 2022) which contains a chapter giving tips on legal writing.

While it is perfectly permissible to use quotations, do so sparingly. If you do use a quotation ensure that it is, for example, to provide evidence to support a point previously made or to express a point of view. Often students use quotations in place of explaining a basic point for themselves. This will not score high marks as it is your understanding/analysis which needs to be expressed not that of someone else.

Relevance and Sticking to the Word Limit

One of the criteria against which your answer will probably be judged is that of relevance. By including in your answer only relevant material you will be demonstrating that you have understood the question asked. What is relevant depends upon the question and the issues raised by it. Only deal with the areas of law that relate to the issues in the question.

If your answer is constrained by a word limit you must be mindful of the consequences of exceeding the word limit. Your coursework will usually indicate the consequences of non-compliance which can range from a mark reduction to an outright failure.

Referencing and Citation of Legal Authorities

You will be expected to reference your coursework appropriately. Three points should be borne in mind. First, to avoid an allegation of plagiarism, it is important to acknowledge the sources you have used in your answer by including sources both in footnotes and in a bibliography. Secondly, as the reader of your answer may wish to check the source you have used you must give a full reference so that the source may readily be found. If you are including in your essay a quotation from a source, it is necessary to give a page reference (or a paragraph number) to precisely identify the source. Thirdly, it is important to ensure consistency in referencing and to this end the Oxford University Standard for the Citation of Legal Authorities (OSCOLA) may be followed (your university should indicate the method of citation that is to be used). OSCOLA is available online at www.law.ox.ac.uk/sites/files/oxlaw/oscola_4th_edn_hart_2012.pdf and is accompanied by a short guide, OSCOLA Quick Reference Guide, which is to be found at the end of the document. This short guide is a good starting point when using OSCOLA.

Coursework Example

QUESTION

'The subject of whether English law does or should recognize a general duty to perform contracts in good faith[1] is one on which a large body of academic literature exists. However, I am not aware of any decision of an English court, and none was cited to me, in which the question has been considered in any depth'[2] (*Yam Seng Pte Limited (A company registered in Singapore) v International Trade Corporation Limited* [2013] EWHC 111 (QB) at [120][3] *per* Leggatt J).

Critically discuss[4] the extent to which the Law of England and Wales does and should recognize a general duty to perform contracts in good faith.[5]

[1]What is meant by good faith? One difficulty when discussing the concept of good faith is that it may mean different things to different people (compare, for example, Pakistan International Airline Corporation v Times Travel (UK) Ltd [2021] UKSC 40). You will need to acknowledge and briefly explore the problems of terminology.

[2]Essay questions sometimes incorporate a quotation which will, for example, contextualize the task or provide a starting point.

[3]Consider whether any source cited in the question might assist in answering the question. In fact, *Yam Seng Pte Limited (A company registered in Singapore) v International Trade Corporation Limited* [2013] EWHC 111 (QB) provides an excellent overview of this area but have there been more recent cases? See, for example, *MSC Mediterranean Shipping Company SA v Cottonex Anstalt* [2016] EWCA Civ 789 and *Bates v Post Office Ltd (No.3: Common Issues)* [2019] EWHC 606 (QB).

[4]The question requires a critical discussion rather than requiring you to write all you know about good faith. Remember PEA!

[5]Remember, there are two strands to this question: a critical discussion of the *current* position and a critical discussion of whether or not there should be a change of direction.

ANSWER GUIDANCE

The role of good faith in contract law is a very topical subject and, therefore, is a prime candidate for assessment. One of the difficulties with the debate on good faith in contract law is that it is clear that good faith may be defined in different ways. For example, at one end of the spectrum some might argue that good faith is essentially a limited negative duty not to, for example, actively mislead a potential contracting party (and, as such, it overlaps to some extent with the law of misrepresentation). On the other hand, some would argue that it is a wider, positive duty which, for example, 'looks to good standards of commercial morality and practice' (*Director General of Fair Trading v First National Bank Plc* [2001] UKHL 52 at [17] per Lord Bingham) or 'commercially acceptable' conduct (compare *Bates v Post Office Ltd (No.3: Common Issues)* [2019] EWHC 606 (QB)).

It is clear that the Law of England and Wales does not *explicitly* recognize a *general* duty of good faith in contract law. However, there are examples of more limited duties of good faith in the Law of England and Wales: for example, under the Consumer Rights Act 2015. Furthermore, subject to these problems of definition, the Law of England and Wales regulates contractual behaviour in other ways (e.g. through the doctrine of undue influence or the doctrine of misrepresentation) which, to some extent, in effect requires parties to act in good faith (see *Interfoto Picture Library Limited v Stiletto Visual Programmes Ltd* [1989] QB 433 at 439 per Bingham LJ).

To what extent, if any at all, was this position changed in *Yam Seng*? Here you should briefly explore the use of implied terms of good faith but note the caution of Leggatt LJ: 'I doubt that English law has reached the stage, however, where it is ready to recognize a requirement of good faith as a duty implied by law, even as a default rule, into all commercial contracts' (at [131]).

You will need to explore why there is a reluctance to recognize an explicit general duty of good faith in contract law in England and Wales.[1] Are the reasons convincing? For example, it is sometimes argued that an explicit general duty of good faith runs contrary to the adversarial nature of contracting (such as driving a hard bargain) but good faith does not necessarily mean a party has to sacrifice their own interests (see D. Campbell, 'Good Faith and the Ubiquity of the "Relational" Contract' (2014) 77 *Modern Law Review* 473). This will set the grounding for the second part of the question: would you suggest that the current position needs to change and, if so, why?[2]

[1] H.G. Beale, *Chitty on Contracts* (34th edn, Sweet & Maxwell 2021) 1–39ff provides an excellent overview of this area.

[2] Express *your* reasoned, argued opinion.

Index

V

W